SECRETS
OF THE NEW
ONLINE
ENTREPRENEURS

SECRETS

OF THE NEW

ONLINE

ENTREPRENEURS

HOW AUSTRALIA'S TOP DISRUPTORS

SCALE UP, SELL FAST
AND STAND OUT

AND HOW YOU CAN TOO

BERNADETTE SCHWERDT

WILEY

First published 2026 by John Wiley & Sons Australia, Ltd

ISBN: 978-1-394-37712-1

A catalogue record for this book is available from the National Library of Australia

Registered Office
John Wiley & Sons Australia, Ltd. Level 4, 600 Bourke Street, Melbourne, VIC 3000, Australia

For details of our global editorial offices, customer services, and more information about Wiley products visit us at www.wiley.com.

Wiley also publishes its books in a variety of electronic formats and by print-on-demand. Some content that appears in standard print versions of this book may not be available in other formats.

Cover design by Wiley
Figure images: figures 3.1 and 3.2: application mitt: © IconArt/ Adobe Stock; bottles (various): © STM 2.0/Adobe Stock

Set in 11/16 pts and Utopia Std by Straive, Chennai, India.

To my parents
Rosemary and David Schwerdt

To my family
Phil, Darcy, Cameron and Maddi

CONTENTS

Books written by Bernadette Schwerdt

Secrets of Online Entrepreneurs

How to Build an Online Business

Books ghostwritten or co-authored by Bernadette Schwerdt

How to Build a Billion Dollar Business by Radek Sali

Catch of the Decade by Gabby and Hezi Leibovich

How to Build a Business Others Want to Buy by Kobi Simmat

How to Manifest Success by Hilton Misso

The Boy with the Suitcase (Holocaust memoir) by Steven Krulis

Misa's Story (Holocaust memoir) by Misa Solar

Books edited or coached by Bernadette Schwerdt

Find. Build. Sell by Stephen Hunt

Earning Power by Roxanne Calder

Empowered by Aviv Palti

ABOUT THE AUTHOR

Bernadette Schwerdt is an award-winning Australian entrepreneur, author and speaker. She is the founder of the Australian School of Copywriting, the head copywriting tutor at the Australian Writers' Centre and is the country's leading copywriting and book writing coach.

She was a former senior account director and copywriter for global advertising agency Wunderman Cato Johnson and created award-winning campaigns for clients such as Apple, American Express, Optus and Colgate.

She has a Bachelor of Business in Marketing, is an accredited MBTI and NLP practitioner and has lectured in marketing and consumer psychology at RMIT, Swinburne and Victoria Universities.

She is the host of the popular podcast, *So You Want to Be a Copywriter,* a judge for the Australian Business Book Awards and a TEDx speaker. She is the author of two bestselling books about online entrepreneurship (*How to Build an Online Business* and *Secrets of Online Entrepreneurs*).

Bernadette was the ghost-writer of the award-winning *Catch of the Decade*, the business biography of the brothers behind Catch of the Day and Menulog, top business coach Kobi Simmat's *How to Build a Business Others Want to Buy*, and leading lawyer and philanthropist Hilton Misso's *How to Manifest Success* and the book editor for Stephen Hunt's *Find. Build. Sell.* She was the co-author of *How to Build a Billion Dollar Business* for Radek Sali, the former CEO of Swisse Wellness, which won the *Australian Business Book Award* for Entrepreneurship. She also wrote the Holocaust memoirs for Steven Krulis and Misa Solar.

Prior to her business career, Bernadette studied acting at the Victorian College of the Arts and appeared in some of Australia's most iconic shows including *Neighbours, The Games, Round the Twist, Winners and Losers* and *Jack Irish*.

She is a trained yoga teacher and was the inaugural in-house mindfulness coach for the Carlton Football Club. She was named in the Top 50 Small Business Leaders in Australia. Her mother still doesn't know exactly what she does for a living.

INTRODUCTION

I've interviewed dozens of founders for three books about online entrepreneurship and ghostwritten five more for entrepreneurs who have built multi-million-dollar companies. I've coached many others to write their books and spent two decades training more than 25 000 people in copywriting and online business through the Australian School of Copywriting and the Australian Writers' Centre. I've also worked as a public-speaking coach for senior executives across dozens of organisations including the Department of Premier and Cabinet, KPMG, NAB and Goldman Sachs.

Alongside that work, I've served as a judge for a range of online business awards and sat on the master judging panel for the Australian Business Book Awards. Earlier in my career, I worked in advertising and marketing, watching how commercial decisions were made when reputations and millions of dollars were on the line.

That breadth of experience has given me a bird's-eye view of how businesses are really built. I've seen the public success and the private struggle, what happens on camera and behind closed doors, and how entrepreneurship has evolved over the last thirty years.

I've distilled what these entrepreneurs shared with me, combined it with my own experience and insights, and translated it into practical tools you can use. Inside you'll find stories, frameworks, templates, scripts, business models, step-by-step guides and Q&As, alongside bite-sized nuggets of wisdom at the end of each chapter to help you put the ideas into action.

The content is both practical and tactical, inspirational and motivational. It explores the enduring emotional intelligence traits that show up in high-performing founders and reveals the modern tools, systems and techniques today's digital entrepreneurs use to turn attention into income.

Why these entrepreneurs?

In these pages you'll meet a wide array of business builders: billion-dollar founders who went all in, lifestyle entrepreneurs who chose small over scale, creators whose businesses run on content, not capital, and not-for-profits using online tools to change lives.

Some are pure online players; others run bricks-and-mortar businesses amplified by digital channels; some are hybrids. Each represents a different pathway into entrepreneurship.

For every founder who started small, another started big.

For every founder who partnered up, another said, 'Don't'.

For every founder who said 'Make a plan', another said 'Wing it'.

There is no single right way to build a business. The founders in these pages have taken different paths, made different choices and paid different prices. They're sharing what they learned so you can make better decisions sooner, avoid the most common traps, and choose the path that's right for you.

Why Australian entrepreneurs?

This book was written for Australian business owners, about Australian business owners, by an Australian business owner.

We all know the American stories of how those 18-year-old Silicon Valley brainiacs barely out of high school became multibillionaires by building apps that went nuts on the NASDAQ.

What we *don't* know are the stories of our homegrown heroes, the stories that tell us how a regular person like you or me from the Sutherland Shire or the Sunshine Coast or South Dandenong took on the big players and won. Those were the stories I wanted to read, so those are the stories I have chosen to tell.

I've had a deep interest in online business for two decades. I sold my first online copywriting course back in 2004 and still remember the thrill of seeing $1000 drop into my account overnight from someone I'd never met. That moment changed how I saw business and I've been dedicated to learning more about it ever since.

It's why I wrote my first book, *Secrets of Online Entrepreneurs*, then my second, *How to Build an Online Business*, and now this one.

We are all online, some are more online than others. No matter where you are on your digital journey, you'll find something of value here.

Why now?

There's never been a better time to launch your entrepreneurial career. Now, more than ever, people are turning to entrepreneurship to build lives on their own terms: to choose how they work, when they work and with whom they work.

People say it's risky to start your own business, that it's much safer to stay where you are, in the job you're in. Once upon a time that would have been true, but not anymore.

With the advent of AI, global unrest and unstable economies, when so many are at the mercy of yet another restructure, redeployment or realignment, many are already living on the edge, wondering and waiting to find out if they have a job today, tomorrow, or ever again.

I would argue that being an entrepreneur is actually *safer* than working for any company right now, because when you know how to manifest something from nothing — which is what all great entrepreneurs know how to do—you will never be at risk. Learning the skills of entrepreneurship is a powerful form of self-protection.

How to use this book

In order to understand *online* entrepreneurship, you first need to understand *entrepreneurship* itself—how founders think, make decisions, deal with failure, handle regret and manage stress.

The opening chapters explore the mindset, behaviours and decision-making patterns that consistently show up in founders who succeed. Once those foundations are in place, we show how to apply those same principles to modern platforms, marketing systems and social media strategies.

I've included examples of how entrepreneurs are using AI to spark ideas and uncover opportunities, but avoided turning this into a how-to guide. AI is moving too fast for static instructions to stay relevant.

The best way to learn AI isn't by reading about it, but by using it. Treat it like the smartest intern you've ever hired: fast and capable, but only as effective as the brief you give it.

The book is divided into five parts, each representing a different phase in the startup journey:

1. Momentum
2. Multipliers
3. Marketing
4. Management
5. Money.

This book offers a comprehensive view of what online entrepreneurship really looks like in Australia right now and how more than 35 of our top online business owners run their operations. Read on and discover how to:

- start small but think big
- spot new trends, turn them into products and get them to market before others do
- increase your capacity for creativity and help you turn ideas into action
- convert passions into profit, do good and leave the world a better place
- pick the right business partners and test them out before going all in
- build a personal brand
- choose the right influencers to take your product to the world
- turn adversity into advantage, take on the trolls and never fear reading the comments again
- protect yourself from being ripped off, taken down, sued or sidelined
- deliver five-star experiences on a rock-bottom budget
- get paid to create content and publish with confidence
- use data to uncover opportunities, manage teams remotely and back your instinct with fact
- hire well, fire faster and create a workplace people love so much they won't want to leave
- measure the metrics that matter and avoid random acts of marketing
- find investors, prepare your business for sale and leave money on the table for all.

This is not a fluffy 'manifest your way to millions' book, where you get to 'dream, believe and breathe' your way to success. These entrepreneurs worked and worried, toiled and troubled, all the way to the top. They got trolled, sued, copied, cancelled, blindsided, burnt out, blown off, caught up and caught out — and yet they *just kept going.*

Writing this book made one thing clear: while the tools and platforms change, the personal qualities that lead to success don't. Every entrepreneur here shared the same defining trait — persistence. They kept going when it would have been easier to quit. So, on that note, why don't we do the same and *just get going*? Happy reading and enjoy the ride.

ENTREPRENEURS AND EXPERTS FEATURED IN THE BOOK

Janine Allis	Boost Juice
Shaun Wilson	Bondi Sands
Radek Sali	Swisse Wellness, Wanderlust, Light Warrior
Matt Rockman	Seek
Adam Schwab	Luxury Escapes
Scott Neeson	20th Century Fox Films, Cambodian Children's Fund
Ronni Kahn AO	OzHarvest
George Calombaris	*MasterChef*, Culinary Wonderland
Kirsten Tibballs	*MasterChef*, Savour Chocolate & Patisserie School
Gabby Leibovich	Catch.com.au, Menulog, Fingertip
Tim Fung	Airtasker
Carla Oates	The Beauty Chef
Meahan Callaghan	Seek, Afterpay, Mecca, Foxtel
Kobi Simmat	Best Practice.biz
Elise McCann & Lucy Durack	Actors; Hey Lemonade app
Kate Halfpenny	*The Age* columnist and author
Glen James	Financial influencer

Kevin Allocca	YouTube
Austin & Lachlan Macfarlane	YouTube influencers
Vince Lebon	Rollie Nation
Nat Kringoudis	Women's health influencer
Adele Samus	Actor and influencer
Nicky Sparshott	Unilever, T2, Procter & Gamble
Valerie Khoo	Australian Writers' Centre
Martin Hosking	Redbubble, LookSmart, McKinsey
Stephen Hunt	Hunt Hospitality
Hilton Misso	Lawyer, philanthropist
Dylan Schwerdt	Pokémon card trader
Kat Moses	MGMT
Pru Corrigan	One Daydream
Melissa Blight	Aster & Oak
Ben Fewtrell	DigiTLC, MaxMyProfit
Michael Potas	Boost Design
Jay Gardam	Wynroy Hot Yoga
Michael Flanderka	Data Interactive

PART 1

MOMENTUM

Starting a business is hard. Knowing what you want from it is even harder.

Do you want a scalable business you can list on the stock exchange for millions or billions, or do you want a lifestyle business that gives you time with the family, a fixed schedule and the freedom to work when and where you want?

Anything is possible. It just comes down to what you want, why you want it and how hard you're willing to work for it. Most successful entrepreneurs didn't have their future mapped out from day one. They started, pivoted and worked it out as they went. Action creates traction, and traction leaves clues. As momentum builds, you will see what works and what doesn't; what energises you and what drains you. The secret of success is to follow your instinct, stay curious and move forward even if you don't know exactly where you're going, and let the results of those actions inform your next move.

1

KNOW YOURSELF

Many entrepreneurs stumbled their way into a business because they were good at something, or an opportunity appeared and they ran with it.

Five or 10 years later, they 'wake up' and realise the life they've built isn't the one they wanted. Their finances, identity and obligations are now tethered to a business they never consciously designed.

Before you set out on your entrepreneurial journey, take a moment to answer these two questions:

What kind of life do you want to live?
What are you prepared to trade to get it?

Everything has a cost, so it's wise to understand the price before you're forced to pay it.

If you want the waterfront mansion, the first-class flights and the boat on Sydney Harbour, you'll need to build a business that can scale. That may mean years of intense output, uncomfortable risks and a level of stress and debt most people can't endure.

If you want a laid-back life, control over your diary and time with the kids, you can build a smaller business and still live well. You may never get the superyacht or the private island, but if those things weren't important to you in the first place, nothing has been lost.

There will still be stress, but it will be proportionate, and you (might) sleep better at night.

There are pros and cons to going big or going small. Both paths are valid, but the price tags for each are very different.

What really matters is *knowing yourself*. What does success mean to you? Can you back yourself when things get hard? What does 'enough' mean to you?

Knowing who you are and what pressure you can cope with is an important indicator of the size and scale of business you might want to build.

Going big has an upside — and a downside

Matt Rockman, one of the three co-founders of the online juggernaut Seek, saw up close what it took to launch and list a multi-billion-dollar business. As the sales and marketing director, he was tasked with finding the clients and generating revenue.

'I worked around 80 to 100 hours a week for years. My wife called herself the Seek widow because I was always away and she had to go to all our social occasions on her own. She understood, but I don't think she loved it.'

The travel was relentless. 'When we listed, we had over 10 000 clients across Australia and Europe. The diaries were in control of me. That's what the job demanded.'

Once he'd hit his goal of listing and the business was flying, it was time to take stock.

'At the end, I felt it was a choice between Seek or my family. I was tired. My lifestyle wasn't healthy and neither was I. Listing gave me the financial freedom to make a choice. I could have stayed on in a pretty burnt-out way, or choose my family and reset. I chose the latter.'

Janine Allis, founder of Boost Juice and Retail Zoo, faced a similar challenge. She remembers that period vividly.

'When Boost Juice began, the business took over every corner of my life. We were surrounded by work 24 hours a day, seven days a week,' she said. 'If you're not passionate about what you do, that level of commitment gets tiring very quickly.'

The pressure was relentless. 'For the first 12 months, I was forever on a plane to visit our store in Adelaide,' she said. At home, she was raising three little kids, 'the youngest being not even one year old', and juggling the demands of a startup that was growing faster than expected. 'It felt like we were living and breathing Boost every minute,' she said.

Things ramped up when the business expanded overseas.

'I was obsessed with getting the international side of the business up and running, but this kept me away from my family for over three months a year. My work–life balance pendulum was angling all the way to the work side. I had developed into a strong, confident businessperson with significant knowledge on how to start a business, but I was losing touch with my husband and family.'

Be careful what you wish for

The daily grind of going big can wear you down. Here's what a typical day in the life of online retailer Catch.com founder Gabby Leibovich looked like.

'I'd wake up, check my emails, drive to the office, and be at my desk by 8 am. I'd solve the problems from the night before, attend a supplier meeting at 9 am, juggle a thousand different balls throughout the morning and eat a hurried lunch at my desk. I'd have more meetings with suppliers in the afternoon, head home at 8 pm, have a quick dinner, kiss the kids goodnight, say hello to my wife, hit the desk for another few hours, answer more emails, get to bed around midnight, read an industry journal for a few minutes, fall asleep, and then get up and do it all again the next day.'

It intensified when he and his brother, Hezi, his co-founder, prepared to list on the stock exchange.

'An international roadshow to woo the investment community sounds like fun. It wasn't. We travelled to Melbourne, Sydney, Auckland and Hong Kong and attended 70 meetings in three countries over seven days — that's 10 meetings a day — saying pretty much the same thing, hour after hour. It was one of the hardest weeks of my life.'

Gabby was so hyped at the start of the roadshow that he even went shopping and bought a fancy suit and tie for the week ahead. 'I wore my nice new outfit on day one and day two, but by day three I'd had enough and just went to the meetings unshaven and dressed in jeans and my black T-shirt with a big Catch logo. I was over it.'

The listing didn't go ahead because the market was too choppy. In retrospect, Gabby was glad.

'We were disappointed because we'd spent hundreds of hours preparing for it and were excited to see how far we could take it, but we were secretly pleased the decision to not list had been taken out of our hands.'

The truth was they never wanted to be at the helm of a publicly listed company.

'We don't always do things in the boring, corporate way. We would have hated having to get approval to do anything and put up with the scrutiny that occurs within a public company.'

They knew who they were and what they valued. Getting that close to going public was a blessing because it showed them what leading a listed entity would be like, and how little they would have enjoyed it. Be careful what you wish for ... or what you list for.

The price of admission

Whenever Radek Sali faced a major decision, he'd ask a simple question: 'What's the worst that can happen?' He leaned on it early in his career when he was offered a life-changing opportunity to buy into Swisse Wellness. The price tag? $14 million. At the time he was their well-paid CEO, but he wasn't in a position to casually borrow an eight-figure sum.

'I could have declined the offer and watched someone else buy in,' he said, 'or I could back myself, purchase the shares and just get cracking on making the company as valuable as I knew it could be.'

Fourteen million dollars was a heavy load at any age, let alone at 34. He went home, discussed it with Helen, his wife and trusted confidant, and asked the only question that mattered: 'What's the worst that can happen?'

'If the business fails,' he said, 'we'll be up for $14 million and be bankrupt. We'll have to live in a caravan in the carpark at Byron Bay beach.'

Helen was undeterred. 'So long as I'm with you, I don't mind where we are.'

He had his answer. He borrowed the money, bought the shares and 10 years later, after an immense amount of work, sold the business for $2.1 billion. They're still in the Byron Bay region, but not in a caravan, or the carpark.

'What's the worst that can happen?' remains his decision-making compass. If you can live with the consequence, go for it. If you can't, walk away.

The real question that sits beneath these other bigger questions is:

- Do you back yourself?
- Do you believe you can hold the downside long enough to reach the upside?

- Do you have sufficient will and skill to see the concept through to completion?

Only you can decide that.

The hidden costs of high-level leadership

Few can speak about being a CEO of a big company with as much authority as Nicky Sparshott. She has led at the highest levels: global chief of transformation for Unilever, CEO of Unilever Australia and New Zealand, Asia–Pacific category head, and board member for ASX-listed companies. She's worked across international markets, led billion-dollar portfolios and chaired major advisory groups. Her résumé gives her rare authority to speak about the costs of leadership and the parts of the CEO job most people never see.

'The real weight isn't the decisions themselves but the emotional load behind them: knowing every call affects people's livelihoods, families and futures. Even as a leader who shares openly with her team, you can never fully offload that weight — because the role requires you to project confidence without arrogance, and vulnerability without instability.'

It's a role that demands constant composure, even when, in her words, you are in a 'semi-constant state of fear' or have moments where you need to leave the boardroom for a few moments to collect your thoughts and find space to breathe.

The pressure is relentless and rarely acknowledged. She's not looking for sympathy, she loves what she does — but few people get to see behind the mask, and the invisible weight of making decisions that affect thousands of people.

The aftermath of admission

There aren't many who talk openly about the serious side-effects that running a big business can have on your health.

When Swisse was sold to Biostime, Radek Sali had a serious physical reaction to the accumulated strain.

'After I had achieved a large chunk of what I'd set out to achieve, I had the freedom to do what I wanted, when I wanted and with whom I wanted. But for every action, there is a reaction. When the craziness stopped, I developed a condition called acute stress disorder, a mental health issue that usually occurs months after experiencing a traumatic event, but can also show up many years later. For me, the effects showed up three or four years after I left Swisse. The trauma affected me in unpredictable ways: I'd play out worst-case thoughts, had trouble sleeping, felt dizzy under pressure, and, eventually, had a panic attack so intense I thought it was a heart attack.'

With support from his wife Helen, his meditation teacher Jonni Pollard, and a return to exercise, rest and good food, he slowly recovered. But the reality remains true: living life at a fast pace and under high pressure has consequences.

High flyers

One of the trade-offs to success is that it makes you visible, and visibility invites judgement. In Australia, outsized success often invites resentment too. If you want to build something meaningful, you will need a thick skin to handle both the admiration and contempt that comes with it. You rarely get one without the other. Having great wealth can sometimes bring out the worst in people, especially in Australia where we love to lop our tall poppies down.

When Seek co-founder Matt Rockman drove his Ferrari down Chapel Street in Melbourne, someone yelled, 'Wanker!'

When he drove a similar sports car down Wilshire Boulevard in Los Angeles, someone yelled, 'I want to work for you!'

Be prepared to cop the flak that comes with success. As Jean Sibelius once put it, 'Pay no attention to what the critics say. A statue has never been erected in honour of a critic.' Criticism is often the price of visibility, and it's rarely paid by those who play small.

The pros of going big

Despite the drawbacks of going big, there are lots of upsides. Having the capacity to make a big impact and leave a legacy are just a few of them.

When you choose to build something big, you're not just growing revenue, you're growing people. Scale creates jobs, launches careers and gives talented individuals a place to find their footing.

Gabby Leibovich saw this firsthand.

'Pretty much every leader of every marketplace in Australia right now is an ex-Catch person: whether it's Myer or Freedom or Kogan, our people are everywhere. It gives me so much pleasure to see all those entrepreneurs now leading very successful businesses, both locally and all around the world.'

Wealth also lets you have a community impact. You can fund ideas, and support causes that matter to you.

Radek Sali's Light Warrior Impact Fund is doing that now. It's a purpose-driven investment group built on the idea that profits should also progress society. It invests in socially responsible and environmentally conscious ventures, and channels a portion of returns into its not-for-profit arm, Lightfolk Foundation. He's using wealth to support vulnerable communities and give back in a way that respects people and the planet.

Martin Hosking used the wealth he created at LookSmart, one of the earliest Australian tech successes, and later through Aconex and Redbubble, the artists' online marketplace, to fund something far more enduring than another venture. Through the Three Springs Foundation, the family entity he co-founded, Martin directed major philanthropic support to establish centres for contemplative studies and consciousness research at Melbourne and Monash universities. His view is that innovation isn't just technological, it's human; that societies advance when people develop greater self-understanding, emotional capacity and connection to the world around them. By backing academic research and teaching in these fields, he's investing in the kind of long-term human development that outlives any single company.

Going big isn't just about what you build; it's about what you enable in others: the people you empower, the ideas you fund, the change you create and, ultimately, the legacy you leave.

The pros and cons of a lifestyle business

Now that you've seen the upside and the costs of going big, it's worth examining what a small — or 'lifestyle' — business can offer, because for many online founders, big is not necessarily better.

Valerie Khoo, the founder of the Australian Writers' Centre, created a lifestyle business that gave her the best of all worlds.

She was a trained accountant working for the big corporates but took the leap into journalism because she was good with words and loved to tell stories.

'I was a freelance writer, working hard and doing well. I was good at what I did, but I was tired of trading money for hours. I'd been working 50 hours a week writing content for a charity, and I couldn't do everything I wanted to get done. That's when I thought: Why don't I *teach* writing? I'm good at deconstructing words, people need help unlocking their potential and I love helping people be the best they can be.'

She offered her first course in 2005. That did well, so she ran another, and then another. 'I took it online in 2007 because I could see that people wanted to come but they couldn't physically get to the classroom.'

Valerie now runs a lean operation with just 10 staff yet offers 75 online courses a year and trains thousands of students, many of whom have become household names in the literary world. The digital systems she set up enables her to scale up yet still control her business without having to engage a large team. She invests in the tech side of the business with dashboards and real-time data systems, knows at a glance what's selling and what's not, and reads every piece of feedback so she can be responsive to what her students are telling her. 'If something needs fixing, it gets done instantly.'

This systematic approach gives her the time and space to do other things. The trouble was, she didn't know what they were. Her friends said, 'Get a hobby.' She said, 'I don't have one.' They said, 'Find one.'

'So, I went looking. I experimented and did lots of short courses in woodwork, crochet and craft, and found I loved oil painting. I loved it so much that I started to put financial targets on how much I could sell. I reached those targets, but realised that I was doing it for the wrong reason. It took the fun out of it, so I stopped setting goals and just did what I loved.'

Making one-off artworks was her passion but she also realised that, like training courses, you are limited by the number of hours you can put in, so she licensed her artwork for commercial sale and found another way to generate passive income.

'My designs now appear on fabric, wallpaper, jigsaw puzzles and greeting cards, and I get royalties. It's nice to see them out in the world because it means more people get to experience them.'

Valerie's core online business is profitable, nimble and creatively satisfying and gives her the time and space to pursue her offline passion.

That's not to say a lifestyle business isn't without its issues. It's often portrayed as calm, balanced and wholesome. It can be all that, but it can still be stressful as Melissa Blight discovered when she set up her home-based clothing business.

Small can still be stressful

Melissa Blight from Aster & Oak runs a purpose-led online children's clothing brand. She's got 93 000 Instagram followers, but a tiny team. She should feel more relaxed than she does.

'There's a lot of stress, sometimes ridiculous amounts, where I find myself questioning every day what on earth I'm doing with my life! Running your own business means you are *on* 24/7. The pressure never really stops. There are constant decisions, deadlines and challenges to face, and if someone is sick or if a supplier falls over, or if anything goes wrong, it's all on me.'

The stress is balanced by the upsides.

'I get to be present for my kids in ways a traditional 9 to 5 wouldn't allow, and I can step back when I really need to. Yes, it makes life busier and more consuming, but it also gives me flexibility that I value deeply.'

She is working towards creating a better work-life balance and reminding herself of the bigger picture — that the business exists to support her family and bring joy to her customers, not the other way around.

'When I can step outside, ground myself in nature, or just take a moment with my kids, it helps me zoom out and remember why I started in the first place.'

If you value freedom, autonomy and presence more than scale, small might be the best way to go.

Go super small

Dylan Schwerdt, 32, was on a footy trip in New Orleans when he saw something in the window of a little hobby store that stopped him in his tracks. It was a pack of Pokémon cards, the same vintage cards he'd collected as a kid, selling for nearly half the price he'd seen in Australia.

He didn't think too much of it. He just laughed with a mate about how cheap they were and kept moving.

Six months later he broke his arm playing footy and was stuck at home, bored and unable to play. He started browsing Pokémon card prices online and realised the gap he'd seen in the United States wasn't a one-off situation. US sellers were listing cards for up to 50 per cent less than those in Australia. He'd been playing with these cards for years and still knew what each card was worth — and that price gap ignited an idea: buy in the United States, sell in Australia and pocket the difference. Some call it arbitrage. He called it card-bitrage.

Dylan keeps the whole operation simple. He sources cards from the United States, then sells them through two channels: eBay and Instagram. eBay gives him reach: a steady flow of collectors searching for specific cards, with built-in bidding and buyer protection. Instagram gives him speed: he posts a photo of the card, names a price and regular buyers DM him within minutes.

What began as a way to make an extra hundred dollars a week soon grew into a tidy side-hustle that slotted neatly around his banking job. He makes over $100 000 a year from the cards and works about 10 hours a week with no staff, no website, no branding, no office and no pressure.

'I mostly do it all while I'm watching TV.' It's just a small, nimble venture that funds itself, and lets him indulge in a little nostalgia for days gone by.

* * *

As you follow the founders' journeys, keep one thought in mind: almost every business, whether it's a lifestyle venture or a global brand, began in the same way: as a small idea, a problem that needed solving, an offhand comment or a moment of frustration; something they saw, heard or felt that they couldn't forget. When in doubt about what to do next, follow the whispers, take action and see where it leads you.

Nuggets of wisdom

▶ Identify the worst that could happen; assess whether you can live with that and then make your decision.

▶ If you want an international business, be prepared for lots of travel, time away from home, hotel food and jet lag.

▶ Money will solve a lot of problems, but it will create problems too. Be careful what you wish for.

2

GETTING STARTED

Long before the awards, the headlines or the global distribution deals, there's often a tiny spark: a moment of ignition where a hunch, a problem, or a dream gets so loud it's impossible to ignore. Few founders begin with scale; they begin with something much more modest: a weekend course in a dusty warehouse, a few saucepans and an old recipe. What sets them apart is their willingness to persist in the face of resistance, to follow the breadcrumbs and solve whatever challenges come their way.

Small team, world-class impact

If you love chocolate, watch *MasterChef* or have stumbled across Foxtel's *The Chocolate Queen,* you'll know the name Kirsten Tibballs. I know her because we spent 13 years standing at the same school gate, waiting for our boys to come out of class.

What I didn't know was that this self-effacing woman had over a million followers on social media. You could say she's popular. I also had no idea she'd had a tumultuous adolescence.

'I didn't really go to high school,' she said. 'I did two weeks of year 7 and then I became very unwell, and I hardly went to school.

At 15, when I was well enough, I left school altogether and started an apprenticeship in a small bakery on the Mornington Peninsula, 60 kilometres south of Melbourne.'

'It was a demanding course,' she said. 'It went from 2 in the morning until 5 at night, six days a week, but I loved it.'

After winning a scholarship to compete in a baking competition in Europe — and winning that — Kirsten travelled the world studying new and better ways to make chocolate and pastry, then returned to Australia and worked as a recipe writer for the high-end chocolate manufacturer Callebaut.

By the time she was 27, Kirsten's reputation was spreading fast. She was approached by a food equipment distributor who saw her potential to teach.

'He asked me to open my own cooking training business within his building and utilise all his ingredients and equipment,' she said. 'Having my own business wasn't even on my radar at that point.'

She started with six students, two tables and a fax machine to take bookings.

'I worked full time during the week, and ran the courses on the weekends,' she said. The classes routinely sold out.

Within five years, Kirsten had outgrown the space and in 2002, she launched her own business, Savour Chocolate & Patisserie School in Brunswick, Victoria, now recognised as one of the world's premier training institutions for pastry and chocolate professionals. Then came the accolades. In 2004, she represented Australia at the World Pastry Team Championships in Las Vegas, winning first in the Individual Chocolates category, and a host of other awards.

Her merchandising arm began when, at the end of each course, she'd wheel out a small cupboard of cooking equipment for students to purchase. The items always sold out, so she scaled up and opened a bricks-and-mortar store at the front of the school. As her student base grew and people around Australia wanted access to her teaching, she started filming her classes and uploading them to her website.

Once the courses were online, the next logical step was to put her entire inventory of kitchen equipment online too. Every bowl, whisk and mould she once wheeled out in a rickety cupboard was photographed, uploaded to the website, and linked directly to the recipes she taught. Students could click on the exact tools they'd seen her use, add them to their cart and have them delivered the next day.

She knew early that if people were going to discover her school, she'd need a public profile. That meant getting herself on television. The challenge was convincing producers she'd earned her media stripes and could perform under pressure. Fortunately, she could. She'd spent years competing in high-stakes baking competitions and international festivals, including cooking on stage at a Las Vegas casino in front of 10 000 people and the world's toughest judges.

She sent out media releases, built a showreel and took every opportunity that came her way: morning television, daytime chat shows, segments on *The Bert Newton Show* as well as features in *The Australian* and *Gourmet Traveller* magazines. Bit by bit, her profile grew, as did her confidence. She could feel the momentum building.

Then the breakthrough arrived: *MasterChef,* one of the most successful cooking shows in Australian history. She was invited to appear as a guest judge, and she's appeared on every season since. That was the moment everything took off.

Kirsten now has 20 000 people in her online cooking community, brand deals with Callebaut, speaking gigs, cooking tours, recipe books, a television show, a retail arm that ships ingredients and equipment globally, and a marketing team that produces high-quality video content on a weekly basis.

'I love teaching people and giving them something to aspire to,' she said. 'It's my passion. It's all I've ever wanted to do.'

She started with just six students and a fax machine and is now a global brand. Proof that when you have a passion and a purpose, profit will follow.

Six ways to validate your online course before you create it

Most content creators and thought leaders want an online course. Get it right and you'll create a valuable income stream that scales. Get it wrong and you've poured time, money and energy into a white elephant that no-one wants.

Here are six ways to test your course idea before you build it.

1 Sell it before you build it
Create a simple sales web page and invite people to join an early-bird offer. If people buy, build the course. If they don't, refine the promise, positioning or product offer.

2 Validate the problem
Publish blogs, emails or posts that answer the problem your course solves. Track comments, replies and questions. If they generate engagement, the idea is strong. If not, the topic may not be as popular as you thought.

3 Run a live workshop
Test the idea as a one- or two-part webinar or live-stream session. Promote it through your socials and email list and see who shows up. Offer it free to remove friction and build the database, or charge a small fee to filter out tyre kickers to test if the demand is real.

4 Create a pilot program

Invite a small group of ideal customers into a beta version of the course at a reduced price. Use their questions, feedback and testimonials to iterate and curate the next version.

5 Check demand for the topic

Use Google Trends to check if demand for the topic is rising or falling. If it's rising, test which words or course titles are more popular, and use that to inform your course name.

6 Audit existing courses

Search online course marketplaces like Udemy and Coursera for similar topics. Courses with 10000 to 20000+ students confirm strong demand. Scan reviews for complaints and tailor your course to offer that point of difference.

From home remedy to global category

Carla Oates had an instinct — you could call it a *gut* instinct — that the recipes that healed her childhood eczema and allergies could do the same for her daughter. As a beauty journalist for *Harper's Bazaar* and *Elle*, she'd tested thousands of products and knew one immutable truth: topical treatments soothed but rarely solved.

So, when her daughter developed similar skin issues, Carla did what she'd always done best. She went back to the kitchen and to the broths, the ferments and the wholefoods that had restored her own health years earlier. She trusted food long before 'gut health' became a buzz phrase, and she trusted her instinct even more.

In 2009, from her Bondi kitchen, with a couple of saucepans, some superfoods and her fermenting recipes, she started experimenting. There were no grand plans at this point. She just wanted to help her child. What she didn't know was that those kitchen-bench experiments would spark a new category called ingestibles and reshape the beauty industry from the inside out.

'I didn't initially know it was all connected to gut health,' she said. 'I stumbled across research exploring the link between allergies and gut health while I was looking for solutions for my daughter.' Drawing on her own childhood health issues, she already believed that food was medicine, and had seen firsthand how what she ate influenced her skin and overall wellbeing.

She researched everything she could, removed processed foods from her daughter's diet and introduced probiotic-rich, fermented wholefoods. Within weeks, her daughter's skin began to clear and her allergies abated.

'Our kitchen looked like a science lab,' she said.

The shift was profound. Carla's long-held belief that good health began from within — as the outcome of an internal ecosystem — became the foundation of her company, The Beauty Chef.

She tested her first home-made ferment on her daughter and the results were so obvious, her daughter's friends wanted to try it. Then their friends wanted to try it, and then their friends, and then the local health stores started calling. Soon she was up to her elbows in ferments, spending her mornings filling jars at the kitchen bench, loading orders into her car and doing deliveries around the neighbourhood, before sitting down to her actual job as a beauty journalist, the job that paid the bills.

'I thought, if I can make a little business out of this and help people, that's enough for me.' Going global was never the goal but she wanted to let people know it was available and that it got results, so she set about building a small website to spread the word.

She'd been quoted $30 000 for a logo and website, money she didn't have, but the graphic designer whose company quoted believed in Carla's idea so much, she reached out after hours and offered to do the entire job for $1000. A few orders trickled in off the website, then a few more. Word continued to spread.

Then came two turning points that put the wind beneath her wings: a feature in *Vogue*, followed by a phone call from Rob Hunt, an agent representing brands appearing on TVSN, the TV Shopping Network.

'We've heard about this incredible purple powder of yours called Glow,' he said. 'Come and sell it on air.'

She demurred for a bit to think it over and then agreed. She went on TVSN as the face of the brand, explained what Glow was and who it helped, and it sold out. Rob even lent her $20 000 to buy the ingredients so she could make enough product to fulfil the orders. After that, Sephora came calling, as did Mecca and Chemist Warehouse. None were without their challenges, but she knew she was onto something and she couldn't wait to see how far she could take it.

'I never thought the brand was going to be anything bigger than selling a few products from home and my website,' she said. From that little Bondi kitchen, The Beauty Chef grew into a pioneering brand that ignited a global movement and redefined beauty from within. With investment from Radek Sali's Light Warrior fund, her next goal is to use that investment to scale up, go wider and turn a homegrown idea into a household name.

Kirsten and Carla both began with almost nothing — six students in a dusty warehouse with a fax machine for bookings, and a few recipes and elixirs brewed in a saucepan on a kitchen bench in Bondi — yet each created something that travelled far beyond where they started. They followed their instinct, solved a problem people cared about, and built momentum by creating new opportunities based on what the market wanted.

Nuggets of wisdom

▸ Start where you are, sell what you know and solve a problem you've got.

▸ Don't rue your past, use your past. Turn your adverse childhood into an asset in adulthood.

▸ You don't need to spend thousands on a logo or website. Create an online presence but focus on creating a great product first and let word of mouth build momentum for you.

3

START SMALL, THINK BIG

It's hard to reconcile a global beauty brand like Bondi Sands with its humble beginnings: two men in a cramped Melbourne apartment, mixing formulas without a lab, funding the business with mortgages and parental loans, and doing everything themselves. Fourteen years later, that same business would sell for $450 million.

It's equally difficult to imagine Boost Juice starting in a suburban kitchen, with a founder juggling three children underfoot while experimenting with juice blends that would later form the basis of an international brand and be worth hundreds of millions of dollars.

Like many standout founders, these entrepreneurs didn't start with scale. They started with instinct. They thought big, took risks most people avoid, and put themselves under sustained pressure that made it impossible for them to back out.

A man, a can and a tan

'I need a tan for the Melbourne Cup, but I don't have time to get one.'

That offhand comment planted the seed for Bondi Sands, a tanning brand that would grow into a $450 million business in just over a decade.

Shaun Wilson was working at RACV in Melbourne's CBD as the Lifestyle and Wellbeing Manager. He was seriously credentialled: a degree in Applied Science, a Masters of Business, a Harvard course in Executive Leadership, and a desire for constant and never-ending improvement buried deep in his DNA.

His friend Blair James took a different path to entrepreneurship. A country boy from Yea in regional Victoria, he established his tanning salon a few years after leaving high school, catering to the young and gorgeous who wanted to look hot for a Saturday night.

But when their mutual friend uttered those memorable words about wanting a fast fake tan, they looked at each other and thought, why can't she get a tan right now? Why can't she do at home what Blair offered in the salon?

They took up the challenge. Blair got to work testing and tinkering with tan-at-home formulas. Shaun buried himself in marketing reports and global trends to see what future demand looked like.

'I wanted to know the market better than anyone,' Shaun said. 'I wanted to understand the customer and where the gaps were.'

The opportunity was obvious. Solariums were being banned due to skin cancer concerns and customers wanted a safer way to tan. Spray-tan appointments were booked out long in advance, and the off-the-shelf lotions were streaky, smelly and expensive. The category was shifting fast, and Blair, after years of running spray-tan salons, could see that demand was building.

Self-tanning was the answer, but the leading brand, St Tropez, was hard to use and distinctly un-Australian.

'No-one had captured the Australian lifestyle in a meaningful way,' Shaun said. 'People around the world saw Australia as having that beach culture, so why wasn't anyone owning it?'

They decided they would. But what would they call it?

St Kilda Sands? That won't fly.

What about Port Melbourne Sands? Still not right.

What beach represented the best of Australia? What name carried global recognition? What about Bondi?

The boys were from Melbourne, but that didn't matter. It had to be Bondi. And so it was on this day that Bondi Sands was born.

They didn't have a lab, so Blair worked in the back room of his salon, tinkering with active ingredients until he found a formula that produced a natural colour. They didn't have a boardroom, so decisions were made in Shaun's study, which Blair eventually moved into when the rent money ran out. Apart from Shaun's father, Garry Wilson — a former Fitzroy player and AFL Hall of Fame star who invested $200 000 to get them started — they had no other investors. To bridge the gap, they mortgaged their homes and invested over $600 000 in total between them. They didn't have staff either, so they did everything themselves: they answered the phone, wrote the copy, maintained the socials, tested the products and even built the website.

The early wins were small: a few loyal salon clients who loved the colour, a handful of stores willing to trial the product, and a modest order from Priceline that felt like a breakthrough. Then came the early loss that nearly cost them the business.

Six months after launching, while the pair were in the United States trying to crack their first international account, messages started coming through on Facebook. 'My skin is turning green!' one message said. 'I look like Kermit the Frog,' said another. One complaint they could understand. But dozens? Something was seriously off.

It was the formula. Their first batch was fine, the second wasn't. They'd altered the formula and rushed the testing, which was how the flaw was missed.

They flew home immediately to stem the crisis. Twenty thousand units had to be recalled. It was the kind of nightmare that ends most startups: bad press, bad product, bad timing. But Shaun went straight to the Priceline team, explained what had gone wrong and promised to resolve it, and he did.

'Priceline was great about it. We pulled the product, paid for the costs, went back to the lab and fixed it. It cost us $330 000 but it was a great lesson. Don't rush it, test it.'

The banks were good about it too. 'Our purchase orders proved we had demand. We told them the truth, they extended our terms and they lent us more money to pay for the stuff-up.'

The product recall also revealed just how powerful social media was. The green-batch complaints turned up on Facebook long before the retailers had even noticed something was wrong. They figured that if customer's complaints could travel that fast and have that power to sink them, those same customers, and the platforms they were on, could also send their marketing efforts into overdrive.

Shaun and Blair weren't social media natives, and didn't know a lot about digital marketing so they were starting from behind.

'We knew enough to know we were bad at it,' Shaun said, 'which is why one of our first hires was someone who lived and breathed social. Tanning is visual, so we had to use the most visual platform, and that was Instagram.'

Thousands of followers quickly became hundreds of thousands.

Then came the moment that changed everything.

In 2018, Kylie Jenner posted.

The post wasn't a gift or a gesture of goodwill from Kylie. It was a brand deal, and a very expensive one at that, especially for a new business still being bootstrapped by the founders with just 20 employees.

'We got in touch with Kylie's people and discovered she had already used and loved our product, so that was a great start. It cost us $300 000 and we got one post in return.'

It was a ride-or-die moment. Everything rested on that one Insta post.

They'd done the maths. Kylie wasn't just a celebrity; with more than 136 million followers, she was the most influential beauty voice in the world. If Bondi Sands wanted to enter the United States with authority, they needed cultural leverage, and Kylie could give it to them.

Shaun and Blair used the post strategically. They were due to meet with Walgreens, the biggest pharmacy chain in the United States — which was another make-or-break moment — and wanted them to see they were a brand worth dealing with. 'I wanted to be on their radar before we had the meeting.'

To achieve that goal, they made sure Kylie's post appeared in the Walgreen buyers' feeds, so by the time the meeting rolled around, they'd already know about Bondi Sands.

The post went live and the internet went wild.

'We had a PR team amplify the content and it got picked up all around the world. It went nuts.'

But behind the glamour, the reality for Shaun and Blair was still grinding. They were heavily involved with everything — answering queries, packing orders, coordinating photo shoots, doing deliveries — working out of tiny, rented offices and borrowing from family when funds were tight. But they kept going because their instincts told them they were onto something and the sales coming in confirmed it.

The world wanted a safer way to tan, they had the formula, the brand and the right price point. The conditions were finally in their favour.

Kylie's post worked. Within a few years, Bondi Sands had become Australia's number one self-tanning brand, with more than 70 per cent market share and distribution across 40 000 stores globally. By 2018, it was the number one tanning brand in the UK, and by 2021, the number one brand in the world. The company added sunscreen and skincare to the range, developed dozens of new ancillary products like tanning mitts, and maintained local manufacturing to keep the quality high. Their US strategy snowballed, cemented by partnerships with global retailers like Superdrug, Boots, Walgreens and Walmart.

In 2023, just over a decade after starting, Kao acquired Bondi Sands for over $450 million. Blair and Shaun pocketed $150 million each, and Garry received over $100 million for his $200 000 investment.

And it all began in a tiny apartment with two friends who saw an opportunity and decided to think big. Sometimes starting small just means starting where you are, even if where you are is nowhere near Bondi.

Three tips to grow the core

Most first-time founders launch too many products too early. The best strategy is to focus on one hero product, test it, build demand and grow from there.

1 Focus on the core
Start with one profitable product. Refine it, improve it and wait to see how it goes.

2 Expand the core
Once the product is established, leverage its strengths by adding tight line extensions that stay close to what already sells.

3 Innovate into new categories
When the line extension succeeds, expand into new product categories.

After Shaun had validated his core self-tanning 'dark foam' product, he extended it to the 'ultra dark foam' product, and then innovated to enter the accessories category with tanning mitts, tanning robes, pillow protectors and more.

Similarly, once Carla Oates had validated her core Glow product, she extended it to Glow Ageless and then innovated to enter the skincare category with Glow Face and other ancillary products.

See figures 3.1 and 3.2 (overleaf).

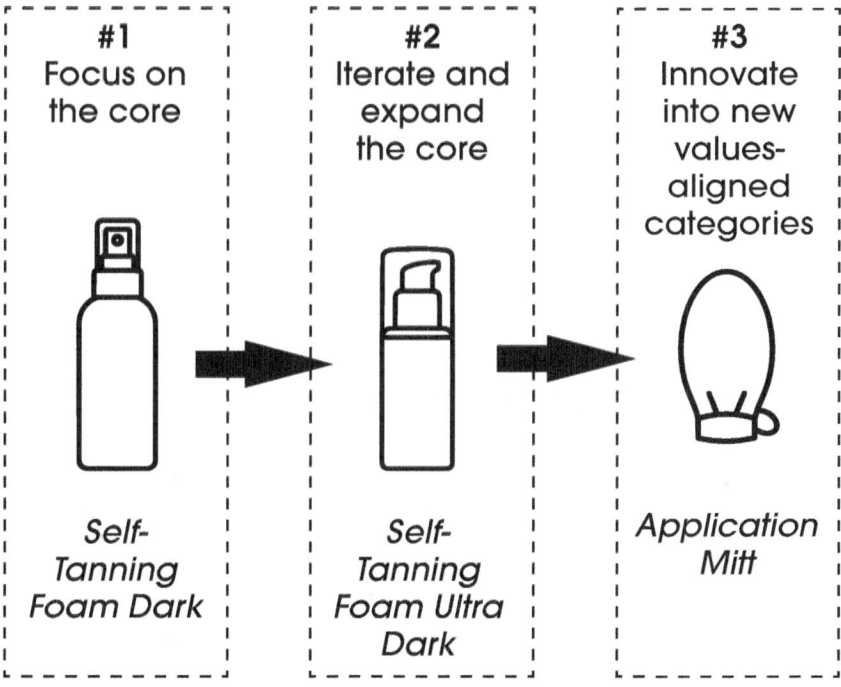

Figure 3.1 the 'grow the core' formula for launching the Bondi Sands products

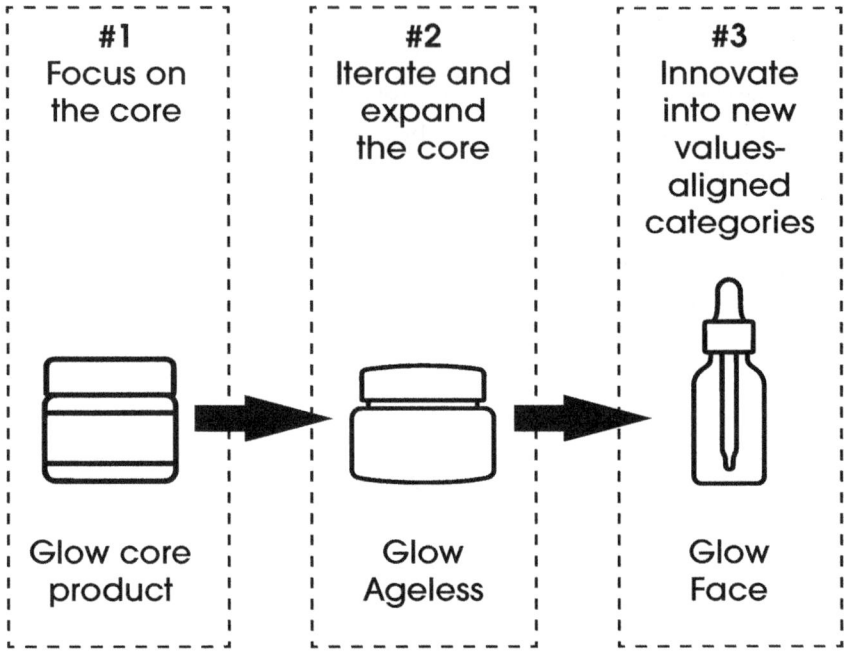

Figure 3.2   the 'grow the core' formula for launching the Glow products

This juice was worth the squeeze

Janine Allis didn't start with a plan, or a degree, or a safety net. She left home in Melbourne's southern suburb of Knox at 21 years of age, with a backpack, a formidable work ethic and enough curiosity to carry her across continents. She worked as a nanny in France, sold timeshare in Portugal, and spent two years as crew on David Bowie's private yacht, mixing with luminaries like Princess Margaret, Robin Williams and Mick Jagger. She studied people long before she studied business, and without realising it, learned the first principle of success: it wasn't so much about *who* you knew but about *how* you showed up.

Six years later, at 27, she landed back on her parents' doorstep with a suitcase in one hand and a baby in the other. Having a baby wasn't part of the plan, but Janine took whatever work she could find to support herself and her baby and got on with living life. Job by job, she built something more powerful than a résumé: belief in her own resourcefulness.

Life changed when she met Jeff, a senior executive at Austereo Radio. Living together within six weeks, married in eight months, pregnant within the year, they shared the same drive, appetite for risk and belief that life rewarded those who took the leap.

The idea for Boost Juice began at home. In 1999, after seeing the explosion of healthy fast food on a trip to the United States, Janine came back convinced Australia was ready for juice bars. No-one believed healthy fast food could beat burgers and fries, but she'd seen the data. She was already a home juicer, blending fruit at her kitchen bench with her toddlers underfoot, adjusting recipes based on whatever her family and friends thought tasted good.

'People thought there was a grand strategy,' she said. 'But it was just me testing juices at home.'

They opened their first store in Adelaide in 2000. It started with a bang, literally. The shop was packed and Janine thought, 'This is incredible. We haven't even started marketing and they're lining up.' Only later did she learn the crowd was there because of a bomb scare in the sushi store next door. When the panic dissipated, so did the crowd.

But those same people came back the next day, and the day after that, and the day after that. Demand was so strong the store was profitable within a few weeks of opening. Every dollar earned went straight back into the business.

Then came the moment that defined the next decade. Jeff secured 18 retail sites with Westfield and landed them with a $5 million liability.

'There was no way we could afford it,' Janine said. 'We mortgaged the house anyway. Fear was a huge motivator. We had everything on the line. At 34, with three kids, losing the house wasn't an option.'

They worked quickly and efficiently, opening 18 stores in 18 months. Janine worked until 1 am most nights, breastfeeding between meetings, learning accounting from a QuickBooks tutor, firing people who didn't fit and solving problems as fast as they arrived. It was exhausting, but as she said, 'No-one gives a shit how you feel. You just do it.'

The setbacks came thick and strong. She was underestimated, overlooked and taken advantage of, but she refused to be a victim. 'Everything that went wrong put us in the best position later,' she said.

By 2004, they were opening a new store every week, with each location generating around $1 million in weekly turnover. Janine was building systems, spreadsheets and processes at a pace that earned her the nickname 'Task Queen' for her dexterous use of Outlook's Task function. That same year, she landed on the BRW Young Rich List; a hilarious result considering she was earning just $35 000 a year, the lowest salary among her small but growing team.

Like Kirsten Tibballs, Janine recognised that an online profile could lift a brand, so she said *yes* to every media opportunity that came her way, which ultimately led to high-profile podcast appearances, *Shark Tank*, *Survivor* and a reality series called *Gordon Ramsay's Food Stars* featuring Janine as one of the lead investors. Every appearance expanded her audience and converted more customers to the Boost mission.

In 2007, she and Jeff formed Retail Zoo, an entity created to acquire and scale complementary food brands. They bought Salsa's Fresh Mex, then CIBO Espresso, then launched Betty's Burgers. In 2010, a private equity firm, Riverside, took a stake; in 2014, Bain Capital bought in, leaving Janine as the remaining founder–owner.

From a single store in Adelaide to more than 900 stores across Australia and around the world, Janine is now Chairman of Retail Zoo, leading a portfolio of well-known brands and is one of Australia's most recognisable founders.

'There's nothing special about me,' she said. 'I didn't finish year 12. I didn't go to university and I'm a shocking speller. If I can do it, anyone can.'

* * *

The founders who prevail are the ones prepared to fail: the ones who take the risks that others won't. They make big bets, paint themselves into corners from which they can't easily escape and do what's required to make it all work. Pressure is what makes them perform, which in turn creates the momentum needed to maintain growth. The costs are commensurate with reward but it's the ability to hold their nerve and find solutions to intractable problems that makes them successful.

Nuggets of wisdom

▶ Listen closely to everyday conversations for complaints and frustrations. Those whispers reveal unmet needs and opportunities.
▶ Clients will often forgive mistakes if you admit to them first. Own them, apologise and fix them quickly.
▶ There's never a perfect time to start a new business. Commit yourself to an audacious goal that you cannot walk away from, and then work like crazy to deliver on it.

4

START WITH HEART

Not everyone sets out to be an entrepreneur, but sometimes people just going about their lives stumble across something they can't unsee: an inequality, an imbalance or a flaw in the system that gnaws at them so persistently they can't keep living like they used to. Something has to shift, it's either them or the world they're living in. When it's both, the groundwork is set for something remarkable to emerge: an upswell that creates a spark bright enough to light up lives far beyond their own.

One child at a time

'My life shouldn't be this difficult,' said the Hollywood A-list actor as he stepped aboard his private Gulfstream jet. His grievance? The crew had forgotten to stock his favourite bottle of Glenlivet scotch.

Those words were directed at Scott Neeson, president of 20th Century Fox and the man behind some of the biggest films in history, including *Titanic*, *Independence Day*, *Spider-Man* and *Star Wars*.

It was July 2003. Scott had wrapped up his contract at Fox and was five weeks away from starting as head of Sony Pictures. His route to Hollywood had been anything but direct. He'd grown up in Elizabeth, a working-class town 30km north of Adelaide, worked in a range of odd jobs, including as a projectionist at a local drive-in, and had zigzagged his way up the studio ladder to become one of the most influential executives in Hollywood.

'It had been a very stressful few years, so I went backpacking through Asia for three weeks to decompress. I ended up in Phnom Penh and was taken to see the garbage dump just outside the city.'

That dump was Stung Meanchey, a landfill known internationally as Smoky Mountain. It was as long as 11 football fields and piled as high as a four-storey building. It heaved with heat, smoke and the sour stench of decay. As Scott took the phone call from the irate actor, he stared out over the landfill and noticed flashes of colour moving through the sludge. At first, he thought they were objects. Then he realised they were children — some no older than four — crawling across the steaming waste, scavenging for something to eat or sell.

He quickly discovered the landfill was more than a dumping ground, it was a gathering place for over a thousand children who called it their 'workplace' and, in many cases, their 'home'. Mountains of food scraps, hospital waste, car parts and human waste formed a toxic maze. Methane bubbled beneath the surface, creating pockets of fire that ignited without warning, burning the soles of the children's bare feet as they searched for anything of value.

'I had seen poverty before, but I had never seen a place like this,' recalled Scott. 'There were kids everywhere. In some cases, they'd been left there by parents who didn't want them. It was like standing at the edge of the apocalypse, staring into the abyss.' Scott met a little girl who lived at the dump. 'She'd never been to school and was ill from malnutrition. She couldn't go because the family relied on the few cents she earned foraging on the mountain.'

Scott understood the complexity of what he was seeing. Poverty on this scale didn't have simple solutions. The world's largest charities already knew about Stung Meanchey. He figured if they couldn't fix it, what chance did he have? But he also knew that complexity didn't absolve him of responsibility. There were things he couldn't change, but there were small things he could. Helping the little girl who stood in front of him was one of them.

What struck Scott most was that the little girl didn't ask for money, or even food. 'She just wanted the chance to go to school.' For Scott, that was the compelling moment that spurred him to take action.

He began by finding housing for the girl and her mother in a nearby village. The shack was located in a run-down part of town where the squatters lived. It was ramshackle and rudimentary, but it had running water. 'I asked the translator to call in on her every few weeks, and to make sure they had regular supplies of food and essentials so she could get to school.' Back at his hotel that night, he replayed the day: the heat, the stench, the burning rubbish, the little girl's request to go to school.

'In under an hour and for less than $15 a month, I had changed the trajectory of that girl's life forever. She was born on that garbage dump and would probably die there. The idea that this was 'someone else's responsibility' evaporated, because what I'd done had actually worked; not as a symbolic gesture, but as a real intervention: a safe house, regular meals and a chance at education where none existed before. I couldn't not help. I couldn't unsee what I'd seen.'

So, he went back the next day and helped another child. He went the day after that and helped another child, and then another and another, day after day, child after child. It didn't take long before he found himself asking the question that would rewrite the course of his life: *If I can change the lives of six children, why not eight? Why not 20? Why not 100?*

The contrast was jarring: an actor raging about his missing bottle of whisky, and children clawing through burning waste to survive. It stripped everything back to its essence. He realised the Hollywood life he'd been living couldn't coexist with what he'd just experienced.

'What I'd seen made it really difficult to return and start my new job. I'd just witnessed these atrocious situations, and then I'd be in a meeting in a palatial office discussing the most trivial things about an upcoming film. It all seemed so superficial.'

The life he had built — the prestige, the pay cheques, the access, the status — quickly lost its allure.

'I'd stare out the window, wondering how those children I sponsored were going, and what would happen to the thousands of others who lived on the mountain.'

In 2004, 12 months after that backpacking trip, he resigned.

It was not an impulsive decision. He had spent a year thinking it through. But as that year came to an end, the thought of what those children were enduring — and how dangerous their lives remained — made it impossible for him to maintain his current lifestyle.

He sold his house, car, boats and possessions, left Hollywood, moved to Phnom Penh and, using his own funds from the sale of his worldly goods, founded the Cambodian Children's Fund.

Twenty years later, he's still there.

CCF now employs more than 300 staff and provides education, healthcare and shelter to thousands of children from Phnom Penh's poorest communities.

The man who once measured success in box-office receipts now measured his life by a very different metric.

'There's a wonderful moment,' he said, 'when you see a child who once had no light in their eyes now laughing, happy and full of hope. That's the real reward.'

Scott uses his Hollywood backstory unapologetically. 'It gets attention,' he said. 'If that story can shine light on what matters, I'll tell it until its currency runs out, or I do.'

What set Scott apart from the hundreds of charities in similar conditions wasn't who he was, but how he used his skills, credibility and experiences to create an impact.

First, he leveraged his business background and personal assets to help establish the fund.

'Everyone tells you that you can't do anything, that things can't be fixed, that it's too complex, but working in Hollywood taught me that anything was possible. I was good at taking complex problems and breaking them down into actionable tasks, creating contingencies and having a long-term plan.'

Second, he amplified his personal profile. With nearly half a million Facebook followers and a contact book with Harrison Ford and Heather Graham on speed dial, he treated his digital footprint the same way any savvy entrepreneur treats a platform: as a spotlight.

And third — the one thing most charities struggle with — data and digital communications.

'Reporting was our strong suit,' he said. 'I was used to being accountable, transparent and managing numbers. People wanted to know where their money was going and who it helped. We did that really well, and it's part of the reason people chose us as their charity of choice.'

Donor Phil Hawkins said, 'What we appreciated most was the timeliness of their online communications. Their emails were clear, comprehensive and outlined exactly how the process worked. We knew exactly what to expect and when. They also kept us in touch with how our sponsored child was going, which made us feel very connected to how our funds were being spent.'

The little girl Scott met on that first day — the child picking through burning waste for scraps — now has a law degree. She is flourishing, as are the thousands who followed her.

A reminder that change begins when one person with heart steps up and chooses to start.

Food for thought

Ronni Kahn's OzHarvest story began with a table laden with exquisite food she couldn't bear to throw away. Her events business staged conferences and expos for the corporate elite. After one lavish night, after all the guests had gone home, she discovered that the mountain of food she had prepared for the event had gone untouched. Her inebriated clients had been so busy drinking they hadn't bothered to eat.

This was nothing new. She had tossed out loads of leftovers before, but something about this night felt wrong. It was the extravagance, the waste — it felt obscene. She couldn't explain why this felt so different, but she just knew she couldn't toss this food out like she'd done before. So, she loaded the trays into the back of her van and drove to the nearest charity she could find. It was well after midnight, but the charity didn't care. They took the food with open arms. They couldn't believe their luck.

A week later it happened again: another gala, another glut of untouched food. She took it to another shelter, and then another. Night after night, event after event, she delivered food across the city.

She asked one charity if they knew of any others who needed help. They hesitated, worried their own supply might shrink. 'There's plenty for everyone,' said Ronni. One charity led to another, then another. She started making a list of who needed what, and where. That was how her database got started.

She ran events by day — 'I still needed to work. I wasn't a rich, bored housewife'— and delivered food by night.

Her database was rudimentary and inefficient, but she felt like she was making a difference, and for the first time in years, she felt better about the work she was doing and the impact she was making.

Her deeper purpose crystallised years later on a trip to South Africa. A childhood friend took her through Soweto — once a place no white person would ever enter — now a sprawling city of millions. As they drove through the streets, her friend, also a social entrepreneur, casually mentioned she'd helped bring electricity to three million people who had previously lived without it.

Ronni was stunned. 'It was like a lightbulb went on inside me,' she said. 'I wanted to know what it would feel like to make that kind of impact on that many lives.'

She flew home like a woman possessed. If electricity could transform a city, food rescue could transform a nation. She started with a single van and a fierce determination to build something that didn't yet exist. The beginnings of OzHarvest were slowly forming, from the simple conviction that when so many people are hungry, perfectly good food should never go to waste.

How OzHarvest scaled into a global movement

Ronni didn't try to raise money for her charity through traditional funding channels. She funded it by leveraging her own business and by securing practical resources like office space and vans from supportive partners.

One van became two, then four, then a fleet. The real turning point came when Ronni discovered a simple off-the-shelf software package called Crittah. Overnight, her team could now see every van on a live map, redirect drivers in real time and collect food before it spoiled. Until then, they'd relied on phone calls, guesswork and luck: an expensive, slow and unreliable way to run a fast-moving charity.

Over time, the software evolved into a bespoke dashboard that tracked every pick-up, delivery, donor and data point, enabling OzHarvest to rescue more food, reach more charities and respond faster than ever.

Today, OzHarvest has almost 400 staff, a fleet of 85 vehicles and operations across every Australian state. Ronni has since shared the model with teams in the UK, Japan, South Africa,

Vietnam and New Zealand, extending a simple idea far beyond anything she could have imagined that first night in her van.

'Feeding people is a gift,' she said. 'I'm just the vessel.'

Her purpose never changed, but the digital tools with which she achieved it, did, and with them, her impact: proof that when mission and method align, one small act of kindness can scale into a global movement.

Some entrepreneurs don't start because they want to, they start because they have to. They can't sit back and wait for others to do what needs to be done. They follow their conscience, and in doing so, step into a role they never planned for but can no longer ignore. By putting service ahead of self, they unlock a capacity that carries them further than ambition alone ever could.

Nuggets of wisdom

▸ Don't wait for permission to do what you think is right. Do it and deal with the consequences later. If your intentions are good, most unintended consequences can be fixed.

▸ Use data to build credibility. Whether it's investors or donors, show them exactly how the money is being spent, who it helps and what impact it has. Transparency leads to trust.

▸ Don't assume you need to buy custom software at the start. See what's available off the shelf and then customise it to suit your needs.

5

START WITH WHY

Business author Simon Sinek talks about finding your 'why'; about how people will push further and endure more when they're driven by something bigger than themselves. Childhood memories can influence our 'why' long before we realise it. Watching a parent struggle, persist or be dismissed can leave a mark so deep it forms the blueprint for how we move through the world. It impacts the work we choose, the problems we try to solve and the people we feel compelled to help. For some, those early experiences become a lifelong call to service.

A lost lifestyle

For Kobi Simmat, that 'why' crystallised early. At 15, he stood on the balcony of his family's five-level home on the Hawkesbury River and watched as the sheriff took possession of his beloved home.

His architect father had trusted the wrong people, made the wrong decisions and lost control of his business. In a single afternoon, the house, the boating lifestyle, the poolside parties and the carefree existence he'd known had vanished. He and his family were cast out, humiliated, suitcases in hand, forced to find a rental far from the community they'd called home.

'You don't appreciate what you have until it's taken away,' he said. 'Losing that lifestyle made me hungry to get it back.'

Getting it back became his goal. At 15, he made himself a promise: when he grew up, he would learn the rules of business so thoroughly that he would not only rebuild what his family had lost, and retrieve that lost lifestyle, but he would also teach other business owners how to protect themselves from befalling the same fate.

He saw how fragile small businesses were and how vulnerable good people were to bad advice from malevolent partners. He vowed to understand the rules of the business game more deeply than most, and help others do the same.

That purpose shaped everything that came next.

He built a business around accreditation, ISO standards and audits — work most people consider dull — but Kobi didn't see it that way: he saw those reports and checklists as a form of insurance; a way to give businesses both a stable foundation from which to grow, and the technical credibility to compete for large-scale tenders that would otherwise be out of reach.

But to protect as many business owners as possible, he needed reach, scale and a megaphone to spread the word about his corporate services and coaching courses, and that's when he hit the marketing wall. He knew he wanted to leverage social media and go big; he just didn't know how to do it.

Then an opportunity arose to attend a London conference with US entrepreneur Gary Vaynerchuk. The trip and ticket cost $100 000. He winced. He could barely afford to pay the rent, but he also knew that if nothing changed, nothing would change.

He slapped the fee on his credit card, got on the plane and went. Gary listened to Kobi's story and cut straight to the truth.

Gary: You're not making enough content. You need to post more.

Kobi: On YouTube?

Gary: On everywhere. How often do you post?

Kobi: Twice a week.

Gary: My friend, we have work to do. You need to get more active on social. By March, three months from now, you need to be posting 1000 pieces of content a week.

Kobi: A week?

Gary: A week. If you want to build a wall, you need bricks. Stop thinking, start implementing.

Kobi didn't fully understand the mechanics of how that would happen, but he understood obligation.

He and his team got to work. Ten posts a week became 20; 20 became 40. Soon they were creating close to a thousand pieces of content a week across LinkedIn, Instagram, (what was then) Twitter and YouTube.

At first, nothing happened, then not much, then something and then a lot. The phone started ringing, emails arrived, web leads spiked. It seemed the more content he produced, the more leads he created. Each post drew people in, each video opened a door, each coaching course gave someone a path forward. It was content at scale, driven by service, anchored in a purpose bigger than profit.

The quality of the early content was average, but it got better, and so did Kobi. People resonated with his honesty, his clarity, his experience. Sales of his consultancy service surged, he hired a team and the business flourished. Eventually, he built Best Practice Biz, a global business improvement and advisory agency so robust it was acquired by a British conglomerate for $20 million.

Kobi knew his why. He never forgot what losing everything felt like, and he never wanted anyone else to feel like that again.

Find your higher purpose

Radek Sali's purpose was shaped by watching his father, Avni, an Albanian immigrant and medical pioneer decades ahead of his time, fight to legitimise integrative medicine in a world that dismissed it. His father saw what others refused to see: that true health came from prevention, not just intervention.

Avni questioned why doctors were given seven years of training to cure disease, yet only one week's training on how to prevent it. When he suggested that nutrition, exercise and mindset could transform wellbeing, he was mocked by his medical peers. But he persisted, and over the decades, contributed to over 300 peer-reviewed papers, and his work became the foundation of modern integrative medicine, which culminated in the formation of the National Institute of Integrative Medicine.

That courage to lead with conviction became Radek's mission.

It shaped how he led Swisse, taking it from 30 staff and $15 million in revenue to 300 staff and a $2.1 billion sale in 10 years.

He fused mission with innovation long before wellness became mainstream, blending science, brand and ambition in a way Australian supplements companies had never attempted before. Under his leadership, Swisse transformed from being a local vitamin brand into a global wellness business.

That shift changed everything. Swisse became one of the earliest Australian brands to embrace celebrity-led influence, signing global names like Kim Kardashian and investing millions in marketing that propelled Swisse onto the international stage. He paired scientific credibility with star power and turned Swisse into a global force by leveraging online marketplaces like Tmall years before other brands knew platforms like this even existed.

Cross-border e-commerce then did what traditional expansion never could: it connected Swisse directly to millions of Chinese consumers and accelerated its rise onto the global stage.

At every step, Radek's decisions were anchored in a clear purpose: improving health outcomes while building a brand bold enough to compete with global giants.

That same instinct to help others lead healthier lives carried him into his next chapter. After selling Swisse, he and his wife, Helen, spent long stretches in Los Angeles while undergoing multiple rounds of IVF. Between medical appointments, they wandered the aisles of Erewhon, the upmarket organic grocer beloved by the Hollywood elite. There he spotted a new category — liquid herbal extracts — flying off the shelves. They were potent, clean, fast-absorbing and rooted in naturopathy and Ayurvedic medicine. It was everything he believed wellness should be.

He didn't want to start a new business from scratch — he always preferred to buy businesses with an existing 'drumbeat', so he searched for a platform with a heartbeat. That search led to Wanderlust, a global yoga community with 1 million members that had run into financial difficulties, but still had an active audience. He bought the brand, revived it and merged music festivals, liquid extracts and wellness education into a new marketing flywheel. He engaged movie stars like Drew Barrymore and Jane Fonda, along with yoga ambassadors, health practitioners and musician activists, to introduce a new product category to the market and deliver a fresh wave of consumers directly to the door and online store of his pharmacy partners.

But Radek's mission ran deeper than just growing the business. He believed companies had a responsibility to lift the collective wellbeing of society, not as a side project, but as a core operating principle.

'Imagine if everyone loved going to work. What would that do to society?' he asked.

That belief shows up tangibly across his businesses. Through Light Warrior Group and Wanderlust, purpose became embedded in how people were employed, supported and empowered. Teams received paid volunteer leave, matched payroll giving, and budgets to contribute directly to causes they cared about. Both organisations actively support First Nations initiatives, women's empowerment, health and community wellbeing, and have formal action plans spanning reconciliation, equal pay, social procurement, pro bono work and B Corp commitments.

Radek has long argued that governments should reward companies that genuinely invest in great workplaces, because when people feel valued and energised at work, that effect ripples outward into families, communities and society at large.

For Radek, it always comes back to priorities. When purpose is the passion and people sit at the centre of decision making, profit follows.

* * *

Some entrepreneurs are driven by opportunity; some by money; others by memories shaped by a defining moment that lodges itself deep enough to influence every decision that follows. When that inner 'why' is clear, work transforms from being something you *have* to do, into something you *want* to do.

Nuggets of wisdom

▶ Post more content. Even if no-one is engaging and there is no evidence that it's working, just keep posting. Do it for long enough, and the tide will turn.

▶ Connect your business with a powerful purpose. It will give you staying power when you feel like giving up.

▶ Don't start a business from scratch. Buy one with an existing heartbeat, or drumbeat. Check out Flippa.com, an online marketplace for buying and selling websites, apps and digital businesses with established traffic and revenue.

6

KNOW YOUR BUSINESS

My teenage son beats me at Scrabble, every time. It's annoying. I'm three times his age, an award-winning author and have been doing word puzzles since before he was born. He's barely out of high school, rarely reads a book and thinks a magazine is a broken iPad. And yet he always wins.

It wasn't always like this. Everything changed the day he did something I'd never bothered to do: he memorised every two-letter word in the Scrabble dictionary. Last night he scored 66 points with a single tile: a Z placed on a triple-word square, played both ways as ZA and ZE. Since when were ZA and ZE words? Since the Scrabble dictionary said so.

Does he have a bigger vocabulary than me? No. Is he smarter? Possibly. Does he know the rules of Scrabble better? Absolutely.

In business, as in Scrabble, success belongs to those who study how the game *really* works. You don't need to be the most talented person in the room to win. You just need to understand the rules better than anyone else in the room.

Understand the rules

James 'Jimmy' Donaldson, aka MrBeast, is the world's top YouTuber and has more than 460 million subscribers. James began posting on YouTube when he was a teenager, experimenting with gaming videos and commentary content. His breakthrough came in 2017 when the video he posted a video of himself counting from one to 100 000 went viral. From there he scaled up his content to incorporate high-stakes challenges, elaborate giveaways and spectacular stunts.

'There's a five-year point in my life where I was just relentlessly, unhealthily obsessed with studying virality, studying the YouTube algorithm,' Donaldson told *Rolling Stone*. 'I woke up. I would Uber Eats food. And then I would sit on my computer all day just studying shit nonstop with [other YouTubers].' He watched thousands of videos, to understand why some were successful and others weren't. He studied the retention curves, analysed the thumbnails and observed the first five seconds of every trending video. The goal? To learn the rules of YouTube; not just the official ones, but the unofficial ones too. MrBeast made it his business to know everything about how the YouTube game worked, and it paid off. As of 2024, his company, Beast Industries, reportedly generated $473 million in revenue. He's yet to turn 30.

If you want to win, don't rely on talent. Learn the rules. The ones who win big are the ones who understand the game they're playing.

Keep asking until you get answers

Janine Allis also believed you have to know everything about your business to succeed.

'During those early years, I made sure that I understood every aspect of every decision I made. I took the time in every area to come to the right decision, from dealing with the franchising and trademarks to working on supplier relations.'

Janine rarely used outside suppliers for advice about franchising, legal and marketing because she wanted to make sure everyone who worked on Boost had 100 per cent focus on Boost at all times.

'I was a total control freak. I needed to know everything. If you thought that running a business required you to have good systems and processes in place,' she said, 'well, multiply that pressure by 10 to get closer to the requirements once you franchise.'

Setting up a franchise is not for the faint-hearted. The Franchise Code of Conduct needs to be followed closely, and you need to have meticulous systems in place that track sales, leads, overheads, marketing costs, wages and more.

'Your business needs to be in great shape before you franchise. And once it is, you need to continually invest in digital systems to keep your business robust.'

She said, 'When you're starting something from nothing, every detail matters. Everything. Even the distance between the blenders matters. If they're too close they'll blow up; too far apart and it disrupts the workflow. I had to make sure every manager had a checklist and every process was clear. That level of detail wasn't my husband's strength, but it was mine. I was in my element, but the pressure to get everything perfect felt enormous.'

So, she did the thing she was really good at: she asked questions, and lots them.

'I stopped caring if the questions made me look inexperienced,' she said. 'I started questioning documents, challenging assumptions, and I realised something surprising: common sense was quite uncommon. I discovered that just being sensible went a long way in getting things done.'

The more she asked, the more she learned.

'I discovered how often the so-called experts got things wrong. I'd put them on a pedestal, but half the time they didn't know as much as I thought they did.'

Bit by bit, she stopped leaning on her husband and other experts, and gradually, day by day, she developed the confidence to tackle the harder problems.

'It was 2000, GST had just come in, and we were off and running. I went out and bought a copy of QuickBooks. Then I hired a QuickBooks expert to come to my home and teach me how to use the bloody thing.'

She laughed at the memory.

'I had no idea about accounting. None. But I was determined to understand the financial and technical sides so I'd know my business inside and out.'

A very long apprenticeship

Vince Lebon never set out to build a global footwear brand. He just wanted to solve a problem. His wife, Kat, nicknamed Rollie, was a flight attendant who needed a shoe that was light enough to pack in a carry-on, comfortable enough for 12-hour days and stylish enough to wear out at night. Most people would have suggested better insoles. Vince didn't. He went down a shoe-shaped rabbit hole. He's yet to come out.

He became obsessed with shoes. He studied the anatomy of feet, the physics of gait, the chemical composition of EVA foam and the way air moved through leather. He cut open soles and peeled apart uppers; he tested every lace, eyelet and outsole, and then tore them down again. He didn't just learn the rules of shoemaking — he ingested them.

When he finally built the first Rollie prototype, a shoe so light it felt like air, it was the culmination of a 10-year apprenticeship built on obsessive attention to details most people never noticed. Vince didn't just know his product; he knew everyone else's too.

His superpower emerged early. In high school he excelled in digital media, particularly Photoshop, and built a portfolio so impressive he was given permission to skip university and go straight into an Advanced Diploma of Electronic Design and Interactive Media. He dreamed of working in a bustling design studio surrounded by animators and filmmakers, but the big 3D animation hub planned for Docklands in Melbourne's CBD collapsed before launch. So, he hit the streets and knocked on every door to find a job. None opened, except for one at a local shoe company. It wasn't quite what he was expecting, but it was better than nothing.

He was tasked with graphic design work, but after six months, got bored and walked into his boss' office to see what else he could work on.

'I like designing graphics,' he said, 'but I'd rather be designing a product.' His boss shrugged. 'Go for it. Design me a shoe collection.'

So, he did. He created a series of shoe designs in Photoshop that looked so sharp and crisp, people couldn't tell if it was a computer-rendered image or the real thing. It didn't matter because the buyers loved them so much, they put down an order for over 3000 pairs, before a single shoe had even been made. His boss was so delighted with what Vince had made, he asked him to stay on as a shoe designer.

Vince spent the next six years travelling the shoe world. He attended trade shows in Europe, visited factory floors in Asia and spent long nights testing and trying what he thought the public might like next. He did what many would call an *apprenticeship.* Then he made Kat her shoe: a lightweight, durable sneaker in a spectrum of rainbow colours to match her personality. It was exactly what she wanted.

To test if others might like the shoe, he set up a tiny stall at the South Melbourne Market in 2012. Within weeks, the entire first collection sold out. What started as a single prototype for his wife became the foundation of his business.

His industry contacts helped him secure global retail distribution almost overnight. When Rollie Nation moved online, Vince built everything himself. He coded the website, designed the graphics, wrote the copy, packed orders, printed labels and hauled the boxes to Australia Post. He had done every job in the chain, so he understood the entire system better than anyone.

People think Rollie was an overnight success. It wasn't. It was the result of 10 years of grind, travel and unglamorous work. Sure, the shoes looked good, but that's not why the brand took off. It succeeded because Vince *understoo*d shoes — the craft, the supply chain, the margins, the customer — better than anyone else in the room. Having sold over one million pairs of its iconic Derby shoes, the brand has transformed from a creative experiment into a high-growth business generating over $10 million in annual revenue. The brand continues to build momentum, earning recognition across the e-commerce industry, including Power Retail's Top 150 Online Retailers and Afterpay's Fastest Cross-Border Growth award. With a dedicated community of more than 111 000 passionate Instagram followers who like and share Rollie Nation shoes, doing that long apprenticeship has paid off for Vince.

Know the jargon

Shaun Wilson didn't have a background in the tanning industry, but he was committed to learning all about it.

While finishing his MBA, he chose the business of tanning as his major thesis; not because he loved bronzer, but because he saw a gap big enough in which to build a global brand. Salon spray tans were high quality but expensive and impossible to book at the last minute. DIY tans were cheap, uncomfortable and delivered poor results.

The opportunity lived in the space between those two options. Shaun made it his business to study it, dissect it and find a product to fit it.

The goal was simple: to create a DIY tan that looked good, was affordable and lasted.

To do that, Shaun went straight to the sources: chemists, formulators, salon owners, retailers, distributors and customers. He and his friend Blair James spoke to every chemist who would take their call, learned the chemistry behind DHA, dye structures, transfer resistance, shelf life and the rules and regulations that made it safe to use. They analysed St Tropez at the top end, supermarket brands at the bottom, pored over global reports and marketing trends, and mapped the exact technical and commercial gaps no-one else had been able to solve.

Shaun understood the tanning category inside out, but he quickly discovered another truth: you don't just need to know the rules of the retail *product*; you need to know the rules of the retail *game*.

'I got a bit caught out in the beginning. I didn't know the numbers that made retail work. I didn't even know what TPR was,' he said. 'I didn't realise if we discounted the product for the retailer, we paid for that gap. I thought the retailer absorbed it.'

Misunderstanding TPR — temporary price reduction — cost him. Every time Bondi Sands ran a promotion, he assumed Priceline or the pharmacies shared the discount. They didn't. He was footing the bill each time.

'The retailer never loses their margin,' he said.

That shock forced him to learn how the retail machine really worked. He studied the four Ps — price, place, product and promotion — until he knew exactly how to offer a $5 at-home tan that felt like an $85 salon tan. He dug into the fine print surrounding trade terms, margin protection, distribution models, ranging costs, planograms, discount structures, points of distribution and the financial mechanics that determined whether a brand survived or died on the shelf.

'All these things were new to me,' he said, 'but you have to work it out financially.'

Before he'd even set foot in a buyer meeting, he'd already mapped Priceline's strategy, Boots' positioning, Walgreens' corporate plans, the behavioural triggers of Gen Z and the digital landscape that would open the category to millions of women searching for a better tan at home.

By the time Bondi Sands launched, Shaun not only knew tanning — he knew the business better than anyone else in the room.

* * *

In a crowded market, where obvious points of difference are hard to find, knowing your business is the one advantage that costs nothing and can't be taken from you. Find the time to understand the rules, regulations, systems and structures that underpin not just your business, but the wider ecosystem around it. Know this better than your competitors and you'll create a compounding, defensible advantage that will be hard to beat.

Nuggets of wisdom

▶ Ask the uncomfortable questions, and keep asking *why* until you actually understand everything you need to know.
▶ Do an apprenticeship in your industry before striking out on your own. Learn the ropes from others and let them pay for your education.
▶ If you need to learn a new skill, hire an expert to teach you.

7

KNOW YOUR NUMBERS

Good entrepreneurs rely on instinct; the great ones validate it with data. Numbers reveal patterns, behaviours and opportunities that gut feel alone can't detect. If you don't know your numbers, you don't know your business, and the market will be an unforgiving teacher.

Find white space

Radek Sali understood this concept better than most. As CEO of Swisse, he was under pressure to lift sales and rebuild the board's confidence. Fortunately, he had invested in his financial education years earlier during his time at Village Cinemas, completing courses in accounting and data analytics. To put his studies into practice, he sought out datasets on a daily basis and devoured them. His goal was to uncover any hidden opportunities that would give him an edge over larger players who lacked the capacity, patience or capability to go as deep into the data. That grounding in numbers gave him the skills to read between the lines, see what others might miss and to present his business cases with conviction.

That preparation paid off.

'I did a deep dive into the sales data to see if it would reveal any insights that would help us find a new source of revenue or growth. That's when I noticed an anomaly: certain pharmacies in particular areas were selling 10 times more than stores elsewhere.'

He wondered why, so he kept digging.

He took to the road with his sales manager to learn more. In a Terry White pharmacy in Adelaide's Rundle Mall, they watched Chinese students loading boxes of Swisse products into suitcases.

'What's going on there?' he asked the pharmacy assistant.

'This happens all the time,' she said. 'They buy as much stock as they can and send it home. The gift of health is huge in China.'

Radek wondered: if this was happening in Adelaide, was it happening elsewhere too?

They spent the rest of the tour looking for sales spikes in Chinese-dominated suburbs to validate their hypothesis. Their instincts were correct. This was not just a one-off spike in sales in Adelaide, or in a few isolated suburbs; it was happening all over the country. Box Hill in Victoria. Chatswood in New South Wales. Robertson in Queensland. This was a trend and, judging from their sales results, it was growing stronger.

'We did some further research into the Chinese diaspora in Australia and the numbers were startling. One million Chinese nationals had migrated to Australia over the past five years; over one million Chinese tourists travelled to Australia each year; and over 400 000 Chinese students enrolled in an Australian educational institution that year,' said Radek.

Radek realised they had just found their next major source of growth: China.

They had unlocked a new export market without having to export it themselves. International students buying the products in Australia and shipping them home were doing it for them.

From that insight came Project Gold, Swisse's move into the daigou economy. (Daigous are personal shoppers who buy goods overseas and send them back home to resell online, acting as informal cross-border retailers.)

To service this new market, Radek commissioned a Mandarin-speaking customer service team and provided culturally appropriate marketing tools and product education for his pharmacy partners.

Then the online marketing flywheel kicked in. Within a year, more than 130 000 independent Chinese daigou sellers were selling Swisse products through the Taobao and Tmall platforms, turning a local vitamin brand into a cross-border e-commerce phenomenon.

That one spreadsheet anomaly became the source of a multi-million-dollar growth engine, and a key driver behind the company's eventual sale to Biostime.

* * *

When you take the time to truly understand your numbers, and commit to getting out from behind the desk and closer to customers, you may discover an entirely new market waiting to be uncovered.

Data equals trust

For Scott Neeson, founder of Cambodian Children's Fund (CCF), data was the backbone that secured the charity's future. His Hollywood backstory may have opened doors in the early days, but it was the transparent, verifiable numbers that kept the charity growing. Donors were inspired by his story, but they stayed because the numbers proved their donation made a difference.

The CCF data showed supporters exactly where their money went, kept the team accountable, and documented outcomes that could be tracked, audited and trusted.

Scott's 2024 Annual Report presented clear metrics about impact and allocation: the organisation delivered a 99 per cent pass rate for Grade 12 students, provided 173 200 meals and gave 56 450 kilograms of rice to 4495 needy cases. It allocated 85 per cent of its revenue to programs and services, 8 per cent to administration and 7 per cent to fundraising. CCF also maintained a four-star, 100 per cent rating from Charity Navigator for many consecutive years.

In addition, it was named a finalist in the 2024 Community Choice Awards, ranking in the top three charities in its financial category, and was the only child development organisation from Asia to be included in the final shortlist.

Another donor I spoke to said, 'We liked CCF because it was clearly well run. They told us when deductions would occur and payments were processed on time. Tax receipts arrived promptly, customer service answered questions quickly and their disclosure policies were transparent. We also received updates about our sponsored child. It gave us confidence in the organisation.'

By publishing audited annual reports, verifiable success stories and evaluation scores, CCF showed that its work was measurable and verifiable. Scott said, 'Transparency is everything. That's why we're dedicated to showing donors where the money goes and how it's used.'

This data-driven digital approach satisfied donors and became a unique selling point that put CCF above the thousands of other organisations vying for the charity dollar.

Track what works

Before he became the co-founder of Luxury Escapes, Adam Schwab was a lawyer, trained to sift through evidence, read the fine print and follow the logic wherever it led. That discipline informed the way he built businesses.

In 2010, Adam and long-time business partner, Jeremy Same, founded their first online business, Zoupon.com.au, which later became DEALS.com.au. Within three years, the business had evolved into the AussieCommerce Group, a fast-growing e-commerce empire spanning 14 brands across food, fashion, tourism and homewares.

The company won Deloitte's Leadership Award, was named the fastest-growing business by the Australian Financial Review and Adam was named Young Executive of the Year by *CEO Magazine*. By 2017 the business pivoted again, this time focusing on travel under the Luxury Escapes brand.

Adam and Jeremy met in high school when they were 15. Their partnership has lasted more than 20 years for many reasons, but one of them is because they stayed in their lanes.

'We're both good at different things and have huge respect for each other's abilities which is why it's worked so well. Jez has a great contrarian take — he's willing to take big calculated risks and can see around corners,' Adam said. 'I tend to handle execution and people.'

What also makes it work is how deeply Adam understands the numbers.

Every day, the Luxury Escapes data and analytics teams deliver a series of reports with thousands of lines, outlining every hotel, tour, flight deal, product and conversion pattern.

'There are about 6000 lines in the key report,' he said. 'We don't look at every line, but there are about 300 critical ones I go through carefully every day.'

He tracks what deals are performing, the margin on each view, the conversion rates, the value of each email sent and the cost of every marketing decision.

The metric that matters most? Conversion.

'For every time someone looks at a deal, I need to know how many dollars in margin we made,' he said. 'If the margin per view is high, the product resonates. If it's low, something's wrong.'

That metric determines everything: which deals get promoted, which channels they use and what and who gets emailed, texted, or contacted through WhatsApp.

'We want to send the right stuff to the right people at the right time,' Adam said. 'Families buy differently from retirees. Couples buy differently from solo travellers. If you get it wrong, you waste money. If you get it right, you scale.'

Luxury Escapes now uses algorithms and personalisation tools to tailor every message.

'We look at a lot,' Adam said. 'But the key thing is how each deal performs. We came from an online deals business. Maximising revenue for every partner still matters.'

Keep your hose clean

Pub baron Stephen Hunt spent a lot of time in hotels but he didn't necessarily want to own one. His goal was to play rugby for Australia. When he realised his talent didn't quite match his ambition, he had to find another path.

It arrived in the form of a $100 backyard bar.

When Stephen was 17, his dad transformed their backyard into a makeshift party zone: second-hand armchairs, eskies, a tarpaulin roof, and party lights.

'He must've wanted us kids out of the house pretty bad,' Stephen said. It worked. Every weekend he and his mates gathered there, and soon the crowd swelled into the hundreds.

His friends helped out: one handled food, one handled drinks, another watched the gate. When they ran low on beer one night, a mate said, 'Why don't we charge two bucks for each can left in the esky'. Stephen did, used the money to buy more cans of beer, sold them too, and finished the night $100 ahead.

'I looked around and saw everyone having the time of their lives because of something I'd created. It was exhilarating.'

His mate turned to him and said, 'I think you should do this for a living.'

'So do I, mate. So do I,' said Stephen.

That backyard bar became the blueprint for a life in hospitality. Stephen spent the next decade working in pubs: clearing glasses, washing dishes and mopping floors. By the time he bought his first venue, he knew exactly how the business worked and what it needed to succeed. His superpower? Numbers.

Pubs live and die by margins, and margins live and die by detail. Stephen knew the cost of every bottle, glass and keg.

'Numbers are the language of business,' he said, 'and if you don't speak it, you're already behind.'

His digital dashboard became the backbone of his empire. Real-time reporting showed him where money was made, where it leaked and what gaps needed to be plugged. That combination of a hands-on pub apprenticeship and numerical fluency made him an exceptional operator, and a compelling target for investment.

When he launched his pub investment fund, a high-net-worth investor tested him by asking, 'What does it cost to serve a single glass of Pepsi?' Stephen didn't flinch. He knew a box of syrup cost $116, so he ran the maths on the spot and delivered the exact figure. The investor was impressed. 'Anyone who knows their business at that level is someone I can trust,' they said. That single answer brought in more than $3 million in investment funds.

He knew his business the way a pilot knows their cockpit. Every number, every ratio, every ounce of alcohol was tracked in real time through reporting software he designed himself.

And nowhere was that obsession with data more important than in the draught beer system. In pub economics, cash flow is king and draught beer is the throne because 35 per cent of revenue comes from it. When you're pouring 30 000 beers on a big night, one weak link can topple the whole system.

Slow service means fewer beers sold. Fewer beers mean missing the rebate. Miss the rebate and the margins collapse. Lose the margins and investors walk away.

And at the centre of it all? A $10 hose.

The beer reticulation hose, the line from keg to tap, is a nightmare to clean, but if it's dirty, the beer tastes terrible, customers complain and a third of your revenue is suddenly at risk. Clean glasses, fast service, friendly staff are all important but if the hose is dirty, none of them matter. That, plus dozens of other one-percenters are the tiny details that not only boost the profit margins, but give Stephen clues for how a pub is tracking.

For example, when Stephen walks into a venue that may be up for sale, he scans for miniscule clues that the owner has stopped paying attention: a broken light bulb, a sticky counter, a sports television switched off, a torn bench seat. These one-percenters indicate value is already leaking, and that's where the opportunity to buy the pub at a discounted rate resides.

It took Stephen 30 years of working in pubs to become an overnight success. But that hands-on experience, combined with an MBA, a leadership course at Harvard and a Graduate Certificate in Applied Finance, gave him the foundation to build the reporting systems his venues still run on today. They allow his staff to operate independently so he can work *on* the business, not *in* it.

Today Stephen oversees a portfolio of pubs and a fund worth more than $100 million.

Investors don't invest in the business; they invest in the owner, and when the owner knows the numbers better than anyone else, they can deliver better outcomes than anyone else.

Check your phone

Jay Gardam, owner of Wynroy Hot Yoga in Adelaide, didn't have to go far to find his numbers. They were sitting on his phone. Jay runs his entire operation through the Mindbody app. Every enquiry, booking and payment is automatically logged, and generates instant reports on attendance, teacher performance, retention rates and revenue per class. Mindbody was acquired by Vista Equity Partners for US $1.9 billion, so the tech stack behind it is serious, and it shows.

'The data is so valuable,' Jay said. 'I can calculate the average revenue per class by analysing every membership type — six-month, 12-month, casual passes — and at all the different price points. Some members come 10 times a week, others three. By dividing total income across all attendance, I get a true picture of what each class earns.' That single calculation tells him everything he needs to know about how the studio is tracking: the profitability of each class, how the instructor is performing, which classes contribute to the bottom line and which ones cost him more than he makes.

Jay ties each teacher's performance to that one metric, so if their class numbers drop, he knows exactly what is going wrong, and how to fix it.

He studies attendance patterns and the source of student enrolments. If new clients arrive via word of mouth, it means the teacher is building loyalty. If the student comes via Instagram, it means his marketing is working. Those insights tell him whether the issue is the teaching quality or the advertising, and how to tweak each to ensure they operate at maximum efficiency.

The app also acts as his marketing engine. It sends automated push notifications to clients who have gone quiet, generates sales reports and promotes one-off events like International Yoga Day. It also monitors attendance without requiring any manual input. All those important functions — operations, retention and sales — sit inside the one dashboard so he can, with one push of a button, generate all the reports he needs to manage the business.

The app lets Jay run his studio without being in the studio, and the data reveals why things work or don't, so he doesn't have to rely on instinct.

* * *

If you want to beat the competitors, take the time to know your numbers: they tell you what's working, what's not, and what can be improved. Instinct might start a business, but numbers keep it growing.

Nuggets of wisdom

▶ Commit to knowing more about your business and industry than anyone else. If you don't have the budget to outspend competitors, deep market intelligence can be your point of difference.

▶ Look for sales spikes or anomalies in the data that might indicate a growing niche or opportunity that you can exploit.

▶ Numbers are the language of business. If numbers intimidate you, do a short course in finance or accounting to build your confidence.

PART 2

MULTIPLIERS

Every breakthrough in business comes from the multipliers: the forces that amplify your effort, extend your reach and accelerate your results. Multipliers are the partners who complement your strengths, the pillars of purpose that pull you forward and the trends you spot before the market does. They're the habits that increase your luck, the creative sparks that compound over time and the decisions that turn small wins into momentum. Once you learn to recognise and cultivate your multipliers, everything grows faster and with far less friction.

8

HOW TO BE A SUCCESSFUL FOUNDER

Having worked with, written for and interviewed some of the most successful founders in Australia, the question I get asked the most is: what do they all have in common? I don't think there is a single trait that guarantees anything, but I do think success leaves clues.

Among the entrepreneurs I've met, I see the same qualities surface again and again, not in everyone, not in the same order, and not in equal measure. But when enough of these traits show up in one person, and they are harnessed correctly, they act like personal multipliers; they amplify effort, compensate for blind spots, and create momentum others struggle to generate.

The top 30 multipliers that matter

While there's no secret ingredient that guarantees success, certain traits consistently show up in founders who build enduring businesses. What follows is a summary of those qualities.

The most successful entrepreneurs are:

1. intensely competitive: they hate losing, to others and to the standard they set for themselves
2. single-minded: they don't get distracted and are committed to completion

3. tenacious: they don't let go until the problem or situation is fixed
4. big-picture thinkers: they aim far beyond what most people do
5. relentlessly positive: they never say die, even when the odds are stacked against them
6. self-aware: they know their blind spots and actively work to address them
7. purpose-driven: they're motivated by something bigger than money or ego
8. persistent: they keep asking until they get the answer they're looking for
9. creatively astute: they see connections others miss
10. radically self-believing: they back themselves, even when no-one else does
11. team builders: they put the company and team ahead of their own needs
12. thick-skinned: they don't take rejection or humiliation personally
13. great at sales: they ask for the order and are unafraid to do so
14. receptive to feedback: they seek it, apply it and don't hesitate to give it to others too
15. punctual: they arrive early, and secure the best seat at the table that gives them the upper hand in negotiations
16. risk takers: they establish the worst that can happen and work from there
17. hedge their bets: they have multiple plays in action so if one stalls or falls, they have optionality
18. committed: they are willing to sacrifice health, leisure (and sometimes relationships) for the wider mission
19. disciplined: they keep fit, physically and emotionally, and take mindfulness seriously

20. motivated by progress: they see money as a scorecard, not just the end goal
21. emotionally resilient: they engage in the tough conversations that bring out the best in their team
22. generous with contacts: they are often happy to help others who have the gumption to ask for it
23. across the details: they know their numbers, the metrics and the minutiae that matters
24. frugal: they don't spend on things that don't add to the bottom line
25. high-energy: they work longer and harder than many would imagine
26. patient: they know a business takes at least 10 years to gain traction
27. stoic: they don't let the team see how badly the stress is affecting them
28. well-informed: they read, listen, network and stay across every shift in their industry
29. coachable: they seek out coaching to build connections, test assumptions and gain feedback
30. flexible: they are willing to change their minds if new insights emerge.

There are two traits not on that list that have an outsized impact on a founder's likelihood of success: heightened creativity and the ability to attract luck.

Most people treat creativity as an accident of birth and luck as an act of God.

I don't.

Alongside all the other multipliers — each worthy of a chapter of its own — these two matter most precisely because they're so often dismissed as fixed or uncontrollable.

My view is simpler and more useful.

You can strengthen the first, and you can deliberately invite more of the second.

Let's start with creativity.

Creativity is not a trait — it's a process

People often assume creativity is binary: you either have it or you don't; that it's a fixed, immutable quality rather than something that can be developed.

The truth sits somewhere in between.

Some people are naturally wired to spot patterns, connect dots and see associations others miss. They link unrelated ideas and recombine them into something new with ease. For others, that ability to make instant connections from unrelated elements doesn't come as easily. That doesn't mean the muse is out of reach; it just means they have to work a little harder to summon it into existence.

Creativity isn't like eye colour in that it's innate and unchangeable. It's more like a muscle: it grows with use, weakens with neglect and responds to concentrated training.

At its core, creativity is intelligent recombination. It takes two existing concepts — be it an idea, product, skill or category — and combines them to create a new and innovative third.

Most breakthroughs look obvious in hindsight because they're built from familiar parts:

- The iPhone was a mobile phone merged with an iPod.
- Spanx was born when lingerie met Lycra.
- GoPro was a waterproof camera strapped to a surfboard.

None of these products appeared out of thin air. They emerged through trial and error — by identifying a problem the founder wanted fixed, and then by moving between different worlds to notice what categories could be combined to create a solution.

When we look at successful creators and entrepreneurs, it's tempting to label them as geniuses, or as maverick outliers who knew more, saw more or had access to a source of secret information the rest of us didn't.

That story is comforting, because it lets the rest of us off the hook. If they're special, then their success is unreachable. If they were born with something rare — more intelligence, more courage, more creativity, more character — then effort becomes optional and fate explains the outcome.

But that's mostly untrue.

Many people I've worked with — founders, writers, designers, product builders, leaders — are ordinary human beings, as flawed, insecure and emotionally needy as anyone else.

The real difference?

They take bigger risks, more often than most, and stick around long enough to find out if their bet pays off.

To be fair, we only hear about the entrepreneurs who win. The rest just disappear, never to be seen again.

If Elon Musk or Mark Zuckerberg had failed early, they wouldn't be billionaires, they'd be footnotes in history, dismissed as slightly odd men with ambitious ideas that didn't work.

Genius is rarely the cause, but it is often the result of years of learning, failed experiments, exposure to different worlds, stubbornness and the discipline to keep going long after things got boring or hard.

We also cling to the myth of the lone genius: the idea that creative breakthroughs come from gifted individuals working in isolation.

In reality, sustained creativity is almost always collaborative and every entrepreneur I have met consistently acknowledges that nothing would have occurred without the support of their team.

The entrepreneurs who flourish are the ones who actively invite creativity in. They share early drafts, take feedback from people they trust, borrow frameworks from other industries, put their work up for public criticism before it's perfect and accept the feedback that comes back.

If it's bad, they don't take it personally.

If it's good, they share the credit.

They experiment and understand that making things badly is part of learning to make them well.

So, how do you get more creative? Can you *learn* to combine two new or unconnected ideas to create a distinct third? Is it possible to train your brain to see patterns that others miss?

The truth is that the gap between those who succeed and those who don't is rarely due to talent, but more so a willingness to look harder, deeper and longer at how separate pieces might come together to create something new.

It starts with working out where good ideas come from.

Where do innovative founders find their best ideas?

Michael Potas is a seriously clever individual. He is the founder of Boost Design, an engineering-led product design company that helps founders and inventors bring their new-to-world ideas to life. As the former Head of Research, Design and Development at Nanosonics, a billion-dollar ASX-listed medical technology company, he is an expert at taking complicated products from concept to completion. If you have a back-of-the-napkin product idea but have no clue how to bring it to life, Michael is your guy. I asked him where the best ideas come from.

'There's a myth that great ideas appear out of nowhere,' he said. 'Most come from two places: from people who've felt the problem firsthand, and people who see what's coming before everyone else.'

He calls them the lived-experience entrepreneur, and the lead-the-market entrepreneur. The lived-experience entrepreneur is driven by a personal pain point they can't ignore, like Canva co-founder Melanie Perkins. She saw how hard it was to use graphic design tools so she set out to make an intuitive piece of software everyone could use.

Then there's the lead-the-market entrepreneur. They're driven by a future opportunity others can't yet see. Tim Fung could see people needed access to local, affordable tradies who could fix something small, or large, and built Airtasker to help them do it.

Once you understand where ideas come from, the next step is to create more chances for them to form. How? By doing more, sharing more and putting more creative inputs — or dots, as I call them — out into the world.

Make more dots

Ask anyone who has written a book, developed a product or formulated a recipe and they'll tell you the act of creating is inherently messy, frustrating and confusing.

The process doesn't unfold in a straight line. It zigs, it zags, it rises and falls; it offers a brief revelation for a fleeting moment, then transmogrifies into something completely unexpected. What once felt pointless and pathetic at the moment of ignition can suddenly — when the conditions are right — morph into a dazzling display of artistic erudition.

In his famous Stanford University address in 2005, Steve Jobs said, 'You can't connect the dots looking forward; you can only connect them looking backwards.' He was talking about life, but the same can be said of creativity.

In her TED Talk, punk rocker and performance artist Amanda Palmer calls creativity 'joining the dots': noticing connections others miss. Palmer suggested we make more dots; Jobs recommended we take the time to connect them. I suggest we do both.

If you want to increase your quota of creative serendipity, the secret is to put as many dots out into the world as you can. Dots can take many forms: a blog, a webinar, a workshop, a line of code, a thank you note, a phone call, a podcast, an email, a question asked at a conference. Put something out into the world that the universe can pick up on.

Up close, those dots may look small and inconsequential, but over time these tiny acts of creativity produce a magnetic field that vibrates with plump potential and random possibilities.

You never know which dot will merge with another to create something significant, or magnificent. You'll also never know when or if they'll ever connect: it could be next week, next year or not at all. It's an utter leap of faith to believe that today's work may matter tomorrow, but that's the nature of creative work. You trust that you will be rewarded in the light for what you do in the dark.

Mathematically speaking, the more dots you release, the more chances they have of finding each other and forming something that looks a bit like luck. You'll know the process is working when strangers make contact saying, 'I heard you on that podcast ...', 'I saw you speak at ...', 'I read your blog ...'.

Those are the moments when those messy, unplanned dots line up and make sense. The result looks obvious in hindsight, but never at the time.

You can't connect what doesn't exist, so have the courage to make the dots, the energy to distribute them and the wisdom to see when they've connected.

And remember, creativity doesn't respond well to force.

Think of it like untangling Christmas lights. If you pull too hard, the knots get tighter, but if you drop them on the ground and let them settle, the knots will slowly loosen of their own accord.

In other words, let go of the timetable for when things *should* happen, and make way for what *might* happen. God's delays are not god's denials. You can only control the inputs, not the outputs.

Just make the dots, have faith and let time do the rest.

Put yourself in the right room

If the doors of perception were cleansed, everything would appear to man as it is, Infinite. For man has closed himself up, till he sees all things thro' narrow chinks of his cavern.
                                                    – William Blake

The most creative entrepreneurs aren't always the smartest in the room, but they are the most courageous. They actively put themselves in unfamiliar environments that stretch their thinking, challenge their assumptions and expand the range of ideas to which they are exposed.

They move between industries, disciplines and communities, collecting perspectives others never encounter. Creativity erupts when categories collide and when different worlds overlap. When you change the rooms you move in, you change the inputs, and that's when innovation flourishes.

Proximity is power. Who you work with, mix with, talk to, matters. We've all heard that your income is the average of the five people you associate with most, but just *being* with others in the right room delivers benefits too. Creativity works the same way. The rooms you enter reconfigure what you believe to be possible.

If you want to be more creative, don't wait for inspiration to strike. Enter the rooms where ideas are already circulating: attend conferences, sit in classrooms, join communities; talk to customers, take courses and work with coaches.

Here are a few rooms that leading entrepreneurs stepped into and walked out of with ideas that changed the trajectory of their business and, on some occasions, led to million- and billion-dollar exits.

The storage room

When I feel like being pampered, Gold Class is my go-to treat. But prior to 1997, this service didn't exist. Going to the movies was a cattle class experience. No service, sticky seats, stickier carpet and a long wait in the queue to buy your choc top and Coke.

The idea that cinema could be an intimate and indulgent experience hadn't been considered until Robert Kirby, the head of Village Cinemas, came along.

Radek Sali worked at Village and shared the story with me of how in 1997, as Melbourne's Crown Casino and cinemas were being built, Kirby wandered past a disused storage room behind the cinema kitchen.

Peering in at the dusty chairs stacked against the wall, Kirby saw what others had walked past a dozen times and never noticed. He recognised a pattern, joined the dots, and applied his version of creativity by merging existing worlds to create a new one.

'Why don't we combine this storeroom with the kitchen and bar behind it and turn it into a luxury cinema? We'll offer food and wine, comfortable seats and screen the latest blockbuster films so people can have a home cinema experience but with five-star service.'

So, he went ahead and built it.

By merging three categories — a bar/restaurant, a cinema and five-star service — Kirby created something that hadn't existed before: Gold Class Cinema (see figure 8.1).

The formula was simple: storage + seats + screen + service = a premium movie experience.

This invention didn't require advanced technology or a radical breakthrough in cinematic innovation. It came from a shift in Kirby's doors of perception, allowing him to see familiar things in a new way.

Gold Class went on to become a runaway success, redefining how Australians — and later the world — experienced the movies.

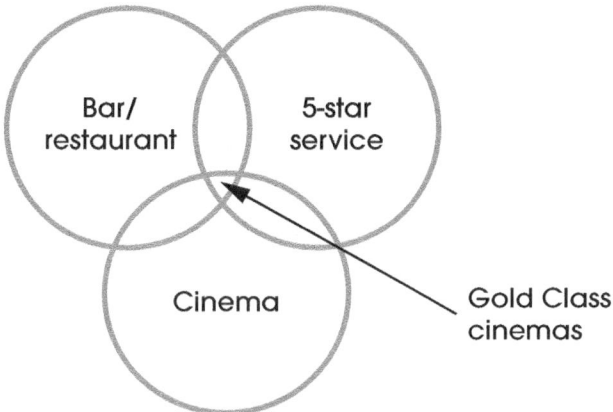

Figure 8.1 merging three categories created a fourth category called Gold Class cinema

The conference room

The best ideas don't germinate when you hibernate; they happen when you circulate. One of the most reliable ways to spark new ideas and foster creative connections is by attending conferences. Trade shows, expos, industry forums, demo days and networking nights expose you to fresh thinking, and the further you travel from home, the more likely you are to uncover something new.

Hilton Misso was a shy and introverted lawyer from suburban Brisbane. After attempting Year 12 three times due to poor health, he finally got into law and joined his father's law firm, Trilby Misso. His father, a dedicated community servant, was instrumental in inspiring the first legal aid service to help the needy, but was content to run his two-person father-son law firm.

Hilton, on the other hand, was a little more aspirational. Despite struggling with low self-esteem, and limited life experiences, he had a bigger ambition: to build a multinational legal practice with offices across the globe that could do more, for more people, and make a bigger impact.

In an attempt to overcome his crippling shyness and improve his personal power, Hilton devoured any success literature he could find. From Dale Carnegie, Jim Rohn and Norman Vincent Peale to Tony Robbins, Napoleon Hill and John Kehoe, he absorbed them all, and was assiduous in applying those principles at every opportunity.

In 1989, he heard about the American Trial Lawyers Association Convention, booked a ticket to the States and went.

The convention exposed Hilton to world-class legal thinking: how to market a firm, attract top talent and build a sustainable practice.

While there, he encountered a pricing model called 'No Win, No Fee' and immediately recognised its power. He knew better than anyone that high legal fees were a major barrier to justice. This model removed that barrier. Clients paid nothing upfront, and if they won, the fees came from the settlement; if they lost, the law firm absorbed the cost.

Hilton brought the idea home and became the first lawyer in Australia to offer the 'No Win, No Fee' model at scale.

The impact was profound. Thousands of Australians could finally access the much-needed legal advice and justice that had previously eluded them. That one pricing innovation put his law firm on the map.

Years later, when law firm Slater & Gordon were on the lookout for acquisitions, they sought out Hilton because of the innovative 'No Win, No Fee' service he had pioneered a decade earlier. After several rounds of white-knuckled negotiation, Hilton sold his law firm in 2010 for an extraordinary $57 million. That one idea, sparked by one conference, transformed a small suburban law firm into a national powerhouse and delivered a multi-million-dollar payday.

The wellness room

Whenever Swisse CEO Radek Sali felt he'd lost touch with the customer or wasn't sure what step to take next, he'd visit his pharmacy retailers to find inspiration. He liked to walk the aisles and watch customers pick up a product, turn it over, put it back, pick something else and eventually put one in their basket. He wanted to understand that zero moment of truth when the action shifted from considering to purchasing.

He'd stop customers and ask, 'Why did you pick that one?' The result was a rich, layered conversation blending market research, product design and behavioural insights. It was design thinking on the run.

He'd also chat with the pharmacy assistants stacking shelves. He couldn't understand why Centrum got more shelf space despite being pricier and less effective. Their answer was simple: 'They have a famous brand ambassador that everyone knows and trusts, they give us promotional posters featuring that ambassador, they put the posters up for us, and they advertise on TV to create more awareness.'

'So, if we did that too, would you give us the same shelf space as Centrum?' he asked. 'Yes, we would,' she replied.

That brief conversation gave him the blueprint for taking Swisse into pharmacies and competing head-to-head with Centrum. It also changed how he thought about marketing.

He looked around at the dull vitamin aisles with their poor lighting, cardboard displays and generic advertisements. Then he wandered into the beauty section, where glossy life-sized posters of Elle and Claudia glowed under perfect lighting, surrounded by vibrant merchandising collateral. That's when it hit him: the vitamin category needed a complete makeover. What would it be like, he wondered, if we merged the vitamin market with the beauty market and created a whole new wellness category? He took action to make it happen. He brought in some of Australia's most recognised celebrities to become the faces of Swisse, including Nicole Kidman, Sonia Kruger and Jessica Mauboy. By blending the credibility of vitamins with the glamour of beauty, he turned wellness into an aspirational lifestyle.

He did it again when he launched Wanderlust. He had just sold Swisse and was looking for his next challenge when he spotted liquid herbal extracts in Erewhon.

'They caught my attention as this was a new category in the wellness sector. They are highly potent, contain a greater concentration of beneficial plant compounds, and are commonly used in herbal medicine for their quick absorption and dosing flexibility.'

In that moment, he knew he'd found his next frontier.

'I could see an opportunity to make them far more potent than most tablets. They would be 100 per cent plant-based — with no synthesised ingredients, no fillers — and more bioavailable.'

Just as he'd transformed the vitamin industry, he planned to do the same for supplements, and is well on his way to doing that.

If he hadn't wandered into Erewhon that day, Wanderlust might never have been reborn.

The community room

In 2017, financial podcaster and adviser Glen James flew to the United States for FinCon, the world's biggest conference for personal finance creators. He went to see what was on the horizon for the financial sector; he came back with a new idea that changed the trajectory of his life. At the time, he was running his financial planning firm and his podcast, *Sort Your Money Out*, was little more than a side project: a creative outlet that blended his love of teaching with his desire to help people master their money.

FinCon changed that. Surrounded by creators seemingly printing money from basic online endeavours, and turning podcasts into global brands, Glen realised he'd been thinking too small.

His new idea was simple: instead of charging thousands for one-on-one coaching and personal advice, he would pivot to a one-to-many model.

He went all in on a new podcast, built around the FM radio format, blending education and entertainment to create an infotainment show. He shut down *Sort Your Money Out* and launched *my millennial money*, later rebranded as *money money money*, possibly one of the first mainstream personal finance podcasts made for Aussies, by Aussies.

Glen said that the breakthrough idea of selling his financial services firm and doubling down on the podcast format to make that his primary channel of communication, came from seeing a gap in the Australian market, and then being inspired from being in the right room, with the right people, and taking action.

It's a clear example of how Glen listens to his market, adapts his format and positioning, and isn't afraid to change course to stay relevant and genuinely useful to his audience.

'A lot of entrepreneurs skip industry conferences because they think they're a waste of money or they know it all already. I don't go for the keynotes. I go for the conversations in the hallway. That's where the real gold is. Someone might not be as far along as me, but they'll say something that sparks a new idea. Those one per cent insights, when you actually implement them, add up fast.'

That one conference inspired an idea that turned his podcasting side hustle into a national platform that delivered him a huge audience, a loyal fanbase and the power to help people at scale.

* * *

Creativity expands in direct proportion to the inputs you feed it. The more rooms you step into, the more dots you collect, the easier it becomes to connect them in ways others can't see. Change the rooms you move through, and you'll change what feels possible — because innovation doesn't comes from thinking harder, it comes from seeing differently.

Nuggets of wisdom

▶ Commit to attending events, conferences or courses related to your sector, or adjacent to it. One new idea or connection could change the direction of your business.

▶ Don't take no for an answer. If you don't like the answer you've been given, keep asking and try new strategies until you achieve your outcome.

▶ Create more dots and send them out into the world: blogs, webinars, books, newsletters and thank you notes are all emissaries of hope that contain the seeds of your creative talent. Eventually they'll connect and create opportunities you could never have anticipated.

9

HOW TO GET LUCKIER

Many people assume successful founders were simply lucky: that they were in the right place at the right time, met the right people, and caught the right wave. There's a sliver of truth in that, but it raises another question: was the luck random, or did they create the dots that increased the odds?

Usually, it's both, but once you understand the ingredients that influence luck, you can dramatically increase your chances of finding it. And the good news is there's a formula you can follow. It's called Mazal.

There's luck, and there's Mazal

Mazal (MZL) is a three-part framework that gives structure to what most of us loosely call luck. The original Hebrew meaning of Mazal was 'constellation' and evolved to mean fortune or luck, as in the phrase 'mazal tov.' We tend to think luck is random. This model shown in Figure 9.1 (overleaf) suggests otherwise. It breaks luck into three practical components, all of which can be influenced, improved and controlled. When combined, they significantly increase your odds of being in the right place, at the right time, with the right capability:

- M: Makom (location)
- Z: Zman (timing)
- L: Limood (learning).

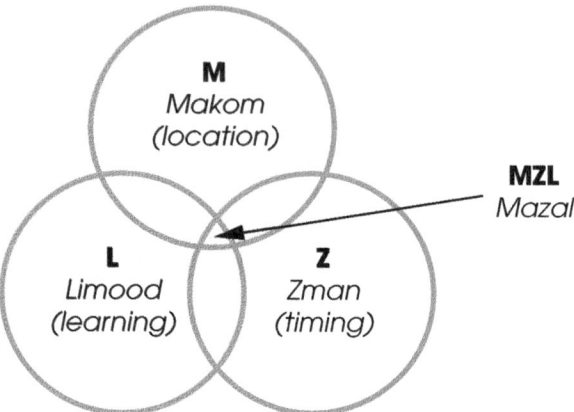

Figure 9.1   the Mazal recipe for making luck

When these three collide, extraordinary things happen. Here's how it breaks down.

M (Makom): Location

Put yourself in the places where others gather. Go to events, conferences and trade shows; join a masterclass, start a podcast, join a coaching group, ask for meetings and mix with others who operate and vibrate at a higher level than you.

Z (Zman): Timing

Timing is everything. It's no accident YouTube, Facebook, Twitter and LinkedIn all launched between 2002 and 2006, the same fertile window that led to the creation of some of Australia's top tech firms: Atlassian (2002), Campaign Monitor (2004) and Kogan (2006). Some seasons are simply ripe for innovation. Being aware of the past and what the future holds gives you an insight into when those seasons are arriving.

L (Limood): Learning

Learning is the thread that knits the other two elements together. Knowledge gives you the confidence to question the status quo and recognise better ways to solve problems. You can increase your learning by increasing your inputs: read books, listen to podcasts, watch webinars, follow thought leaders, study your competitors. The more you absorb, the more you'll know.

Mazal isn't magical thinking; it's about being intentional in thought, word and deed. When all three align, it looks a lot like luck.

Source: Thank you to Lior Shorman for sharing this concept, as referenced in Gabby and Hezi Leibovich's book, *Catch of the Decade.*

Catch a big break

Gabby Leibovich, the co-founder of Catch of the Day, is a man of action. When he wants to achieve something, he rattles every door until one opens. If it doesn't, he tries the side door, then the back door — and if all else fails, he'll climb in through the window.

By following his Mazal recipe for making luck, he turned a series of closed doors into a string of multi-million-dollar deals.

Catch of the Day didn't begin as the market darling it eventually became. It started as an online daily deals site that the best brands didn't want to know about. No-name brands didn't have a problem being listed, but the luxury brands weren't willing to see their prestigious products sold online. 'It will ruin our reputation!' they cried. Hard to believe, but that's how people thought back then.

One of the toughest segments to bring on board was the personal computer market.

Back in 2008, Australia's PC market was tightly controlled by a handful of distributors, the most powerful being Ingram Micro.

Gabby discovered in an industry journal that they were hosting a strictly invite-only trade expo. He didn't get an invitation, but that didn't stop him from going.

'I ironed my suit and fronted up to the Melbourne Exhibition Centre. They didn't let me in the front door so I went around the side. They didn't let me in there either, so I entered through the loading dock.'

He arrived with a box of brochures outlining the Catch 'deal of the day' premise and worked his way around all 80 suppliers, pitching his premise to anyone who'd listen. The biggest names in tech were there: Toshiba, Asus, Canon, HP, Lexmark. Most of them demurred, but Toshiba took the plunge.

They handed Gabby 8000 laptops and said, 'Go for it'. The deal launched at midday and by 4 pm they had sold 4000 laptops: that's 1000 an hour. Word spread quickly. Within hours, every PC supplier in the country wanted to list.

More deals followed. The standout came soon after. In a single hour, Catch sold $1.5 million worth of Samsung TVs.

'Our little team gathered around the computer, staring at the screen in disbelief as these numbers rolled in. It felt like a parallel world, but it was real. That was the day our reputation was made.'

So was Catch's success due to luck, or did Gabby deliberately assemble the ingredients that made opportunity look like luck?

On the surface, it seemed accidental. Look closer and you'll see Mazal in action.

Let's unpack what happened:

- *M (Makom): location.* Gabby put himself in the right place. He showed up uninvited to the Ingram Micro conference, armed with flyers and confidence. By being in that room, in the presence of all those major suppliers, he positioned himself at the epicentre of opportunity.

- *Z (Zman): timing.* He struck at the perfect moment. The 2008 financial crisis was biting, suppliers looking to shift old stock were seeking new distribution channels and listing on Catch was an easy solution to a complex problem.
- *L (Limood): learning.* Gabby was a voracious reader of industry journals, trade publications and retail updates. He'd spent years studying the electronics industry and understood what suppliers wanted. When he read about the event, he made it his mission to be there, to educate them on his concept and offer them a deal he knew they couldn't resist.

What looked like luck was actually Mazal in full flight. Right place, right time, right learning.

Do the work

Kevin Hart, the comedian, said it best: *Everyone wants to be famous, but no-one wants to do the work.* Actress and social media creator Adele Samus did the work.

A fashion retail assistant by day and a content creator by night, Adele is skilled at turning everyday conversations and complaints she hears in-store into comedic scripts for her social media skits. She promotes her talent the unglamorous way: by showing up, doing the work and creating chances for the right people to find her.

The compounding effect of turning up and doing the work has paid off. She's had brand collaborations with travel companies, leading food chains, makeup brands and fashion lines, signed with an agent, secured stunt jobs on major productions and even worked on Ryan Gosling's movie *The Fall Guy.*

'My most exciting brand collaboration was with Klook, a travel experiences company. They sent me and my then boyfriend to Disneyland. All I had to do was create content of us having a great time. It wasn't hard because we were! It was one of the best weeks of my life.'

Was landing the brand collab of a lifetime and a role in a Hollywood film a fluke, or did Adele actively create the conditions for luck to find her? When you map her actions against the Mazal model, it seems like she's taken the reins into her own hands and made her own luck.

She nailed *location* by getting her videos into the right feeds. She wrote her own scripts, filmed and edited everything herself and treated every post as a chance to be discovered.

She honed *timing* by studying her Insta analytics. She learned when her audience was online, what they watched and shared, and posted when attention was highest.

She doubled down on *learning*. She took stunt, acting and accent classes. She studied the art of Instagram and TikTok including how to use captions, music, trending sounds, editing and hashtags — and used each lever to widen her reach.

When the dots aligned, the luck arrived.

Get on the road

Swisse's breakthrough in China wasn't due to a single lucky moment; it was the compound effect of a thousand creative observations, experiments and decisions.

As Radek puts it: 'People often ask if our success was due to luck, hard work, serendipity or a combination of all three. I think it's the latter. But I think you can make your own luck; you just need to give yourself every chance to take advantage of it.'

The chain reaction started with *location*.

If Radek hadn't been in pharmacies often enough to notice Chinese students bulk-buying Swisse vitamins, he wouldn't have created Mandarin-language training and merchandising material for local

Chinese-owned pharmacies, a small gesture that signalled respect, recognition and relevance.

Then came *timing*.

Years before Swisse ever entered China, Radek thought big by investing in global ambassadors like Nicole Kidman and partnering with the Australian Olympic team. He didn't know if or when those big investments would pay off, but he trusted that when the time was right, his courage would be rewarded. When China suddenly opened its doors to international wellness brands, their leading online influencers already knew Nicole was Swisse's brand ambassador, and that was all the proof they needed to give Swisse their endorsement too.

And then came *learning*.

By staying curious, paying attention to the sales data and watching online behaviours, Radek learned that the diagous were active buyers of his product, and witnessed the surge in Taobao influencers sharing Swisse products. This led to an unexpected sales force: 130 000 Chinese micro-influencers selling Swisse directly to their networks. This turbocharged sales and was ultimately responsible for the rapid escalation in the price of what nutrition brand Biostime was prepared to pay for Swisse.

* * *

Luck will always play a role, but as William Blake observed, unless the doors of perception are opened, most people will see the world through 'narrow chinks'. Founders increase the odds of creating luck by showing up, making more dots, stepping into new rooms, and acting when opportunity appears.

Nuggets of wisdom

▸ When you feel stagnant, indecisive or can't get clarity about what to do next, go on the road and visit customers, suppliers and colleagues. It will expand your mind and spark your imagination.

▸ Get clear about who you want to influence, why and what their motivations would be to say yes to your request. Find them online, make contact and have the courage to ask for what you want.

▸ Do a deep dive into the data. White space opportunities show up in the anomalies. If you aren't competent or confident with data analytics, enrol in a course to teach you how.

10

HOW TO FIND YOUR PASSION

You can have all the luck in the world, but if you're selling the wrong product or service, your chances of success are slim.

So, how do you know if an idea is worth pursuing?

Start with the problem you're solving. Is there genuine demand? Is it a *hair-on-fire* problem — something people urgently need solved, or just a nice-to-have? Do you have a clear unique selling proposition that sets you apart? Is the total addressable market (TAM) big enough to make the effort worthwhile? Can this market afford to buy it? Can you make a profit from it? Have you tested demand by trying to sell it before you build it?

That's a lot to cover, but before all that, you need to answer an even more important question:

What do you want the business to *do for you*?

Do you want power, wealth and a first-class lifestyle? Or do you want a smaller business that offers you freedom, flexibility and the chance to work on something you care about?

Before you think about marketing, business models or making money, get clear on *that*, because everything else flows from it.

Play to your strengths

If you want to build a business others want to buy, most entrepreneurs concede it will take at least 10 years to generate enough traction for it to become attractive for acquisition.

So, with that timeframe in mind, what will that something be that will sustain you for a decade or more? Will it be something that sparks your passion and delivers a small but meaningful return? Or something that you are not overly passionate about but generates a monster profit? They're not mutually exclusive, but they don't necessary correlate either.

I have coaching clients whose passion is 'making money'. They don't actually care that much about what they sell, so long as it makes them money. They are the lucky few. Many, including myself, need passion to maintain their momentum.

Based on Isaiah Berlin's essay, the *Hedgehog and the Fox*, and later adapted by Jim Collins into the Hedgehog Process, this Triple P Model of *Passion, Proficiency* and *Profit* provides a simple framework for choosing what to sell, based on the three factors that drive long-term success.

The Triple P Concept (see figure 10.1) asks three questions:

1. What do you love doing? (Passion)
2. What are you skilled at? (Proficiency)
3. Who can pay for it? (Profit)

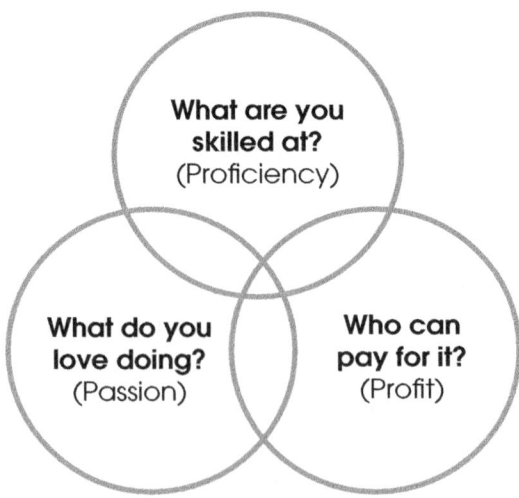

Figure 10.1 the Triple P Concept

When all three circles overlap, you'll find your sweet spot — the rare point where passion, excellence and economic potential meet. Businesses built from this intersection are not only more profitable, but more sustainable, because they're fuelled by motivation, capability *and* demand.

Where passion meets profit

The Triple P Concept works on a number of levels. You can use it to find direction in your own personal life, or go bigger and use it to identify what direction your overall business should take.

I used this process with my copywriting students because it helped them find the right places to network.

Colleen, one of my copywriting students, was a single mum looking to build a flexible copywriting business. I took her through the process. 'What do you love watching or reading about in your spare time? What lights you up?' She said, 'I love food, wine and tourism.' I asked her to pick the one she loved most. She chose wine. The way forward was now clearer. She jumped on Seek.com, found a wine-writing content role, applied, got it, and now spends her days writing about wine. The three elements aligned. She understood wine, was able to write about it, and found a company willing to pay for her unique blend of skills.

Building the business model for Retail Zoo

Janine Allis' trajectory also mirrored the Triple P Concept. After enjoying significant success with Boost Juice, she held an off-site retreat for her staff where she asked a simple question: 'What are we really good at?' The team discovered that what they were good at wasn't just their 'fluffy bits of marketing' — it was their 'boring' back-end.

'We were great at business, franchising, IT, design, development, legals and finance. These back-end departments gave the business the strong infrastructure required to grow. My annoying focus on every detail and refusal to outsource these departments were the keys to building these cornerstones into the foundations of our business.'

That revelation formed the basis of their next business venture, Retail Zoo, an entity that invested in or bought complementary businesses that Janine and her team could add value to. That led to investments in Betty's Burgers, CIBO cafes, Salsa's Fresh Mex and others. Those founders got Janine's expertise and contacts, she got their entrepreneurial energy and passion. A win-win for everyone.

Figure 10.2 reveals how this correlates with the Triple P Concept.

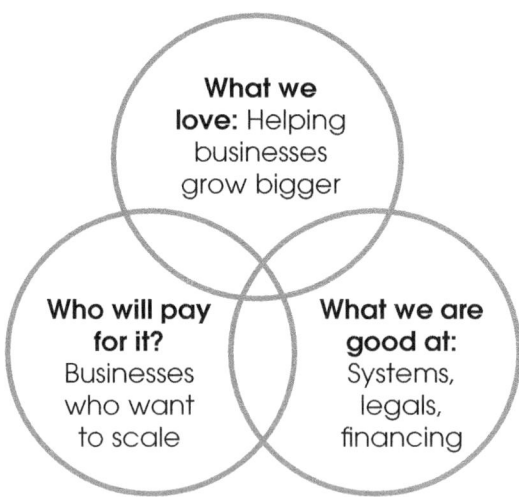

Figure 10.2 the business model for Retail Zoo

If you're struggling with what direction to take, look for the intersection between what you love, what you're good at and what the market values. It will light the torch that will illuminate the next steps you need to take.

What if the passions you have don't pay?

Is it idealistic to think we can make a living from pursuing our passion? Business coach Kobi Simmat thinks so. 'We get fed a lot of nonsense about how it's possible to make money from your passions: that we can do, be and have whatever we want and be paid handsomely for it. That's somewhat true, but only somewhat,' he said.

He's not saying passion is irrelevant, he's just saying it's not *enough*.

'It's true *if* you're truly gifted at something and have a lot of luck. It's true *if* you've got inbuilt grit, or have rich, well-connected relatives to support you during the down times. But the idea that we're *all* on a level playing field, and that passion alone will get you there, is simply not true.'

Kobi is adamant the 'follow your passion' movement has led too many people astray.

'You can make money from anything, but you need to work out how much money you actually want to make. If you want enough to cover school fees and a trip to Bali each year, pick a lifestyle business built around your passion. If you want to build something you can sell for an eight-figure sum, you may need to pick a different product.'

He wishes someone had said to him when he was younger that you shouldn't make your lifestyle fund your business, but make your business fund your lifestyle. 'I would have done things a lot differently and got to where I was going a lot faster.'

Kobi is blunt: build the economic engine to support your lifestyle, not the other way around.

What if you can't pursue your passion?

I met a young law student at the gym. We got chatting and I asked her what she wanted to do after graduation. She'd wanted to be an astronaut, but reality intervened in the form of asthma and short-sightedness. That was the end of her dream. Or was it? Instead of giving up, she merged 'space' with 'law' and enrolled in a space law degree at Adelaide University, which was handy, because South Australia is home to the Woomera test range and Australia's growing space-tech sector.

It takes time to work this stuff out. The Triple P Concept fast tracks that thinking, and helps you identify what you should be doing far more quickly than relying on trial and error alone. Figure 10.3 offers a popular meme showing how many creatively confused people approach life choices.

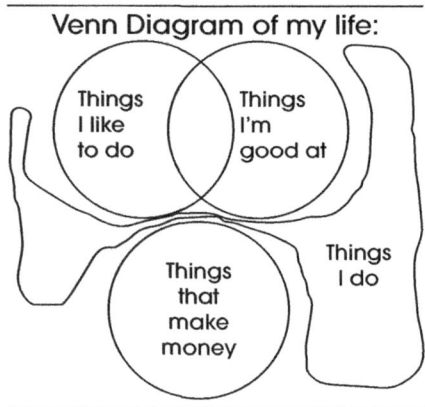

Figure 10.3 here's how some people make their career choices

Want to go big? Here's how

If you like the thought of staying small, that's great.

But if you want a business that can grow, function without your involvement, and eventually be sold, you may need to shift your identity and how you spend your time.

'You'll need to stop building a business around what you do, and start building it around what the business *needs*,' said Kobi. 'The skill that gets you started is rarely the skill that takes you to scale.'

Most businesses stay small for one reason: the founder never stops being the 'technician'.

Being the technician means you keep doing all the work.

The hairdresser cuts the hair, the accountant does the tax returns, the lawyer writes the contracts. 'They stay in the weeds because it feels safe, they're good at it and it's what they know. If your goal is to have a lifestyle business, that's fine. Keep being the technician,' Kobi said.

This is the mindset shift that separates entrepreneurs who grow, from those who grind. To build a business that's valuable, sellable and not dependent on you, you'll need to move through what Michael Gerber, author of *The E-Myth*, calls the three phases of entrepreneurship:

1. *Technicians* drive most of the revenue by doing it all. They make and sell the product, design the systems, do the marketing, manage sales and handle administration.
2. *Managers* turn vision into action. They lead people, manage projects and keep the team accountable to KPIs.
3. *Owners* are the visionaries. They create the big picture, inspire the team, build partnerships and turn ideas into valuable assets.

'If you're still a technician three years in,' Kobi said, 'you're wallowing around in work that won't get you the result you want. That said, you don't have to give up all the technician work. With the right systems, you can do more of it, on your terms, and get paid more for it. Your technical creativity can be codified.'

Think Andy Warhol and his legendary studio, The Factory. He trained dozens of acolytes to create art in his distinctive style and sold each 'Warhol' artwork for millions of dollars.

Kobi learned this in the hard-nosed world of accreditation, where only systemised businesses survive. After analysing thousands of manuals and processes about Australia's most successful businesses, he distilled a repeatable five-step system to create his own coaching and accreditation business, BestPractice.biz, which he later sold for $20 million.

You do you

If you're trying to match your skills to the right online business model, the list of income-generating models in table 10.1 will show you what's possible. There's something here for every personality, budget and appetite for risk. Explore the options, find what fits and start building a model that makes sense for you.

Table 10.1 ideas for online business models

Income model	What it means	Example + financial estimate (excluding fees)
Affiliate	Earn commissions by promoting other people's products or services.	Start a home-fitness blog and link to exercise equipment on Amazon. If 1000 readers buy a $300 treadmill through your affiliate link and your commission rate is 5%, you earn $15000 (1000 × $300 × 5%).
Amazon Associates	Earn by linking to Amazon products.	Write reviews on kitchen gadgets and link them to Amazon using your affiliate code (e.g. 500 sales at $50 = $25000 in product sales. At a 5% commission, you earn $1250).
Amazon FBA (Fulfilment by Amazon)	Sell physical goods on Amazon. Amazon handles storage, shipping and returns.	Import pet accessories from China and sell them via Amazon Prime (e.g. sell 2,000 units at $40 each = $80000 revenue. (After product costs, fees, shipping and ads, profit might be $15000 – $25000.)
Amazon FBM (Fulfilment by Merchant)	Sell products on Amazon. You handle your own storage, packaging and shipping.	Create handmade jewellery, list it on Amazon, and fulfil orders yourself (e.g. sell 800 units at $30 profit per unit = $24000 profit).

Income model	What it means	Example + financial estimate (excluding fees)
Digital Product	Sell downloadable assets such as templates, eBooks or stock photos.	Create Canva templates for Instagram and sell them via Etsy or Gumroad (e.g. 2,000 downloads at $19 = $38 000 in revenue). With 80% margins = $30 400 profit.
DropShipping	Sell physical products that are shipped by a third party. You never hold inventory.	Set up a Shopify store selling custom water bottles and fulfil via a dropshipper (e.g. 500 units × $25 profit = $12 500 profit).
eCommerce	Sell physical products online through your own store or marketplace like Etsy.	Create a brand of baby clothes and sell via your Shopify store (e.g. 1000 items sold at $20 margin = $20 000 profit).
Newsletter	Monetise a newsletter with sponsorships, ads or paid subscriptions.	Start a newsletter about tech trends and charge $300 per sponsor slot (e.g. 3 sponsors x $300 + 50 paid subscriptions at $10 = $1400/month).
Substack	A freemium email newsletter platform with optional paid subscriptions.	Offer subscribers access to job listings. (e.g. 1000 paying subscribers at $8 per month = $8000 per month.)
Patreon	Offer exclusive content to paying subscribers on a monthly basis.	Offer subscribers access to bonus content. (e.g. $10 per month x 500 patrons = $5000 per month.)

If you want to grow your business, you may need to spend less time doing, and more time leading. You'll also need to shift your identity from technician to manager to owner and find a business model that suits your personality, stage of life and tolerance for risk.

Nuggets of wisdom

▶ Before you choose your business idea, do your research to ensure you can solve a meaningful problem that delivers you a pay-packet that matches your aspirations.

▶ Be realistic and honest with who you are and what you want so you don't choose the wrong business idea for the right reason, or vice versa.

▶ Make a list of all the activities you don't like doing and turn them into job descriptions. Post them on a jobs board to find someone who can do it for you, so you can spend more time doing the things you enjoy.

11

HOW TO FIND THE RIGHT BUSINESS PARTNER

Starting a business is deceptively simple. Just register a company, buy a domain, build a website, open a bank account and you can be up and running within days. That low barrier to entry generates optimism, energy and big ideas, and that's good, because energy is the critical fuel that generates momentum in those early days. But the ease of starting also creates a dangerous illusion: if getting going is so easy, then *keeping* it going must be easy too. It often isn't, and what that ease of entry doesn't prepare you for is the long haul, because *sustaining* a business is much harder than it looks.

If you take on a partner, it can make this growth phase a lot easier, or a lot harder, depending on how and who you partner with. If you do bring a partner on, choose carefully. The right choice could help you achieve more than you ever expected in record time, or it could cost you everything you've ever worked for.

Choose carefully

This gap between starting and sustaining is where many founders come unstuck, and it's amplified the moment a partner enters the picture. When this happens, you're no longer just running a business, you're managing a relationship. You need to work out roles, responsibilities and remuneration. You also need to establish a vision for the work you will say yes to and the work you will decline, the way money will be spent and the people you will hire.

What begins as a shared ambition to build something meaningful can slowly turn into tension and stress, and in some cases, litigation. A quick scan of the business pages shows no shortage of legal disputes between former partners. That's rarely how anyone expects it to end, but the seeds of dissent are almost always planted at the start.

I saw this play out with two school mums I knew. They met on day one of term 1 in grade 1. A few coffees turned into a friendship, and before long they decided to start a tutoring service for primary school children. One was a talented marketer, the other was a gifted teacher. On paper, it looked ideal.

By term 2 the partnership had imploded. These two ladies now had to endure 12 years of school pick-up trying to avoid each other at the school gate. It was bound to occur. They hopped into the relationship too quickly without stopping to answer the most basic of questions: What do you want from this? What are your values? What does success look like? Who will do what and what resources will we need?

Their experience highlighted a deeper truth. Partnerships don't fail just because people clash. They fail because assumptions don't get tested, roles are ill-defined and values aren't aligned. The strongest partnerships aren't built on finding people who are like you, but on finding people who complement you, with clear expectations set from the very start.

That same principle of choosing well applies to your personal life too. One of the most consequential documents you will ever sign is not a shareholder certificate, but a marriage certificate.

'The person you marry will be one of your most important business partners so choose carefully right there,' said Janine Allis.

Janine Allis' husband Jeff has been her partner in life and business and credits him with being a significant reason for their success.

'He is the perfect partner for me. We are very different, but our skillsets are very complementary. He's my biggest fan and supporter and I'm his. When I doubted myself, he was there to reassure me. When I came home stressed out of my mind, he was there to put it all in perspective. When we sold our family home as collateral for the business, he was there to say we would make it work. Without this support, we could not have achieved what we have.'

The strongest partnerships create space for each person to play to their strengths, without ego or overlap. That principle becomes even more powerful when both parties know exactly where their lane starts and ends.

The power of two

Adam Schwab's career is a masterclass in choosing the right partners, from co-founders and staff, to suppliers, investors and collaborators.

After studying law and commerce and a brief stint in mergers and acquisitions at law firm Herbert Smith Freehills, he teamed up with school friend Jeremy Same. Together, they launched a backpacker apartments business, before pivoting to a corporate apartment enterprise and eventually creating an ecommerce platform called DEALS.com.au, 'one of many Groupon clones', as Adam puts it. When they noticed that travel deals consistently outperformed everything else, they spun that insight into Luxury Escapes, a multi-billion-dollar travel business that now employs more than 600 people.

Prior to that, the pair founded a food delivery platform called MyTable (which later became part of Menulog, which was acquired by Just Eat for almost a billion dollars). 'The best businesses I've been part of are the ones where the *partnership* is the advantage.'

Everything about Luxury Escapes grew from a deep alignment with its partners. Hotel groups trusted the brand enough to offer premium inventory at great prices. Customers trusted the company enough to pay them in advance, often a year before travel. Adam often said, 'Our job was to sit in the middle and make sure everyone won: the customer, the hotel and us.'

On his partnership with Jeremy, 'We both want the same thing. It's a bit like a marriage. If you have one partner in the marriage who's frugal and the other is a spendthrift, the marriage is probably doomed. We're both frugal, so it works. We don't pay for business class. When we go to a restaurant, we do the sums to work out if it's better to do the banquet or the à la carte.'

Jeremy lives overseas, but he's still very involved in the business.

'He's very aware of what's going on, but he doesn't love the operational stuff whereas I do, so that's what makes it work. We've got this yin-yang partnership where we're really balanced. You don't want to keep count of who did what. If you have a partner who says, "I worked seven hours, you worked five hours", that won't work. I'd rather say, "I love doing this stuff. You love doing that stuff. How do we achieve the best result?" That's the essence of a great partnership.'

One partnership that has stood the test of time, even after the partners left the building, was the Seek.com trio of Andrew and Paul Bassat and Matt Rockman.

'We got lucky,' said Matt. 'There was a huge amount of trust and respect between us. We divided up the core parts of the business for each of us to run, so we could get on and build out our various departments without having to worry about what the other was doing. It was somewhat siloed, but it worked. The journey wasn't easy, but it was made easier than it might have been because of who we were and how we complemented each other.'

Brothers in arms

For Gabby Leibovich, there was no better partner than his brother.

'I've been very fortunate to have my brother by my side the whole way. We are very different people. I love traditional marketing. Hezi loves digital marketing. I like public speaking. Hezi likes to be behind the scenes.'

That difference in perspective turned out to be a strength.

'As a solo founder, you'll always be the smartest person in the room. But when you have two people with contrasting opinions debating the merits of a decision, you almost always get a better result. When you have two co-founders and they both think alike, one of them is not necessary.'

They later brought in a third partner, Nati Harpaz. 'There were lots of scenarios where one of us beat the other two by having a fair and intelligent argument. We firmly believed that no one person had all the answers, but by putting our heads together and collaborating, we had a better chance of finding the right one.'

Their partnership was based on unconditional trust. 'After it was proposed we should build a brand-new, $20 million, 23 000-square-metre warehouse, Hezi approved the proposal with a WhatsApp message that said, 'Sounds good!'

Similarly, when Hezi went off to start Scoopon and EatNow, Gabby approved it with a message saying, 'Cool!'

'It doesn't matter if we're making a $2000 decision or a $20 million decision, we trust each other to do the right thing by the business.'

Gabby and Hezi have also partnered with two younger co-founders to launch a new venture called Fingertip, a web-building platform.

'It's our idea, but we hired two new people to bring it to market. We suffer from FOMO and need to attach those ideas to younger people who have the energy and drive to take it to the next level.'

How to make 1 + 1 = 3

When Hezi and Gabby Leibovich teamed up with Matt Dyer to co-found food delivery platform EatNow, it was growing fast, but too fast for comfort. The startup was burning through $200000 a month, and although sales were strong and the future looked bright, the pressure to halt the losses was intense. At one point, competitor Menulog came knocking with an offer to buy EatNow for $10 million.

'If we took this deal, it would have stemmed our cash burn, recouped our losses and even made a tiny profit.'

But they still said no.

Rather than selling out, the brothers doubled down. They worked harder, moved faster and grew the business. A year later, Menulog came back with a very different message. This time it wasn't, *we want to buy you*, it was, *we want to merge with you*.

Dan Katz, one of the co-founders of Menulog, said to them, 'We're both knocking ourselves out and losing a lot of money in the process trying to compete. Why don't we merge, list or sell the businesses together? We are worth so much more together than separately.'

The brothers always believed in the principle that 1 + 1 = 3; that the sum of the parts is greater than the whole, so they went ahead with the deal.

In February 2015, the two companies merged, negotiated a 30 per cent split to the EatNow team, and a 70 per cent split to Katz and his co-founders, making Menulog the clear market leader in Australia's food delivery space. Four months later, UK food giant Just Eat came along and offered to acquire Menulog for an astonishing $855 million. That was a deal they could all say yes to.

Many of their team members became instant millionaires, and the EatNow co-founders who'd once been on the brink of closure were now part of one of Australia's most lucrative tech exits.

Menulog has left Australia now, but for Gabby and the team, they are definitely not forgotten.

Stay in your lane

After years of building, losing and rebuilding businesses under the hot glare of the public eye, George Calombaris has learned one lesson the hard way: talent matters, but who you partner with matters more.

'Partnerships', he said, 'aren't about doubling your effort, they're about multiplying your strengths.' After years in the spotlight, he's no longer interested in working with just anyone. 'I only want to work with great human beings,' he said. 'Life's too short to work with people who don't share your values.'

When he teamed up with leading chef Shannon Bennett to create Culinary Wonderland, it gave George the freedom to focus on what he does best: food. Culinary Wonderland is an online membership community that connects food lovers with some of the world's best chefs. As Creative Director and Partner, George curates what appears on the platform, drawing on his restaurant experience, culinary aesthetic and extensive network. More than 100 renowned chefs, including Peter Gilmore and Matt Moran, have joined, giving members direct access to their collective expertise and creativity.

'We both knew our lanes,' George said. 'Shannon handles the business; I focus on creativity.'

That same clarity shows up across his hospitality ventures. George is deeply involved in the creative and operational detail of his venues, from the big-picture thinking down to the smallest practical decisions. He knows the architectural layout, the kitchen design and how it all fits together to create a streamlined kitchen experience for those who work in it. He's in venues daily, plugging in fridges, walking the cool rooms, checking what's stocked and what's not.

He sweats the details others might miss. 'Tonight, I'll spend a couple of hours marking up the plans for my Adelaide venue,' he said, 'deciding where the storeroom sits, where the ovens will go and how the kitchen will function under pressure. I even specify exactly where the magnetic cutlery catcher will sit inside the rubbish bin. If a waiter accidentally throws a spoon in with the waste, the magnet catches it so it doesn't get thrown out in the rubbish. That's the level of detail I get involved in. I'm a bit obsessive-compulsive about that stuff.'

The difference is that he doesn't have to do everything. 'It's great knowing I've got someone like Shannon at the helm of the business side,' he said. 'I trust him implicitly. He's great with numbers, detail and operational oversight.'

For George, that's the benefit of a great partnership. Each person stays in their lane, plays to their strengths and lets the other do the same.

Hardened by battle

His long-time friendship with investor Radek Sali, who partnered with George when he invested in the MAdE Group, was tested when it was revealed that wages had not been paid to staff. When the media storm hit and George was painted as a modern-day robber baron, the business imploded.

At the time, Radek served as chairman and majority shareholder. George was a shareholder but did not have a controlling interest in the company. The discovery of underpayments and the subsequent remediation were undertaken collectively by the directors and shareholders, acting as a board.

'I learned a lot from my time with Radek. We both lost a lot of money and I lost my reputation which was irreparable and the impact of which continues to this day. We're still mates, which is unheard of as partners. Most partnerships don't survive the tough times,' he said. 'We did, and that's rare.'

He's quick to admit that in his younger days, he mistook friendship for partnership. 'I used to think being mates was enough,' he said. 'It's not. You need people who'll tell you the truth, not what you want to hear.'

These days, George is selective. 'I don't need to be everyone's mate,' he said. 'I choose people I want to go to war with, and who'll still be there after. You need people around you who don't lose their heads when things go wrong. I've had partners who panicked, and that just makes everything worse. The best ones are calm, steady and stoic and they make you feel like everything's under control, even when it's not.'

For him, a great partnership isn't built on money or fame. 'It's built on honesty, humility and heart. The older I get,' he said, 'the more I value loyalty, honesty and kindness over skill.'

Radek Sali believes you've got to get to the tough conversations with a potential partner as quickly as possible to find out how you both respond when times get tough.

'Get to the bad stuff quickly,' he said. 'Find out who they really are and how they operate when they're under pressure. Everyone's on their best behaviour at the beginning of a deal but it's when things go wrong that you'll see their true colours. Can you fast-forward the bad bits? Not really, but you can do scenario planning to predict what could go wrong and how you'd both react.'

The hacker-hustler-expert trio

At some point, if you want to grow, you'll need to bring other people into the business. The goal is not to hire clones of you, but people who make up for the skills you lack.

One useful way to think about who you should partner with is through the simple archetypes of the hacker and the hustler. The hacker builds the product and makes sure it's technically sound. The hustler finds the customers and raises money. It's not a rigid formula, but it's a practical way to think about how work and responsibility are shared inside a young company.

This division of labour has underpinned many of the world's most successful startups.

At Microsoft, Bill Gates built the technology while Steve Ballmer drove commercial growth. At Facebook, Mark Zuckerberg focused on the product while Sean Parker and later Sheryl Sandberg scaled the business. Apple paired Steve Wozniak's engineering with Steve Jobs' marketing vision. It's widely acknowledged that balancing technical and commercial talent gives startups a far better chance of success.

I've augmented that model to include a third role: the domain expert. In many businesses, the hacker and the hustler can build and sell, but they don't always have deep industry knowledge of the sector in which they operate. They may lack the context, judgement and pattern recognition that only comes from working inside a specific sector. The domain expert fills that gap.

I call this the anatomy of a startup (see figure 11.1).

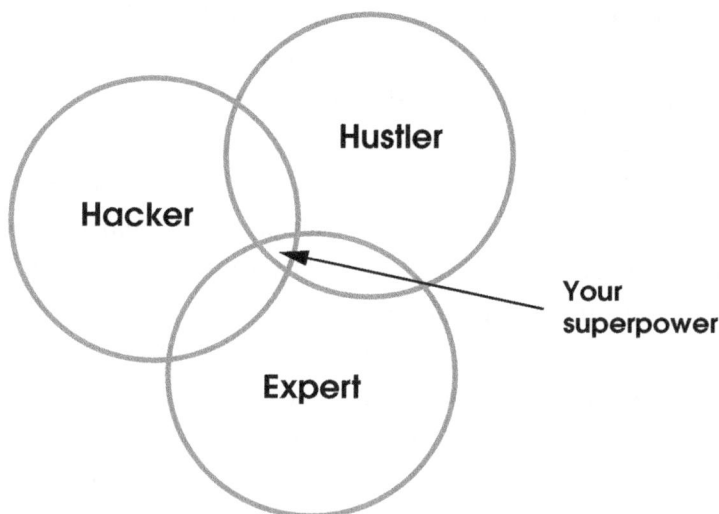

Figure 11.1 the anatomy of a startup

With the right skills and appetite, that domain expert may become the CEO, a neutral voice who can arbitrate between the hacker and hustler co-founders. They can resolve trade-offs, keep decisions grounded, manage egos and stop personalities from pulling the company off course. When all three roles are in place and values are aligned, that three-way partnership becomes more than functional: it becomes formidable, and creates a significant competitive advantage in its own right.

The power of three

Many first-time founders become obsessed with their product: what it is, what it does and how clever it is. They spend months perfecting features, refining the design and crafting the offer.

What they don't spend time on is working out who will actually buy it, how those customers will find it and who they will need to bring in to help make that happen. Distribution is not nearly as exciting as product development, but it's usually the difference between a promising idea and a scalable success.

That was the position Shaun Wilson and Blair James found themselves in when they launched Bondi Sands. They had spotted a gap in the market, created a high-quality product at the right price, wrapped it in a compelling brand story and created the website to facilitate sales. Orders trickled in and the feedback was great, but what they were missing were sales at scale.

Shaun knew the direct-to-consumer model could work in the short term. It would help them test pricing, refine the offer and tighten their sales process. But he was thinking bigger. Real growth meant getting stocked on pharmacy shelves, with a national rollout and the serious support that a retail network could throw behind it.

Rather than knocking on doors himself, Shaun did his research to find a retail sales specialist who could help him gain access to those retailers, and found Craig Stewart.

Craig had been General Manager at Revlon and understood retail from every angle. He knew how to get meetings, structure deals and speak the language buyers used: planograms, sell-in, sell-through, rebates, margins, discounting, points of distribution, lifetime value. Shaun could have picked all that up in time, but it would have taken too long. He was on a mission to go big and fast and Craig was the missing link that could help him do it.

Seen through the anatomy of a startup lens, the roles were clear. Blair was the hacker, focused on making the product. Craig was the hustler focused on making sales. Shaun sat in the expert role as CEO, holding the vision, making the calls and keeping the team aligned. It was a very productive trio, as captured in figure 11.2.

Figure 11.2 Bondi Sands' anatomy of a startup

They now had the right mix of skills to turn the business from a side hustle into a serious vehicle for achieving their global ambitions.

* * *

Choose partners for the skills they bring, not the convenience they offer. Intentional partnerships with the right people can transform an idea into a scalable business.

Nuggets of wisdom

▶ If you don't have a partner but want one, research the business accelerators in your area. Many offer matchmaking services to help you find the talent you're missing.

▶ Be nice to your competitors and suppliers. They could be your partners one day or a candidate for a takeover. Keep the communication channels open and maintain good relationships.

▶ Avoid equal (50/50) shareholdings as they can lead to deadlock when disagreements arise. A 51%/49% split creates accountability, enables faster decisions and reassures investors that the business can move forward.

12

HOW TO MAKE A PARTNERSHIP WORK

When partnerships work well, they are great, but when they don't, they are diabolical. Just look at the fallout of the Atlassian co-founders.

The Atlassian split between co-founders Mike Cannon-Brookes and Scott Farquhar marked the end of one of Australia's greatest business partnerships. Friends since university, they built Atlassian from a dorm-room idea into a US$50 billion software powerhouse. But after 23 years, their differences became too great to bridge.

When partnerships go wrong, it creates emotional and financial turmoil. It shows up in legal fees, distracted leadership, stalled momentum and staff uncertainty, which can deter investors from getting involved. The smartest founders don't rely on goodwill alone. They work together to predict in advance what might go wrong and have a pathway to resolving it if or when it does.

A recipe for resentment

If you want to start a business partnership, business coach Kobi Simmat's first piece of advice is 'don't'.

'I know it's controversial to say you shouldn't partner with someone to build a business,' said Kobi. 'Every accelerator and angel investor preaches the opposite, but I don't see any evidence that business partnerships lead to overwhelming success.'

He's worked with over 10000 businesses and believes the primary reason why partnerships fail is due to resentment. 'One partner feels that they've put in more effort, or one is more set on rapidly growing the business than the other, or one partner puts in the bulk of the seed funding and thinks that absolves them from doing any of the work.'

He believes that's why partnerships, like marriages, have a seven-year shelf life. 'It takes that long for the rot and resentment to kick in.'

Besides resentment, the other predictable reason why partnerships fail is because two 'technicians' decide to pair up and start a business. Kobi said, 'Unless both have a high degree of emotional awareness and take active steps to minimise conflict, two technicians as partners is a guaranteed recipe for failure.'

The school mums example mentioned earlier were both technicians, which is partly why that partnership fell apart so quickly.

Do you need a partner at all?

Despite the detractions of having a partner, there are real advantages to having one. You share the risk, so if one falls ill, the other can step in; you broaden the skillset and strengthen decision making and it sets you up to attract investors. Investors almost never back solo founders. Their logic? If you can't convince one person to join you, then you're unlikely to be able to convince a customer to buy from you either.

The cynics say an investor's preference for co-founders is pragmatic: if one founder burns out, goes rogue or gets sick, there's another to keep the lights on. Others say it's because they get two sets of hands for the price of one.

Being clear eyed about who you partner with, and why, is essential for future proofing the business. As Kobi said, 'It's about starting with the end in mind and understanding everything that could go wrong and having a plan to prevent it, or mitigate it, if it does'.

Top tips for building a strong business partnership

If you are committed to having a partnership or you just know you can't do it alone, follow these five principles outlined by Kobi and you'll minimise the likelihood of conflict and increase the chances of success.

1 Have an exit plan

Before you go into business together, have an in-depth discussion around values, goals and money. You'll need to cover topics like how to resolve conflict, what you'll spend money on, who will do what and how success will be measured. Create an exit plan, or a pre-nuptial of sorts, as to how you're going to get out of it, before you get into it.

2 Write a dis-agreement

Most founders write a shareholders' agreement, but very few write a *dis-agreement*: a document that spells out what happens when things go wrong. The best time to create it is early on in the relationship, while goodwill is still good. Here are some questions Kobi recommends you cover off in the discussion:

▸ What are the 10 scenarios that would make this partnership untenable?

▸ If we have a disagreement, what is the exact process for resolving it?

(continued)

- In what situations would that process fail?
- What could I do or not do that would cause you to resent me?
- What is our shared definition of success?
- Why will *this* partnership work when so many others fail?
- What steps will we take to dissolve the partnership if we must?
- If there's no money in the bank, who pays for the dissolution?
- Who carries responsibility for any outstanding debts?

3 Create a structure

To reduce the risk of conflict, Kobi suggests five strategies to keep your partnership on track.

- Create an organisational chart for the business, with clear lines of reporting.
- Write clear job descriptions as to who will do what, by when, and what each will be paid.
- Develop a performance review process to objectively assess the progress of each team member, including the partners.
- Establish an advisory board that meets monthly and is independently chaired.
- Agree on a third-party mediator to moderate conversations if you can't agree on important decisions.

4 Meet regularly

The worst thing you can do when conflict sets in is to ignore it. It won't go away, and if you're both conflict avoidant, it will almost certainly get worse. Schedule regular conversations and have a documented process for discussing grievances. These meetings need to be diarised and attended. As time goes on, one or other of the parties may want to reduce the cadence of the meeting. Don't let that happen.

5 Get comfortable with uncomfortable conversations

It pays to have some self-awareness around your own behaviour before you start criticising your partner. If you still feel that the situation is untenable and they're not pulling their weight, you may need to have a tough conversation with them to sort it out. Here's a script Kobi uses to deal with these kinds of conflicts:

▶ *Script: part 1 (outline the problem)*
'Hey, I'm not good at having uncomfortable conversations. I feel awkward about something that I need to talk to you about. I don't know how to say it succinctly because I'm still getting used to having these discussions. But in short, I need to let you know that I am starting to resent you, and that the current state of play is not working from my side. I need to have a conversation with you about working through that. Here are the five things I'm concerned about...'

You then outline your concerns, tell them how you want the situation to be different and detail the actions and behaviours you want to see.

You follow up with:

▶ *Script: part 2 (offer a solution)*
'For this partnership to be successful, I need you to exhibit these behaviours and carry out these actions. Is that something you can agree to?'

(continued)

> If they say no, then you'll need to work your way through each item of concern, identify what part of it they disagree with, and find some form of compromise. If they still disagree, you need to flag that the relationship cannot work, and that you'll need to continue running the business with a dysfunctional dynamic, or part ways. It won't be a pleasant conversation, but calling it out early can save a lot of heartache later.

Partnerships can multiply your inputs and double your impact, but they can also multiply your resentment, risk and regret. If you do bring someone in, do it with the dis-agreement document in place, and the values and vision clear. If you start strong, you maximise your chances of finishing strong.

Nuggets of wisdom

▶ If you have a partner but don't have a dis-agreement document drawn up, take time to make one. Even if things are good now, they might not be forever.

▶ Don't wait for conflict to be inflamed. Jump on small grievances early, speak your truth honestly, own your role in the conflict and take the time to listen to their side of the story before sharing yours.

▶ If you can't afford a third partner, or a CEO, put together an advisory board to act as the arbiter to help the two technicians stay on track and in their lane.

13

HOW TO BUILD A LIFESTYLE BUSINESS

Some founders are energised by big teams, fast growth and the prospect of a blockbuster exit. For others, just imagining that level of intensity has them reaching for the smelling salts.

They value control over their time, the freedom to choose who they work with, and a business that bends around their life, not the other way around. They don't want layers of staff, board meetings or investors tracking their every move.

On paper, a lifestyle business offers a cleaner path: fewer operational layers, less politics and a closer relationship with customers. It's an elegant alternative to the venture-backed grind.

But that simplicity is deceptive. A lifestyle business still requires the founder to make tough decisions about what to sell, who to, for how much, as well as decisions about how to defend your turf when competitors move in and play hard ball on pricing.

If you get those decisions wrong, you won't get freedom, you'll get a second job from which you can never escape.

That's where the concept of '1000 True Fans' comes in. This business model is often presented as the shortcut to independence: build something small, find your tribe and the rest will take care of itself. It sounds simple, and it can be, but it only works if you understand the maths that sits beneath it.

The truth behind the 1000 True Fans concept

The '1000 True Fans' idea has inspired a generation of entrepreneurs to launch their lifestyle endeavours with confidence. Created by *Wired* magazine's former editor, Kevin Kelly, the premise was that if you want to make a six-figure income doing what you love, you don't need millions of followers to make it happen, you don't need to be on social media every day and you don't need to exchange cash for clicks.

All you need is 1000 people who love what you do enough to buy from you consistently. For example, if the 1000 fans each paid $10 a month, that's $10 000 a month, which is $120 000 a year. So far, so good.

Gabby Leibovich is a fan of this concept.

'It's harder to start a big business now than it was. You can start a side hustle and make a decent living, but those big ideas, big platforms and big pay days that were common back in the early 2000s, are getting harder to find. What worked then, won't work today.'

He should know. He's been at the forefront of Australian e-commerce since it first took off in 2004. Back then, there was less competition and far less tech know-how available to the masses, and the only ones who could pull off those big tech exits were those with deep pockets, IT expertise or industry contacts. You needed a robust website, a big tech stack, a crack team of highly paid creatives, and a team of customer support staff just to keep things moving. Those resources weren't available to everyone, but the few who had them, and knew how to manage them, did well. Companies that built early and scaled fast, like Seek, realestate.com.au, Wotif and Carsales .com.au, were the big beneficiaries of being first movers in markets that barely existed.

But then everything changed. The tools of creativity became democratised, and suddenly everyone could access what the privileged few once had.

Fiverr, Freelancer and Upwork opened the door to affordable designers, developers and creators.

Kickstarter, eBay and Etsy gave founders access to worldwide markets without needing to build a sales team from scratch.

Then Zendesk, Get Friday and other platforms that came along offered access to low-cost admin, customer service teams and affordable global talent. This was followed by Canva who turned every founder into a graphic designer.

Meta's Facebook Ad Library pushed the shift even further. For the first time, anyone could see every ad running across Facebook and Instagram, each ad searchable by keyword, competitor or industry, giving small business owners the inside running of what ads to run before they spent a dollar.

AI has now erased almost every remaining barrier to entry. Automation, optimisation, content creation and campaign testing can all be done in minutes. You can build and launch an online business in a day for almost no cost. The tech used to be the barrier to entry, now, it's the accelerant.

The consequence? When the tools of distribution and production opened up, everyone piled in. The barrier to entry vanished, and along with it, the ability to stand out. Now, anyone can *start* an online business, but with millions of competitors, it's almost impossible to be *found*.

That's why the 1000 True Fans model has struck a chord. It's based on the simple premise that you don't need masses of customers to build a viable business; you just need a small group of people who value what you do, who will buy from you repeatedly, and keep doing so, year after year.

Kelly's concept rests on two simple assumptions. First, you need to 'own' the customer. When you sell directly to your customers, you keep the margin instead of handing slices of it to the platforms and intermediaries. Second, depth beats breadth. It's far easier, and more profitable, to serve a small group of people who genuinely care about what you do, than to chase the attention of millions who don't.

Figure 13.1 maps the 1000 True Fans idea onto the classic long tail curve popularised by Chris Anderson in *The Long Tail: Why the future of business is selling less of more.*

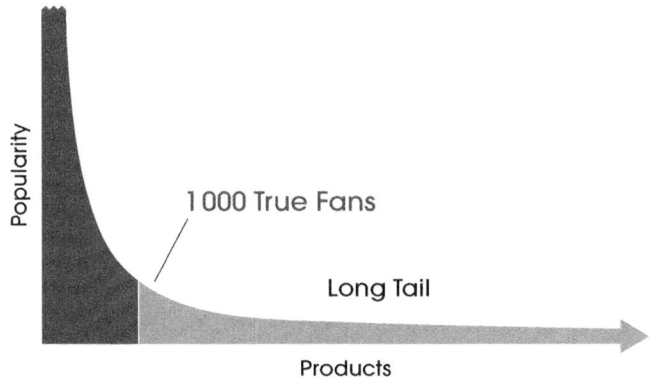

Figure 13.1   the 1000 True Fans model

At the top of the curve are global superstars like MrBeast and PewDiePie. A handful of Australian creators sit there too, including Fortnite gaming influencer, LazarBeam and Aussie mum Sarah Magusara, each with 18+ million-strong followers. Very few ever reach this level.

Below them is the long tail: the thousands of niche creators who rise and fall according to the shifting trends and tastes of the audience of the day.

This is where Kelly places the sweet spot: building a business around the 1000 people who know you, trust you and will buy whatever you release.

For lifestyle entrepreneurs just getting started, the 1000 True Fans is a comforting idea. It reduces overwhelm and gives you the confidence to have a go. But the reality is far more complex because most people ignore the maths that underpin it. To end up with 1000 *paying* customers, you don't need to begin with 1000 people — you need to begin with *hundreds* of thousands, as summarised in figure 13.2.

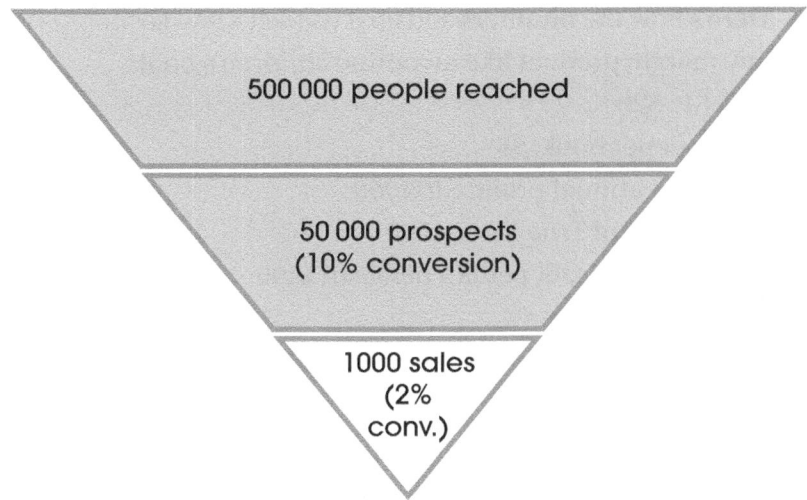

Figure 13.2 how many people do you *really* need to reach to get 1000 customers?

Here's how the numbers stack up.

If your advertisement or post reaches 500 000 people, only a slice of them, maybe 50 000, will stop long enough to actually engage with what you're offering. That group is your real audience. With a standard conversion rate of around 2 per cent, 50 000 prospects translates into roughly 1000 customers.

And that's only for a single sales cycle where just one product is purchased. It doesn't factor in churn or the ongoing effort needed to keep people engaged so they keep buying year after year to deliver you that annual six-figure income. The dream of 1000 True Fans is achievable, but only when you consistently reach enough people for those 1000 fans to emerge.

Does 1000 True Fans stack up for every business?

The 1000 True Fans idea works well when your fans buy high-margin products. Low-margin products make the model problematic.

- **Here's how the numbers** add up if you sell a low-cost, low-margin product like an online children's book:

  RRP: $20

  Profit per book: $5

  Target annual profit: *$100 000*

  Number of True Fans: 1000

  Required profit per fan per year: $100

  How it works:

  Books required per fan per year: $100 ÷ $5 = 20 books

  The maths:

  1000 fans × $100 per fan = *$100 000 profit* per year

  Target profit per fan: $100

  Books required per fan: $100 ÷ $5 ≈ *20 books per True Fan per year*

  The flaw is obvious: you could make *$100 000 profit per year,* but few fans will buy 20 books a year from the one author. Low-margin products make the True Fans model almost impossible to sustain.

- Here's how the numbers add up if you sell a high-cost, high-margin product like an online course:

  RRP: $2000

  Profit per course: $1000

  Target annual profit: $100 000

  Number of True Fans: 1000

  Required profit per fan per year: $100

  How it works:

  Each fan buys one $1000-profit course every 10 years, or one in ten fans buys one course per year

  The maths:

  100 course sales × $1000 profit = *$100 000 profit per year*

Asking a small percentage of loyal customers to buy a premium course occasionally is realistic. Asking them to buy dozens of low-value products every year is not.

What matters isn't how much revenue you generate; it's how much profit you keep. Books or low-priced products require unrealistic purchasing behaviour. Premium courses, services or memberships make the model work, allowing you to reach the same income with far fewer fans.

That's not a reason to avoid low-margin products. It's simply a reminder to be realistic about the income they can generate.

* * *

The 1000 True Fans model can work if you want to build a lifestyle business, but only when you understand the margins behind it. It pays to run the numbers first, or you'll be wondering why the six-figure income doesn't show up.

Nuggets of wisdom

▸ Do the sums to work out what you want to earn per year, how many products you need to sell, what profit you can make and how many people you need to reach to achieve that.
▸ Check out Meta's Library to get a blueprint for the successful ads that are circulating. Why reinvent the wheel when you can already see what's working and what's not?
▸ Lifestyle businesses live or die on customer lifetime value. Prioritise products, services or memberships that people return to regularly, not things they buy once and forget.

14

HOW TO PREDICT WHAT PEOPLE WILL WANT NEXT

Nothing in business stays still for long. Tastes change, technology advances and platforms rise and fall. What feels permanent today is obsolete tomorrow. The smartest founders watch the trends and study the swing of the pendulum so they can position themselves ahead of the wave rather than chasing it. That's what the Pendulum Principle is about: understanding where attention is moving, how the market follows and the opportunities that movement creates. Keeping ahead of the swing helps you choose an offer that's timely, relevant and needed. You want to arrive ahead of the crowd, not after they've left.

The Pendulum Principle

People often ask, 'What's the next big trend?' or 'Where do I look for what's coming next?'

One of the simplest ways to predict what's coming next is to understand the concept of the pendulum (see figure 14.1, overleaf).

Trends don't move in straight lines. They swing back and forth. What becomes popular is eventually taken too far; people grow tired of it, and demand starts drifting in the opposite direction.

The market swings from one extreme to the other, and on every swing, it passes through a middle ground that no-one is fully serving yet.

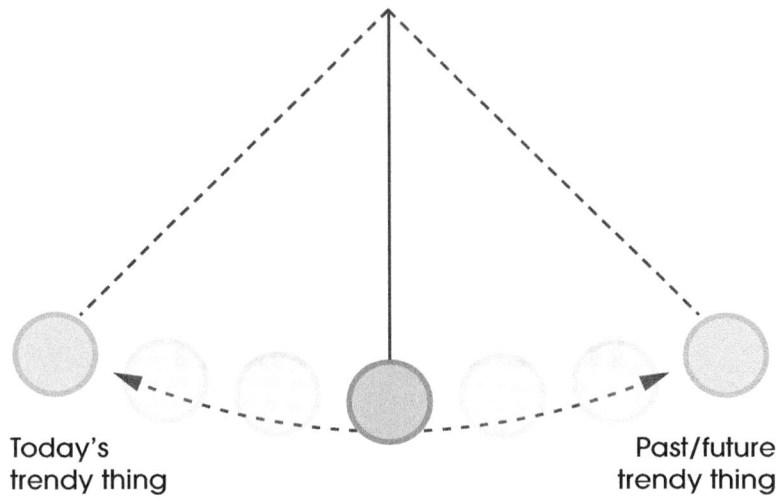

Today's
trendy thing

Past/future
trendy thing

Figure 14.1 the Pendulum Principle

That middle ground is where the sweet spot for opportunity can be found.

From noise to silence

To understand how the pendulum principle works and to take advantage of the lessons it can impart, it's helpful to ask this one question: 'What do we have too much of already?' For example, at the moment, anyone living in suburban Australia would agree we have too much noise. We are greeted most mornings with the sounds of leaf blowers and lawn mowers, dogs barking and the beeping of reverse parking. The online noise is even louder. Notifications pinging, phones ringing, inboxes overflowing. Add to that the white noise of fake news, deepfakes, clickbait and an endless conveyor belt of social media content that floods our feed, it's clear that we're drowning in stimulation. Whenever the pendulum swings too far to one extreme, the opportunity lies in whatever sits on the opposite side. On the other side of noise is silence, and the need for that is growing.

That demand is showing up in the form of a wide range of products and services that were once on the fringe but have quickly become mainstream: noise-cancelling headphones, sensory-deprivation tanks, soundproof hotel rooms and silent retreats are just a few that come to mind. Those who spotted the trend early on, and snared that first-mover advantage, became big winners. The Calm app, for example, released in 2012, just four years after the App Store launched, is now used by over 100 million people and it is currently valued at $2 billion.

Others are getting in on the quiet act. Cruise companies offer digital-detox holidays; quiet cafés provide secluded corners where conversation is off the menu; trains offer quiet carriages; nightclubs stage silent discos. Major retailers like Coles and Woolworths have formally introduced 'quiet hour', where lights are dimmed and noise is reduced to make shopping more comfortable for people with sensory sensitivities.

Tim Gurner, property developer and hotelier, cottoned onto this trend years ago, and in response, set up Saint Haven, a series of ultra-luxury wellness clubs dotted across the well-heeled suburbs of Australia. They offer cryotherapy, hyperbaric oxygen therapy, red-light treatments and meditation spaces, all curated to create a sense of sanctuary and stillness. In a world filled with noise, Saint Haven provides the opposite — the chance to retreat, reconnect and reflect — and it's coming at a high price too, with premium membership tiers costing more than $400 a week. Silence has become the new status symbol.

To anticipate the next trend, we need to understand the broader cultural pattern driving these shifts. The opportunity sits where the pendulum is about to land, and the founders who win are already there.

Table 14.1 (overleaf) shows where attention sits now, and where the next openings are forming.

Table 14.1 the top seven reversals creating new opportunities for entrepreneurs

#	Pendulum swing (what we are moving towards)	Emerging opportunity (counter-swing)	Why it matters / where you can innovate
1	Noise, overload, constant stimulation	Silence, focus, sanctuary	The 'silence economy' is booming. Stillness is a new luxury. It offers simplicity, whitespace and digital sabbaticals.
2	Mass sharing and performative self-promotion	Privacy, intimacy, digital discretion	As trust erodes, audiences crave private, authentic spaces. Small, safe communities (Discord, Signal and Geneva) will outperform open platforms.
3	Automation and AI abundance	Human craft, emotional intelligence, connection	As AI slop floods the market with soulless, emotionless content, storytelling based on trust and artistic intuition will be seen as a premium offering.
4	Algorithmic infinity scroll	Curated, finite, slow media	'Slow content' is rising: Substack newsletters, private podcasts and niche print zines will rise up. Proof-of-human badges and behind-the-scene creation will cut through digital fatigue.
5	Quantity and reach metrics	Depth, retention, meaningful engagement	People are tired of vanity metrics. Membership communities will be built on returners, not followers. Non-fungible tokens (NFTs) will offer personal rewards for long-term loyalty.

#	Pendulum swing (what we are moving towards)	Emerging opportunity (counter-swing)	Why it matters / where you can innovate
6	**Centralised platforms**	Creator-owned infrastructure	Founders are moving off-platform: they want to own their customer lists and digital real estate, and have control over how and when they get used.
7	**Multiple identities**	Private and public identities	Tools that let people choose what to reveal, to whom, and when, will grow as constant online exposure becomes fatiguing.

Trends don't appear out of nowhere. They start as small ripples, gather momentum and sometimes crash over us before we even realise what's happening. The real skill lies in knowing which waves will rise, which waves will crest and which ones to ride.

Five unconventional ways to spot future business trends

Spotting future trends starts with noticing the small signals everyone else overlooks. Here are five ways to spot business trends before they go mainstream.

1 Track job boards and emerging roles
Watch what new positions appear on LinkedIn or Indeed. Roles like Prompt Engineer, AI Ethics Officer or Sustainability Data Analyst signalled where AI was heading before mainstream Australia realised it.

(continued)

2 Watch domain name registrations

New clusters of domain registrations (such as those ending in '.ai' or '.bio', commonly used for artificial intelligence, life sciences and eco-focused brands) often point to emerging industries before the market and the media catch on.

3 Read academic journals

Focus on the *acknowledgements* and *funding sources*: they show who's financing research that will likely commercialise within three to five years.

4 Monitor trademark and patent filings

Search databases like IP Australia or the United States Patent and Trademark Office (USPTO) for clusters of new filings. Patents reveal what companies are investing in long before the products hit the market.

5 Study Kickstarter's 'Almost Funded' projects

Don't just look at what succeeded; examine what *nearly* made it. These ideas show strong consumer curiosity but reveal gaps in execution. Read the comments to see what stopped them: cost, timing, trust or tech. Spot what needs fixing and bring it to market.

How disruptors create new markets

Every major disruptor solves one problem and accidentally creates 10 more. When an industry is shaken up, new frustrations, inefficiencies and unmet needs emerge, and those gaps become the perfect openings for the next wave of entrepreneurs. The trick is to watch what the giants do, study the fallout and look for the small but meaningful problems that appear around the edges.

It's hard to compete with a major disruptor; but you can build a complementary business alongside it by turning those everyday frustrations it creates into lucrative business opportunities. For example:

- Uber turned every car into a cab → Splend built a business leasing cars to ride-share drivers who wanted a car but couldn't afford to buy one.
- Airbnb turned every spare room into a hotel → Smart-lock companies turned lost keys and digital locks into a new category of property tech.
- Zoom turned every lounge room into a boardroom → Tools like Miro and Mural helped teams collaborate when they were no longer in the same room.
- Afterpay turned every retailer into a lender → Risk-scoring companies emerged to decide who should be approved and who shouldn't.

So, how do you spot the problem that lurks underneath?

Almost every good idea starts the same way: with someone wondering if there's a better way to get something done. One simple question that unlocks it is:

> *Wouldn't it be great if...?* It's one of the fastest and most practical ways to turn small frustrations into profitable business ideas.

Here's how that question turns little thoughts into big businesses:

- *Wouldn't it be great if...*
    ... you could split the bill with friends after dinner, with no need for awkward conversations or chasing up of payments?
    Solution? Splitwise
- *Wouldn't it be great if...*
    ... you could use the camera on your phone to check your skin for melanomas?
    Solution? SkinVision

- *Wouldn't it be great if…*

   … every time you bought a coffee, the spare change went straight into an investment account?

   Solution? Raiz
- *Wouldn't it be great if …*

   … you could find local, trusted tradies to help you with odd jobs around the house?

   Solution? Airtasker.com

What you start with may not be what you end with

In 2004, Adam Schwab and his school friend Jeremy Same were looking for a way to exit corporate life and enter the world of entrepreneurship. They didn't have high expectations; they just wanted to replace their incomes from Freehills and ANZ, have more fun and run something of their own.

Their first venture, renting out high-end backpacker apartments, grew fast. One apartment became two, then 10 and then 50. But the market conditions changed, rents rose, landlords hesitated to lease to them and the model became difficult to scale.

So, they moved upmarket, launching Living Corporate Apartments, an executive version of the same concept. That hit $2 million in turnover and while the business was profitable, it wasn't scalable either.

Spotting Groupon's rise in the United States, the pair incubated an Australian version, originally named Zoupon. They renamed it DEALS.com.au, and it too grew quickly, but realised a business selling local experiences wasn't as scalable as they'd hoped.

These challenges revealed a new niche: high-value travel packages for luxury hotels across Australia and Asia. They moved into travel, initially offering small packages, and then expanded into full luxury holidays. Within two years Luxury Escapes was born.

That little backpacker-apartment idea evolved into one of Australia's most successful travel businesses by doing one thing well: joining the dots. Adam and Jeremy solved one problem after another, stayed flexible and moved with the pendulum, constantly pivoting instead of clinging to their first idea.

Some of the world's most successful startups began as one thing and morphed into another. Slack was an internal chat tool for a failed gaming company before it became a workplace messaging platform. YouTube was a dating site before it became a video platform. Shopify was an online snowboarding store before it became an e-commerce platform.

Your first business may not be your final business. The innovators are the ones who adapt, pivot and go where the market takes them.

Why big is not always better

For the past two decades, success in business has been framed as a race: grow faster, scale harder, dominate your category and exit big.

But as automation and AI take over more of the grunt work, and mass production turns more products and services into commodities, a different kind of advantage is emerging.

In a world saturated with speed, noise and homogeneity, what stands out is the opposite: businesses that are small enough to offer a human experience.

More entrepreneurs than ever are trimming their sails to build sustainable, personal businesses, with the needs of their audiences — not investors — at the centre. Ambition can seduce us into believing we must go big or go home. That works for some, but not for everyone.

When content is mass generated, emotionless and identical, people gravitate to what feels handcrafted, personal and authentic.

If small businesses can't win on scale, price or reach, they have to win somewhere else. The most reliable place to do that is in the services they offer, where the experience becomes part of the product.

Five-star experiences on a one-star budget

Kobi Simmat learned this concept early, as an 18-year-old waiter working at Cottage Point Inn on Sydney's Hawkesbury River. His boss, Dan McKinnon, taught Kobi to ask customers a question that has informed his career ever since:

What else can I do to make this experience exceptional for you?

'Dan showed me that great service isn't about price or prestige, but about how you make the customer *feel*. He'd walk past a table and ask, "What else can I do to make this experience exceptional for you?" That question taught me real service is anticipating what people need and caring enough to deliver it.'

Fast-food giant McDonald's gets this concept. It may be a one-star restaurant, but it delivers a five-star experience by being consistent on multiple levels: the food is hot, the staff are friendly, and if there's a problem, they fix things quickly. That consistency breeds reliability, reliability builds trust and trust builds loyalty.

You don't need to be a billion-dollar brand to offer a five-star service

I took a taxi to the airport a while back. The driver was late, he got lost getting there, the car reeked of fried food and he talked on the phone the whole way. Compare that with the Uber I took on the return journey. The driver:

- texted me to let me know he had arrived
- got out of the car, put my luggage in the boot and opened the door for me
- offered to turn the radio off, up, down or to my preferred station
- asked me if the temperature was to my liking

- didn't engage in conversation until I initiated it
- had a bottle of water, mints and a packet of tissues in the side pocket of the door.

This driver turned a basic cab ride into a luxury experience to rival that of a high-end town car. He understood what it was to be 'of service' and had asked the question, 'What would a five-star version of this cab ride look like?' Other than the mints, water and tissues, all of those five-star flourishes cost him zero to offer.

Of course, I gave him a five-star rating, a generous tip and took his personal business card to book him directly the next time I needed a cab. Good service is the best form of business development.

We're at the dawn of a new era of automation, and soon the human will be removed from the entire customer experience. So, what can you do in your business to offer a five-star personalised service that doesn't cost much, yet delights the customer? In a world of chatbots and agentics, the most powerful thing you can do is make someone feel seen.

How to compete with the big players when you're small

The little club that could

Kobi Simmat has been part of boating clubs for as long as he can remember. He witnessed first-hand how a small, determined club that believed it *could* win, triumphed over a larger, complacent club that assumed it *should* win. (The club names are fictional but the stories are true.) Here's what happened.

The Grand Marina Yacht Club was one of Sydney's finest boating clubs, with panoramic views of the Hawkesbury River, multiple dining rooms, a cocktail bar, a wedding venue, and a calendar jam-packed with black-tie events.

Just down the river, the Riverside Yacht Club offered a very different experience. Tucked deep in a national park, accessible only by a long, steep road, it lacked glamour, space and prestige. Membership was dwindling, and closure seemed inevitable.

But instead of giving up, the locals who loved that little club got together and asked a simple question: *What could we offer that the big club couldn't?* The club looked at its current customers—mostly families with young children—and decided to double-down on those it already served and become the best family-focused yacht club it could possibly be.

The club members then asked the breakthrough question: *What would a five-star version of that look like?*

That shift in thinking unleashed a wave of innovation. They introduced affordable family memberships, built a playground, upgraded the BBQ area and created a members' lounge. They hosted pontoon parties, Sunday happy hours, kayak races, and fishing days for parents and kids.

Within a year, the club had reinvented itself. Membership hit capacity, events sold out and profitability returned. Many members said they could have easily afforded the more exclusive club but chose Riverside because it *felt like home*; it *felt like they belonged.*

The little club succeeded because it aligned with where the pendulum was headed: away from prestige and performative towards offering an experience that felt authentic, local and human. By knowing who they were, what they did best and what made them different, they built a brand that put the needs of their patrons over their need to be prestigious.

In doing so, they proved two things: you don't need to be the biggest to win, and you don't need five-star prices to offer a five-star experience. You just need to ask the right question—What would a five-star version of this look like?—and commit to delivering it for your ideal customer.

How to find your niche

What the Riverside Yacht club did instinctively is what the unique competing space (UCS) model explains strategically.

The UCS model, conceived by George Tovstiga in *Strategy in Practice*, offers a simple way to help you find your gap. As shown in figure 14.2, it maps three things: what customers want, what you offer and what competitors provide.

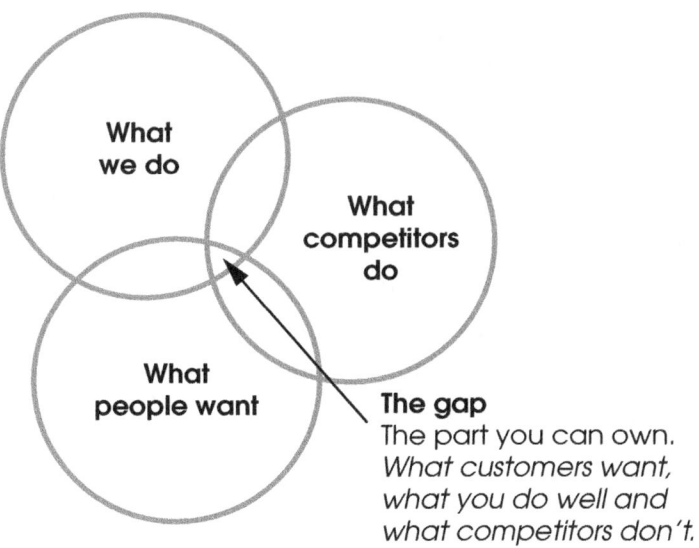

Figure 14.2 opportunity resides in the gap between what customers want, what you offer and what competitors provide

The opportunity sits in the centre, where your strengths overlap with customer demand and where the competition falls short. That's your UCS: the space you can own.

Riverside Yacht Club found their UCS by knowing who they were, what they offered and what their members valued. While the bigger club chased prestige, they focused on people.

Bondi Sands' UCS

Shaun Wilson's Bondi Sands used the UCS process to create a product that was aspirational, affordable and A-grade in quality. Nailing that triple-A sweet spot was difficult to achieve, but they did it.

Here's how.

1. *Step 1: They made it aspirational*
   They placed themselves at the heart of high-end culture through Ibiza beach clubs, Coachella activations and European fashion shows. The message? This is the tan brand of choice for the rich and famous.
2. *Step 2: They made it affordable*
   Aspirational and affordable rarely coexist, but they made it work by working closely with their chemistry team to create a low-cost, high quality formulation. The result was a $20 bottle that delivered four applications at $5 a pop, compared to $65 a bottle for rivals like St Tropez.
3. *Step 3: They made it A-grade quality*
   None of the above would have mattered if the product underperformed, but it didn't. Bondi Sands matched the quality of competing brands priced three times higher.

They reinforced this Triple A offering by linking online and offline channels into a single system:

- Live events and fashion sponsorships created offline aspiration.
- Influencers and PR created online social proof and five-star reviews.
- Online and offline systems merged into a streamlined pipeline, bringing new customers to the pharmacy door and their online store.

In isolation, they had nailed each wedge: aspirational, affordable and A-grade quality. Where the three converged became the engine that turned the brand into a global phenomenon. Figure 14.3 illustrates where those three forces intersected to form Bondi Sands' UCS.

Figure 14.3   Bondi Sands' UCS

This process of finding a unique competing space and servicing it in a five-star manner is not just reserved for the big brands. The same model works just as well for small brands, sometimes even better. The big brands may have scale, but small brands have speed. The rule is the same for both: spot the gap and build a better experience around it.

How to use the five-star experience as a competitive advantage

Aster & Oak

Aster & Oak's online store for organic baby clothes shows how a five-star intention, applied to every touchpoint, can help a small business outshine larger rivals with bigger budgets.

Melissa Blight launched the brand in 2014. She was looking for baby clothes that wouldn't irritate her son's eczema-prone skin. She couldn't find what she was looking for, so she set about making the products herself.

From day one, Aster & Oak's greatest advantage was its personal touch. Everything was handcrafted. Melissa sourced the organic fabrics, sketched the original designs, wrote the copy, tested the materials and inspected every item before it left the house.

The brand grew by obsessing over the five-star details bigger players overlooked: softer fabrics, safer dyes, hand-drawn prints by real artists, compostable packaging, authentic photography and a clear, coherent identity. Melissa's early growth came from word of mouth, loyal stockists and great reviews.

As the business grew, another challenge she faced was whether to maintain her ethical ethos or go down the 'cheap and nasty' path.

'When you're under financial pressure, it's always tempting to cut corners, but I've never been willing to sacrifice our values or quality. Sticking to our ethos has been hard at times, but it's also the reason people trust us and why the brand has lasted.'

Melissa also learned that when it comes to suppliers, bigger isn't always better.

'I assumed the top advertising agencies would deliver because they had the biggest names,' she said. 'Instead, they burned through our budget with very little to show for it.'

She switched to smaller local agencies, saved tens of thousands, and finally got the attention and care her brand needed.

Now, with more than 93000 followers on Instagram, Aster & Oak continues to grow on the strength of its distinctive, vintage-inspired, five-star approach. It demonstrates that when you care about the details, customers notice and will often pay a premium for it.

How to use functional mapping to deliver a five-star experience

It's one thing to talk about creating a five-star experience; it's another to know *where* and *how* to apply it. That's where functional mapping comes in. Most people think of their business as a single product or service, but in reality, it's a series of interconnected actions. By breaking down your business into the small, isolated steps, you can see where the system works, where it breaks down and how you can improve it.

How to use functional mapping to your benefit

Red Barrel is a fictional online wine retailer but based on a real brand. They had a massive range, fast delivery, great customer service and hundreds of five-star reviews. When a new competitor

151

popped up offering discount prices, their once dominant position came under attack. They needed to get back to basics to find a way to compete without blowing their budget. They did it with the help of functional mapping.

They took a step back and documented each action, breaking the entire process into a series of clear steps. For example, they: sourced stock from wineries, photographed the products, uploaded the listings to the website, wrote emails to promote the deals, packaged up the goods, despatched the goods and sent follow-up emails for post-sales campaigns.

At each point in the process, they asked the same question: *What would a five-star version of this look like?*

To test the theory, they applied the five-star thinking to the *packaging* step. This process is often overlooked as a customer touchpoint and treated as a back-office function.

First up, they swapped the boring brown cardboard box for a multi-coloured box. They ditched the polystyrene packing peanuts and replaced them with shredded straw to give it that vineyard vibe. They wrapped the wine in branded tissue paper to create a sense of celebration and added a handwritten thank-you card from the customer service manager. They also included a tasting note with a matching recipe, plus a QR code on the note which linked to a short video of the owner talking about the wine.

With minimal cost and effort, they created a comprehensive 'touch' and 'texture' experience that transformed the routine packaging step into a five-star experience.

Offering excellence isn't one amorphous act of service, but the sum of small, consistent upgrades applied across every touchpoint. Individually they seem minor, but collectively, they change how a brand is experienced.

The upside of automation: The new competitive frontier

Let's not make automation the enemy of everything that is happening now. AI is the workhorse that steps in when speed and accuracy matter most. For example, when your car has been damaged and you're trying to organise repairs and get updates on quotes, you don't want to sit on hold or chase callbacks. You want clear answers, fast. That's where automation earns its place. It sits at the other end of the pendulum from human-centred service. Some moments call for empathy, others demand efficiency, but the best businesses know how to deploy both.

Digital marketer Ben Fewtrell sees this daily. One of his smash repair clients received around 2500 phone calls over a three-month period and was missing close to 20 per cent of them. When calls rang out, the customers often moved on to the next repairer they found on Google, which undermined their marketing spend and created unnecessary frustration. To counter this, Ben installed a Voice AI agent that answered calls instantly, routed callers to the right person, booked quote and repair dates, provided job updates and answered common questions. There were no delays, no missed calls and it relieved pressure on the front-office team.

Michael Flanderka, CEO of Data Interactive, sees the same shift. He built 'Toby', an AI assistant for an eye surgery clinic, and trained 'him' on every question a patient could ask: procedures, prices, risks, recovery times. 'Toby' handles the standard enquiries so staff can focus on the patients who genuinely need human reassurance and personalised care.

* * *

When it comes to AI, machines win on speed, but humans win on connection. The advantage belongs to entrepreneurs who know when to use each. Blend them well and you build a business the algorithm can't beat.

Nuggets of wisdom

▶ Complete the UCS for your business and find a point of difference that others can't match.

▶ Document every touchpoint in your customer journey. Rate that experience and see what you can do to turn each step into a five-star experience.

▶ Contact an AI automation expert or consultancy and book a meeting. Tell them what you do, and how, and ask what recommendations they have for automating those processes.

PART 3

MARKETING

Marketing used to be the domain of the biggest, most cashed-up brands. If you didn't have deep pockets or access to mainstream media, you were largely locked out. That's no longer the case. Influencers and content creators have changed how brands are built and discovered, and they're doing it without waiting for approval from traditional gatekeepers.

For startups and small business owners, this shift is good news. You can now grow a brand, generate sales and test what works without spending a fortune. The tools are faster, cheaper and far more measurable than ever before. You can see what's working, cut what isn't and double down on what is.

Part 3 looks at how to leverage the significant power of creators, and how to become one yourself.

15

HOW TO BE A SUCCESSFUL SOCIAL MEDIA CONTENT CREATOR

The most powerful media channels in the world no longer belong to networks, publishers or studios. They belong to individuals. Across every sector, from gaming, beauty and wellness to fashion, film and fitness, creators are building global audiences, and forging valuable brand collaborations in the process. Let's discover how the creator economy really works, and what it takes to succeed within it.

The real powerbrokers of the creator economy

There is an event happening near me right now at one of the city's big sports stadiums. Twenty thousand people, mostly young men smelling of Lynx, are watching their gaming heroes battle it out in the Valorant Champions Tour (VCT). After three gruelling weeks of play, two teams of five will go head-to-head. One team will walk away with $1 million in prize money.

I've never heard of any of these gaming superstars. My 19-year-old son has, and so have the 139 000 people watching live on Twitch, a streaming platform that draws massive online audiences.

I look on, stunned by the scale of the audience, the devotion of the fans, and the intricate sponsorship ecosystem built around something I didn't even know existed.

It makes me wonder what else is going on that I don't know about. As it turns out, there's quite a lot.

A few kilometres away, 30 000 young girls are packed in a concert hall watching a K-pop band I've never heard of being streamed live from Seoul.

An email pops up that lets me know a Brisbane-based wellness coach I follow is hosting a Facebook livestream on 'The Power of Manifestation' for 5000 of her followers. Each has paid $250 to attend. That's $1 250 000 for a two-hour event. (Now, that's what I call manifestation!)

These events remind us of something important: vast, thriving creator worlds are operating in plain sight making serious money, and many of us have no idea they're even there.

We no longer live in a monoculture, where everyone watches the same shows, follows the same celebrities or is introduced to the same idea at the same time. Today, influence lives in echo chambers and in parallel worlds where pockets of people are having experiences that are invisible to the wider world.

Everywhere you look, creators are commanding global audiences and cashing in big time, and just because we haven't heard about them, doesn't mean they don't exist.

That's why it pays to explore beyond your own feeds and familiar platforms. The most interesting ideas, audiences and opportunities often live in worlds you haven't thought to visit yet. If you do, you'll discover a flourishing economy of people making a small fortune off the back of their social media following.

Pru Corrigan is a talent manager at One Daydream. She manages some of Australia's busiest social media superstars. 'There is serious money, power and influence in this space,' she said. Some make over $100 000 a month.'

'Each influencer has set rates depending on their followers and back-end insights,' explains Pru. 'They get paid to create a range of content such as Instagram posts, Stories and Reels, TikToks, YouTube videos, stage appearances, vox pops and other formats. They generally don't get paid for the amount of time they spend on something or the quantity of words they write, but for a mix of what they might create for the client.'

With the potential to earn six figures in one month, it's easy to see why influencing has become the career of choice for the next generation of founders.

Kylie Jenner and *that* $300 000 post

The right influencer can change the fortunes of a brand overnight, something that Bondi Sands co-founder Shaun Wilson found out for himself.

'Marketing hasn't changed in hundreds of years,' he said. 'The most effective form is still referral. Social media just scaled it.' Bondi Sands built its strategy around that insight, working with a wide range of influencers who shared genuine stories about why they loved the brand.

Bondi Sands went big from the outset and approached uber influencer Kylie Jenner.

It was a risky move. Her fee, more than $300 000 for just one post, was enormous for a home-grown brand that had started a mere three years earlier. The good news was Kylie already used the product and liked it. She'd stopped using solariums, cared about skin protection and loved their signature dark foam tanning product.

'That was critical for us,' Shaun said. 'We'd only work with someone who was using the product.'

The post of Kylie posing with the can of tan in her bathroom mirror went viral almost instantly. Sales went through the roof, five-star reviews flooded in and Bondi Sands became the go-to brand for a new generation of sun-smart women who wanted an instant tan.

Timing matters

For Bondi Sands, the real test came when the brand set its sights on the United States. Landing a national pharmacy chain there can make or break a consumer brand. Shaun's chain of choice was Walgreens. With more than 8000 stores, Walgreens offered instant national distribution, credibility and scale. A successful range review would put Bondi Sands in front of millions of customers overnight and fundamentally change the direction of the business.

The backstory as to why Bondi Sands hired Kylie is instructive. Shaun had a meeting scheduled with Walgreens shortly after the Kylie Jenner post went live. The timing was deliberate and the stakes were enormous. Walgreens doesn't take on brands lightly. They expect proof that a company can fund serious co-operative marketing, generate immediate consumer demand and support the operational needs of a national rollout. This meeting was Shaun's one shot to prove Bondi Sands could meet those expectations.

The Kylie Jenner post was more than a tactic to generate sales and headlines. It was a calculated move designed to prove that Bondi Sands could create demand at scale, convert attention into revenue and attract a new demographic of customers into stores.

Shaun had done his homework. He'd studied Walgreens' corporate plans, understood their Gen Z focus and sun-care strategy, and arrived with a tailored pitch. That alone would have been sufficient to get a decent hearing. But Shaun went further. He took the time to research who the Walgreens buyers were and boosted Kylie's post directly into their social feeds. It was a paid, hyper-targeted push aimed at one audience only: the decision-makers who would be sitting across the table from him.

By the time Shaun walked into the room, the Walgreens buyers already knew the Bondi Sands story, and it shifted the dynamic. He was no longer just another small challenger brand asking for distribution. He was a global brand with proven sales offering them a chance to partner with a credible firm who could bring them a new cohort of customers.

Walgreens liked what they saw and offered Shaun a $10 million opening order, and a nationwide rollout over 8000 stores, which was exactly what he wanted.

It was one of the biggest wins in Bondi Sands' history, engineered from a single post, amplified by global PR and delivered into the right hands at the right moment. It put them on the map and they've never looked back.

Look bigger than you are

Like Bondi Sands, Swisse started locally but thought globally. Radek Sali knew he couldn't outspend the giant pharmaceutical companies, so he had to outthink them. With limited marketing dollars, he focused on creating the perception that Swisse was bigger than it really was, because the pharmacy buyers needed to know that the brands they ranged had the financial and operational capacity to support a national rollout and contribute to a co-operative marketing campaign.

Instead of taking out individual billboards across the country, and spreading the marketing budget across multiple markets, Radek studied where all the pharmacy buyers for the vitamin category actually travelled — their commute routes, the roads they took to the airport, the freeways they took to their various head offices — and then bought billboards in those locations.

As buyers went about their daily business, they'd spot a Swisse billboard on the drive to work, another on the way to the airport and then another at the terminal entrance. What was, in reality, a modest media spend centred around a small geographic region suddenly looked like a full-scale national campaign.

When Radek walked into their offices, the overwhelming response he received from the buyers was, 'Wow! You're everywhere.' He wasn't. They just thought he was, and that belief opened doors, won shelf space and laid the groundwork for their bigger goal, which was to get ranged in the major grocery stores.

The moral of the story? You don't need to *be* big; you just need to *look* big.

The road to Hollywood

Another small brand punching well above its weight is the Macfarlane Bros. Long before Hollywood came calling, these two Brisbane-based YouTube creators learned how to look bigger than they were by using short-form video, strategic distribution and disciplined consistency to build a global audience from their bedroom.

Now on the fast track to becoming high-powered film directors, Austin (22) and Lachlan (25) are taking the YouTube world by storm. They've amassed over one million YouTube subscribers, 700 000 TikTok followers and 250 000 on Instagram and continue to attract the attention of fans and fellow film directors alike.

Their niche is making high-impact, 20-second mini-movies for pop-culture fans with an emphasis on creating dazzling special effects that turn their home-made movies into cinematic epics. It's no wonder brands like Warner Bros., Google, Apple, Amazon and Adobe have enlisted the duo to make branded content to promote their products.

It all began with a Christmas present.

'When I was 10, I got a video tripod for Christmas and that kickstarted my interest in film,' said Lachlan. 'I posted my first video on YouTube when I was 11.'

His brother Austin soon caught the filmmaking bug and began helping him shoot and edit videos. Together they took it further, enrolling in a film course at university. They picked up internships on television sets and in post-production houses, worked as online editors and spent time in advertising agencies. After work, they'd go home, head to their makeshift studio and keep working on their own videos.

Their first Spider-Man TikTok was simple and fun, but it wasn't a breakout video. What came next was.

A short sketch built around a Flash parody of the 'fastest man alive' gag was the video that changed everything. It racked up millions of views and unexpectedly sparked a global trend, with creators recreating the format using other films and pop-culture scenes.

That was the moment it clicked.

'We realised it wasn't just about what we were making, but about where we were placing it,' Lachlan said. 'We'd been uploading to YouTube for years, but it was only when we started posting on TikTok that the growth really came.'

From there, they leaned into the kind of content that travelled fast on short-form platforms: cinematic visual gags, superhero parodies, behind-the-scenes fake-outs, and tightly edited sketches designed to surprise viewers in the first few seconds.

Two years later, in 2024, they returned to Spider-Man with a far more ambitious production, using advanced visual effects to show themselves climbing walls and firing webs from the sides of buildings — a full-circle moment from those early experiments.

They'd been around long enough to understand the shift. TikTok didn't just reward good ideas. It rewarded timing, format, and knowing exactly what your audience wanted.

'With YouTube, you have to market your video with the title and thumbnail, and you have to get people to click on it and stay watching. With TikTok, the audience just gets served your content, so as long as you make a good video, you'll see the results. We don't get too stressed if one doesn't land, because we can make another one the following week.'

After that first successful Flash parody video landed, they posted one video every week for about a year and they credit that consistency as the critical factor that helped them grow their audience. Their largest audience is on YouTube, but TikTok fast tracked their early growth and put them on the influencer map.

The big view counts didn't arrive overnight.

'In 2022, our videos weren't doing so well and our views dropped quite a bit. That was an important moment for us because it made us realise that whether our videos were successful or not, we just loved the art of making them and would keep going no matter what.'

Their pinch-me moment arrived in 2024 when they were invited by Warner Bros. to fly to Ireland as brand ambassadors for *How to Train Your Dragon*.

'Sitting there watching Bill Pope, the cinematographer behind *The Matrix*, *Spider-Man*, and Edgar Wright's *The World's End*, directing his camera team was surreal.'

Another standout moment came when they were flown to London to attend the screening of *Wonka*, the 2023 musical fantasy prequel to *Charlie and the Chocolate Factory*. 'We were there to hear the director speak, and then suddenly Timothée Chalamet walked in as a surprise guest. It was mind blowing. We've always dreamed of being film directors,' Lachlan said. 'So, to be invited onto real sets and watch how Hollywood productions come together was incredible.'

They've worked with the team from the hit comedy trio Aunty Donna on a web series called *The Worst That Could Happen*.

'It's a genre-bending anthology that drops ordinary young characters into extraordinary situations, blending comedy, sci-fi and light horror to explore modern fears, ambition and identity,' said

Lachlan. The series is live on YouTube, with vertical short-form edits across Instagram, TikTok and YouTube Shorts.

They were behind the camera for this one, which is where they prefer to be.

'Long term, we want to be a team of brother film directors,' said Lachlan. 'But it's our work as social media creators that's enabled us to learn our craft, meet directors and attend the red-carpet premieres of some really big movies.'

The Macfarlane Bros have achieved so much in 10 years, it'll be fascinating to see what they achieve in the next 10. And to think it all started with a tripod and a camera. A small start that created a big result.

A week in the life of an influencer

Influencers often get dismissed as lazy, superficial or lucky. But those who work with them behind the scenes tell a very different story. Beneath the glamour and gloss is skill, determination and a commitment to creating great content. As Pru Corrigan explains, the reality is far more complex than the stereotypes suggest.

Pru has been in the PR business for longer than most. After years in fast fashion, she felt burnt out and exhausted by the relentless pace. She could see that mega brands like Sephora were about to arrive in Australia so she seized the moment and launched a PR agency dedicated to beauty brands, and within a few years, was representing global heavyweights like Sephora, The Body Shop and Marc Jacobs Beauty.

By 2015, her focus had shifted from gifting products and samples to magazine editors, to targeting social media influencers instead. Then, in 2018, a new opportunity arrived when influencer Ellie Gonsalves asked Pru to represent her. That one partnership sparked a new service of helping social influencers attract brand deals.

After years of negotiating deals on both sides of the table, Pru has a clear view of how the influencer economy actually works, and why the common assumptions about it are so wrong.

Here's her take on the biggest myths about influencers, and the truth behind them.

Myth #1: They don't work hard

Fact: 'They do. Influencers are constantly creating, editing and engaging. Their audience expects daily updates, and disappearing even for a day can mean losing traction. Most work 40-hour weeks, or more, to maintain their following and meet client deadlines.'

Myth #2: They're airheads

Fact: 'Many are exceptionally talented. They weave products naturally into mini-films that entertain and persuade, which would take full-service agencies weeks and big budgets to produce. They're one-person marketing teams who intuitively understand how script, story and sound merge with brand to create a sales-driven narrative. They are technically very clever and strategically very astute.'

Myth #3: They show a fake life

Fact: 'Most share a real, curated version of their lives that cover the major milestones: dating, weddings, divorces, babies, jobs and even mental health struggles. They edit out the boring bits to maintain the narrative tension, but the rest of it is their real life.'

Myth #4: They're one-hit wonders

Fact: 'The top creators have been building their audiences for a decade or more. Some started with nothing and just showed up and kept posting, even when no-one was watching. They took the time to learn how the analytics worked, adjusted their content accordingly, and kept learning, commenting and sharing their stories, day after day, even when they weren't being paid to do so.'

* * *

Strip away the stereotypes and you see the truth: the influencers who last aren't lucky — they're disciplined creators who treat social media as a business and have the long game in mind.

How a digital superstar spends their week

After speaking with multiple influencers and their managers, a clear pattern emerged that debunks the myth that social influencers spend their days lying around taking selfies and sipping matcha tea. They're busy creating content and keeping it all together. What follows isn't one person's routine, but a composite snapshot that paints a realistic picture of how a busy, in-demand creator might spend their week. Some will be busier than this, others less so.

Sammy, 28, is a top health and lifestyle influencer. She's had brand deals with:

- Lululemon: yoga gear
- Charlotte Tilbury: makeup
- Carman's Kitchen: muesli
- Uniqlo: casual wear
- Stanley: drink bottles
- WelleCo: supplements
- Grey Goose: vodka.

Here's what a week in the life of Sammy might look like.

Activity
Day 1 Alarm goes off. Re-check the Lululemon campaign brief and confirm the day's deliverables. Throw on the client-supplied outfit and start mentally storyboarding the morning's content.
Film the 'Get Ready with Me' (GRWM) scene using Charlotte Tilbury products. Shoot multiple takes. Capture B-roll of the products for reels.
Arrive at the yoga studio for the Lululemon event. Complete the session, film sponsored clips and selfies. Tag the brand and re-record transitions.
Return home. Approve content from yesterday's shoot, respond to client comments and write the copy for the captions. Edit footage and send for approval. Go to the gym, have dinner, prepare outfits for tomorrow.
Day 2 Eat breakfast (featuring WelleCo supplements), film that content, send to client. Check analytics from last post.
Change into new outfit from Uniqlo. Film a quick 'Outfit of the Day' (OOTD) transition reel while getting ready. Do hair and makeup, and drive to the event.
Attend PR lunch for a new Stanley drink bottle launch: meet client, do stage Q&A, greet fans, shoot content. Pose for stills, tag other creators, record a short testimonial clip for brand feed.
Sit in the car and re-edit Lululemon content based on client feedback. Re-send to client. Post stories with 'Day in the Life' (DITL) snippets to maintain engagement. Meet friends for dinner at a restaurant.
Day 3 Meet with accountant and agent for the six-monthly review and planning session. Drive to Grey Goose cocktail launch. Conduct light and sound check, meet client, film content, do a live radio interview. Capture behind-the-scenes clips for TikTok, tag collaborators, reply to DMs from followers. Update drink bottle content and schedule posts from yesterday's launch.

Activity
Day 4 Attend film premiere, walk red carpet, capture transition shots and crowd reactions, watch the movie. Draft caption ideas while sitting in the cinema.
Drive home, check emails, edit Grey Goose launch content, post film premiere content, open package from new client and film an unboxing video. Reply to comments, and tag all relevant sponsors before midnight upload deadline.
Day 5 Test out new Charlotte Tilbury products for upcoming shoot. Write scripts. Prepare for tomorrow's trip to Sydney. Film a 'Pack with Me' (PWM) segment. Feed the dog, go to gym, have dinner with partner, have a shower, and go to bed.

As you can see, Sammy's real life and her social media content are so seamlessly intertwined it's hard to know where one ends and the other begins. Her life is the raw material, but the skill lies in how she wields the camera. What looks effortless on screen is based on careful planning, creativity and commercial discipline.

Kat Moses, founder of MGMT, runs her own talent agency spanning Sydney and Los Angeles, and represents some of the world's most successful social media creators. She's quick to point out that no two influencers work schedules are alike.

'Everyone is so different,' she said. 'Some do the majority of their work from 6 pm to 2 am. Others treat it like a day job, sitting at their desk by 8 am and wrapping up at 6 pm. They make their own hours.'

Managing the day-to-day minutiae of a social media superstar requires high-level organisational skills.

'There's a mountain of administration that takes a lot of time,' Kat explains. 'Do we have the contracts? Are the creative briefs signed off? Have the products arrived? The creators spend hours editing their footage and often juggle five or six projects at once, all with tight deadlines. I often get messages from creators at 2 am saying, "Just finished editing, I'm going to bed now. I'll sleep till 11, then call you." It can be an all-day, all-night kind of job.'

They also need to keep up with fast-changing platform demands. Pru Corrigan said, 'Not every platform is going to be relevant to their personal brand or what their clients want. What you create on Instagram may not perform on TikTok, and what you create on TikTok may not perform on YouTube, so they may need to create three or four different types of content to put out on all these platforms. That's a lot of work.'

* * *

To the uninitiated, influencing can look easy. A post goes up, the likes roll in and the money flows. But behind every post and perfectly placed ring light is a lot of planning, discipline and graft. The best creators treat what they do like a real business. They show up consistently, hit deadlines, pay attention to what their audience want and work hard to stay relevant in a fast-moving digital world.

Nuggets of wisdom

▸ Use proven social media content formats like unboxings, before-and-afters, day-in-the-life clips, tutorials, Q&As, reviews and behind-the-scenes posts. These ready-made content formats give you a template to work from, so you can focus on what you say, not how to frame it.

▸ Don't wait to be discovered by a social media agent. Find your own paid social media work by registering with influencer marketing platforms like Tribe.co, fabulate.com and grapevine.ai. Register on multiple platforms, follow the prompts and you could be on your way to being a paid content creator.

▸ Improve your tech knowledge to create better content. Learn the skills that will make your content worth paying for: editing, lighting, sound, captions, composition and simple analytics. Shift your identity from being someone who posts to someone who produces.

16

HOW TO BE AUTHENTIC

In a world where it's increasingly difficult to sort the real from the fake, and the artificial from the authentic, it seems our best bet is to present to the world the person we really are. That said, showing our true personality, foibles and vulnerabilities is confronting, especially for those who value their privacy. But if we want a slice of the social media pie and the financial benefits that come with it, the experts I interviewed were unanimous with their advice: we need to show what our lives are really like.

A masterclass in authenticity

I recently watched a talk from *The Hollywood Reporter* featuring a host of amazing male actors. The moderator, Lacey Rose, asked each performer their reason for acting.

Timothy Simons: 'Because there is no ceiling to the amount of attention I need...'

Sacha Baron Cohen: 'Because I can't do anything else.'

Jim Carrey: 'Because I'm broken in a lot of pieces and acting gives me a chance to reconfigure those pieces into a thousand different things that are positive for people to watch ...'

Jim's was the most searingly honest answer, and captured the hearts of everyone at that table. What happened next was equally illuminating. That disarming revelation broke open the conversation and gave each man permission to speak openly about the *real* reason they became actors.

The chat quickly turned from a talk fest of self-promoting narcissism, to a rich, nuanced, deeply moving expose of broken childhoods, abusive parenting, loneliness and longing. The masks fell away and the resulting conversation made for riveting viewing. It took that brave, wise, broken Jim Carrey to give voice to the vulnerable truth of why he does what he does, which gave the others the courage to do the same.

That's the power of authenticity. When one person is brave enough to speak the truth, it lowers the defences of everyone else, creates space for honesty and changes the emotional temperature of the room.

The question a business owner needs to consider isn't whether they can be authentic online; it's whether they want to be, and whether they're prepared for the trade-offs that come with it. That choice circles back to the core question at the heart of this book: what do you actually want from your business, and what are you willing to put on the line to get it?

I asked leading talent manager Kat Moses how an entrepreneur could make themselves more marketable as a social media influencer. The topic of authenticity came up again.

'Look at popular stars like US influencer Alix Earle. She showed up as her authentic self and consistently posted on TikTok for years sharing candid, unfiltered content about her life, beauty routines and college experience. For a long while it seemed that nothing was happening, and then the tide turned and she just blew up. She's now one of the biggest female influencers in America.'

The thornier question for influencers isn't whether authenticity works, but what it costs. When you put your opinions and personal life up for public consumption, you invite connection — and criticism. Managing that tension isn't easy, and it can take a real toll on mental health, as journalist Kate Halfpenny discovered in a very public and confronting way.

The pros and cons of reading the comments

Kate Halfpenny is nothing if not authentic. Her columns in *The Sydney Morning Herald* and *The Age* routinely outrank the others because she is radically honest.

One column she wrote almost broke the internet and it nearly broke her too.

She thought the column was a stock-standard Saturday piece. It turned out to be anything but. A year earlier, she and her husband Chris had moved to Ocean Grove, 95 kilometres south-west of Melbourne, from inner-city Collingwood for a sea change, only to realise a few months later that they may have made a mistake. They loved their seaside retreat, but missed their city life, so they rented a tiny one-bedder in Parkville, just north of the city, as an urban bolthole to stay in when they came down to Melbourne. Little did she know but that one column documenting her reverse sea change was about to blow up her life.

When she woke on Sunday, her phone was full of messages from friends concerned about the 1000 comments the article had generated on Facebook alone, an extraordinary amount for that masthead.

Kate's revelation that she'd had the temerity to both rent *and* own properties had stoked the fires of outrage. People accused her of single-handedly causing Australia's housing crisis, of pushing up property prices, of denying them the right to secure and safe housing, and overall contributing to widespread societal decay. The vitriol escalated to threats.

> *We are going to find your children and kill them.*
> *We're going to bash your mum.*
> *We hope your dogs die.*

'It was awful, and so out of proportion to who I am and what I do,' said Kate. 'I was scared for my safety. For a few months after that, I made sure I double-bolted the gate and checked all the doors. If people are sufficiently motivated, they can track you down in real life. That's what made it feel so scary. You just don't know what people might do.'

Kate was no stranger to exposing her life. She had written openly about her husband's alcohol addiction, her divorce from her first husband, family fights, her waning sex life and passion for Botox, but this particular column hit a raw nerve.

She coped in the only way she knew how.

'I stood in the shower and sobbed. I did the whole, "Why are people so unkind?" Kamahl kind of thing for a bit. But I eventually realised the best approach was to ignore my phone, eat loads of chocolate, go boogie boarding, walk the dog, do craft and make my husband say, "I really love you" five times a day.'

The trolling was traumatic but it didn't deter her from continuing to share her life and opinions in her columns.

'If you're a writer, you have to be prepared to go really deep and raw and hard. If you don't, what's the point? You're just putting something generic into the world that adds nothing to the conversation. If you're going to go there, then bloody go there. If you're not prepared to do that, don't write about yourself.'

Gaining perspective helped her stay strong. 'I had to remind myself that I'm not performing a public service. I'm writing 680 words on a topic I hope people find interesting. I'm one woman sitting in a converted backyard garage, listening to Gang of Youths and looking at the lemon tree.'

There was a happy ending. Buried among the thousands baying for her blood was one reader who saw potential: Martin Hughes, a co-founder of Affirm Press. He admired how her columns polarised so many readers and attracted so much attention, and offered her a book deal to write her memoir. That book, *Boogie Wonderland*, is now out in the world, and Kate's on the festival circuit sharing the story that once caused her so much grief. Proof that sometimes good really can come from bad.

Does she still read the comments?

'Never. Otherwise I'd never write again.'

The Streisand Effect

In 2003, Barbra Streisand tried to have an aerial photograph of her Malibu home removed from a public archive. Prior to complaining, the image had been downloaded six times. After she sued the photographer, it was viewed over half a million times in one month. Her attempt to suppress the photo had the opposite effect. That's the Streisand Effect at play: the harder you try to bury a story, the bigger it becomes. It's a lesson every public figure and content creator eventually learns. When you're misrepresented online, you're forced into a no-win dilemma. Fight it, and you feed the fire, and drive more eyeballs to what you don't want them to see. Ignore it, and it feels like you've surrendered and they've won. It's a zero-sum game.

One woman who did fight back was Indy Clinton, an Australian social media influencer and mum of three, known for candidly sharing the messy reality of family life. She's amassed over 1.5 million followers on TikTok, and around 650 000 on Instagram. Clinton also faced online backlash, most notably after a story about a cosmetic procedure on her nose triggered negative comments about her appearance. She responded publicly and confirmed she'd hired a private investigator to track down the anonymous trolls who persisted in targeting her.

Few want to take that kind of extreme action to tame the trolls, but for some, like Indy, they feel they have no option but to fight.

What's the solution? Not read the comments? Pretend it hasn't happened? Turn your phone off?

I asked Pru Corrigan, founder of talent management agency One Daydream, for her insights on how to manage negative commentary.

'For some influencers, asking them to not check their comments is like saying, "Don't look at your test results from the doctor". The comments are where we get the results; it's how we know what's going on. You can block them for your mental health, but if you're a professional influencer I think it's important to face it head on.'

Adele Samus — influencer, actress and stunt woman — uses her comments as a source of new material.

'Comments give me great ideas for my comedy skits. They spark my imagination and give me a direct insight into what happens to other people,' she said. 'That's the reality of social media. If you're putting yourself out there, you're going to get all sorts of stuff coming back.'

Knowing others are going through it takes the sting out.

'Hearing from my other influencer friends about the comments and DMs they get blows my mind. We just laugh at them and choose not to take anything personally because it happens to everyone.'

Glen James, financial podcaster and host of the *money money money* show, sees it differently.

'It's really unhealthy to read comments. I don't like Googling my name. That said, it is important to keep up with what your audience is thinking and saying. I'm very active in our Facebook group because that gives me a real-time pulse check of how I'm doing.'

Like Adele, he sees those comments as a source of free market research.

'Most brands have to pay a market researcher to find out what listeners are thinking. I've got a real-time focus group of 52 000 people on Facebook. If a post goes up and one person says, "You're boring, and this is crap", that doesn't mean it's true. But if 10 people in a row say, "You're boring and this is crap", then it probably is, and I would take steps to fix that.'

Focus on what matters

You know you've made it when you've got a Reddit thread under your name. Chef and former judge on *MasterChef* George Calombaris experienced the blowtorch of public opprobrium when it was revealed he'd inadvertently underpaid his staff at MAdE Establishment. He didn't need to go looking for comments; they found him.

'At the worst of it, my friends would text me every day saying, "Have you seen this?" It was pretty relentless. It went on for months and the memory of that time lingers on and will stay with me for the rest of my life. Even now, years later, when my phone pings, my adrenaline spikes. It's a form of PTSD that's triggered by the sound of my phone.'

He sought solace from his close friend, Ange Postecoglou, a man criticised on a global scale by some of the most ferocious people on the planet: soccer fans.

'Ange told me the media always ask, "What's Plan B?" And he says, "Plan B is getting Plan A right". Soccer fans will always have something to say, but if I waste energy worrying about the noise from the grandstands, I'm not giving my best to the people who matter: my team and coaching staff.'

George tries to follow that approach.

'If I give 100 per cent of myself to the people who matter, I know I've done my best. If I start reading what people say — you're fat, you're dishonest, you ripped people off — I get in a rut and I can't be of value to my team or my family. Despite everything that happened, I've had incredible people come up and say the most beautiful things. I'm strong, I can deal with it, but lots of others can't, and I feel for them, because too many people are taking their lives because of this.'

The lesson from those who've lived through it is clear. When the stress is high, the only way forward is to keep your eyes on the work in front of you, control the controllables and give everything to the people who actually count.

How to turn trolls into traction

Kirsten Tibballs, host of *The Chocolate Queen* television show and *MasterChef* guest judge, has over a million followers on her socials, yet remarkably, and fortunately, gets very little online hate. What's her secret?

'I don't do a great deal of talking in my videos and I don't share my opinions, which probably helps. I get a bit of trolling on YouTube, but it's not personal. It's more, "That's not how I would make chocolate mousse", rather than "Your hair looks terrible". People who share opinions get more feedback. I don't generally get that, which is bizarre, but good. I know that's not normal. I'm very lucky.'

When criticism does appear, her response is pragmatic.

'My belief is that even if you get trolling and you can engage with it, you're still winning because they're building your algorithm for you.

You're getting a reaction. I don't worry about what people think. If I did, I wouldn't do anything. My advice is, do what you need to do, be independent, be individual and if you get trolls, look at it as a positive and say, "Thank you for boosting my engagement".'

* * *

As a content creator, you'll need to grapple with the everyday pressure that comes with putting yourself up for public discussion. You need to decide what you will share, what you won't and how to deal with the blowback if or when it arrives. The key is to be intentional, think big, maintain perspective and plan how you want to show up, for whom and why.

Nuggets of wisdom

▶ Set boundaries. Decide in advance how much of your personal life you will reveal online and stick to it.
▶ Create a brag book. Collect a scrap book of complimentary client quotes and reviews to bolster your spirit if the negative trolling gets too much.
▶ Choose your moments. Don't read the comments when you're feeling tired, vulnerable or fragile. Wait until you're in a stronger headspace and have a mantra ready to deflect the worst of it. 'This too shall pass,' 'Not my monkey, not my circus,' and 'This is not about me,' all work well.

17

HOW TO BUILD YOUR PERSONAL BRAND

Everyone has a personal brand, whether they like it or not, and whether they've paid attention to shaping it or not. As Jeff Bezos said, your brand is what people say about you when you're not in the room. So, who's shaping your brand — you, or someone else? The entrepreneurs who take personal branding seriously don't wait for others to tell their story. They take care in curating how they show up, what they stand for and how they're remembered. They do the ground work to craft a backstory that their audience can connect with, their customers can recall and the media can promote.

The power of storytelling

Every successful entrepreneur has a log cabin story. Janine Allis had a great one: a single mum down on her luck looking for direction finds fame in the healthy fast-food sector and creates a business worth hundreds of millions. It was a story worth telling. The challenge was learning how to tell it.

How Janine Allis learned to tell her story

'In the early days, I felt like I was two people,' she said. 'There was Janine, the founder of Boost Juice, and then there was "Janine", the PR tool I had to use to get people to understand what Boost was about.'

She had worked for United International Pictures on a range of different movies, and had a solid background in PR, so she knew the basics for how to tell a story. But as a constant student, she reached out to experts to not only help her refine the story, but to communicate it more effectively. One such expert was Simon Hammond, founder of Hammond Thinking. He understood that it wasn't just about the story you told, but the emotion you elicited. 'His presentations contained videos, humour and sadness, and as all great entertainers know, if you can make them laugh, cry, or both, you have got them,' she said.

With a clearer story and the confidence to tell it authentically, Janine became a highly sought-after keynote speaker, then went on *Shark Tank*, competed on *Survivor* twice, and co-hosted *Food Stars* alongside Gordon Ramsay. All of that media exposure strengthened her personal brand, which in turn shone the light on the Boost brand and created the polished media superstar we see on our screens today. When she learned how to communicate who she really was, people listened, and her personal and business brand grew exponentially.

With over half a million followers on LinkedIn, Janine doesn't have to rely on the largesse of mainstream media to distribute her message. That's the real leverage of a personal brand. When you build it properly, visibility compounds, momentum builds and you get to control the narrative of who you are, what you stand for and what you want people to know about you.

Could you pass the four-word test?

Everyone wants the upside of a high-profile personal brand: the book deal, the TV appearances, the TED Talk. But those opportunities don't turn up just because you want them. They turn up because you've spent time educating the media about who you are, what you do and why you're the best at it, and you've wrapped it all up in a 10-second sound bite.

When TV and event producers source guests for chat shows, podcasts and speaking gigs, they have a dozen or more bios on the table, and very little time to read them. They need a quick way to answer that critical four-word question: 'What do you do?'

The speakers who stand out are those who can distil a lifetime of work into a short, sharp sound bite. *She's the juice lady. He's the resilience guy. She's that Olympic swimmer.*

A friend of mine is a senior entomologist with a Harvard doctorate in biosecurity and invasive species. When she appeared on a morning radio show, she was introduced as 'the bug lady'.

She was slightly deflated to witness her comprehensive body of work flattened into a one-sentence label, but that compression is also what gets people booked. If you can't distil your superpower into something memorable, you won't cut through.

Shouting your accomplishments from the rooftop is difficult for some. It feels egotistical and self-serving, but the uncomfortable truth about social media is that those who spruik their accomplishments profit more than those who don't. It can be galling to watch loud, self-obsessed personalities reap the rewards, but clicks are currency. As Michael J Fox once put it, 'The more you've got, the more you get.'

If you decide to step into the social media arena, it helps to do it deliberately and for a reason that's bigger than your ego. Being in service to a cause, an audience or a mission will carry you further than slavish self-promotion ever could. Just know the trade-off, because once you become visible, you don't get to opt out. Fame isn't reversible, and anonymity, once lost, is very difficult to retrieve.

The one-liner pitch template

The secret of success is to prepare your pitch before you need to deliver it. Making it up on the spot will cost you opportunities. Here's a personal branding framework that the founders of companies like Uber, Canva and Airbnb use to raise money, retain staff and attract media attention. It instantly communicates *what you do, who it's for, and why it matters*:

Here's the formula: 'We [do what] for [who] by [how] so they can [outcome]'.

For example:

- 'We provide on-demand rides for everyday people by connecting them with nearby drivers through an app so they can get where they need to go quickly and safely.'
  → Uber
- 'We make design simple for everyone by offering an intuitive drag-and-drop platform so they can create professional content without a designer.'
  → Canva
- 'We connect travellers with local hosts by providing a trusted online marketplace so they can experience the world like locals.'
  → Airbnb

Top 10 ways to build your personal brand

Here are 10 practical, proven ways to build a personal brand that helps boost your business and brings in media opportunities.

1 Own your digital real estate
Create a Wikipedia page for yourself, buy your personal website domain (e.g. janesmith.com) and secure consistent handles across all social platforms (e.g. @janesmith). You are the brand so take steps to own your digital real estate before someone buys your name and tries to sell it back to you for a fee.

2 Define your one-liner
Get good at delivering your one-line pitch. If a producer, journalist or prospect asks, 'What do you do?' you should be able to deliver a cogent answer in under 10 seconds.

3 Find your USP (unique selling proposition)
Identify what makes you different from others in your sector — it could be your backstory, achievements, a special methodology or unique perspective — and weave that into your one-liner pitch.

4 Work the 7-4-11 rule
Consistency across channels builds familiarity, credibility and momentum far faster than one-off bursts of content. Aim to create around seven hours of content across four platforms (LinkedIn, YouTube, email etc), through at least 11 touchpoints (blog, webinar, newsletter etc).

(continued)

5 Become a public speaker

Being a keynote speaker is a wildly efficient way of increasing your reach. Why speak for an hour to one person, when you could speak for an hour to 500 people?

6 Write a book

A book turns your ideas into a permanent asset and positions you as a credible voice in your field. It also protects your IP. The root word of *authority* is *author,* so if you want to be seen as one, write a book.

7 Share your failures

People love hearing how founders failed, and then prevailed, so don't sugarcoat the bad stuff or pretend it didn't happen. Turn those setbacks into stories. They are the ones the audience will remember.

8 Conduct an online audit

Google yourself. It's confronting, but it's best you see what's coming up before your clients do. If you don't like what you see, publish more content to push what's there down to page 2 of Google.

9 Get found by AI

If you want tools like ChatGPT to recommend you, make it easy for them to understand what you're known for. Publish clear, authoritative content on credible sites that consistently link your name to a specific area of expertise.

10 Collect and showcase social proof

Testimonials, case studies, media mentions, awards and endorsements build trust fast. Display those badges on your website, LinkedIn profile and speaker bio. When others vouch for you, you don't have to.

Your personal brand won't just emerge. It needs to be crafted and be directly connected to what you sell and how you'll derive income. It takes time to get clarity around who you are, what you stand for and what you'll speak about. Once you've got that clear, everything will unfold with greater ease: your website copy, book topic, keynote speeches, newsletters and social content.

Nuggets of wisdom

▶ Slice and dice your content. Record one high-quality webinar, then repurpose it using AI. A single session can become a blog post, email newsletter, social posts, short video clips and pull-out quotes.
▶ Get skilled at writing search-optimised and AI-optimised copywriting. Learn how to write clear, keyword-driven copy so your content ranks in Google and on AI platforms for the terms your audience is already searching for.
▶ Practise public speaking wherever you can. Actively seek out speaking opportunities to build confidence and credibility. Rotary clubs, schools, universities and industry associations are always looking for speakers.

18

HOW TO CHOOSE THE RIGHT INFLUENCER FOR YOUR BUSINESS

Working with influencers for the first time can feel overwhelming, but once you understand the hierarchy, the pricing and the metrics for success, everything becomes easier. When you know the right questions to ask, and know what success looks like, you can make strategic decisions that will grow your brand, generate sales and build your following without wasting money, time or effort.

The hierarchy of influencers

Not all influencers are created equal, and each type plays a different role in your marketing strategy. Figure 18.1 (overleaf) shows the five levels of influence, from global celebrities at the top through to everyday creators and brand advocates at the base. As you move down the pyramid, audience size decreases but trust and engagement often increase. The key is to choose the tier that matches your goals, budget and target audience.

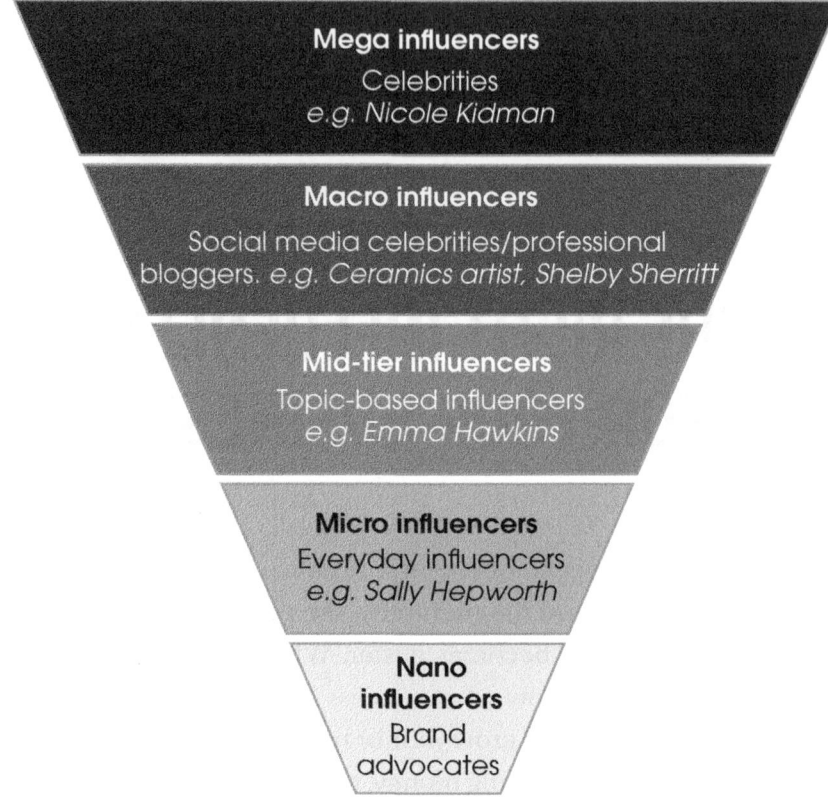

Figure 18.1 the five levels of influence

Understanding influencer marketing

Figure 18.1 shows examples of five tiers of influencers based on fanbase size:

- *Mega influencers:*
  - *Example:* Actress, Nicole Kidman
  - *# followers:* 1 000 000+
  - *Benefit:* Massive reach and instant awareness. Best for global campaigns and brand visibility, but not always direct sales.
- *Macro influencers:*
  - *Example:* Ceramics artist, Shelby Sherritt

- – *# followers:* 250 000–1 000 000
- – *Benefit:* They have a broad reach but are more accessible and affordable than A-list celebs.
- • *Mid-tier influencers:*
  - – *Example:* Emma Hawkins, lifestyle influencer
  - – *# followers:* 75 000–250 000
  - – *Benefit:* Strong reach with high trust and engagement. Big enough to move the needle, small enough to feel credible and affordable.
- • *Micro influencers:*
  - – *Example:* Author, Sally Hepworth
  - – *# followers:* 10 000–75 000
  - – *Benefit:* They have smaller but highly engaged audiences who see them as peers, making their recommendations feel personal and trusted.
- • *Nano influencers:*
  - – *Example:* Anyone you know, like and trust
  - – *# followers:* 1000–10 000
  - – *Benefit:* They have a smaller reach but are a highly trusted voice. They are ideal for grassroots campaigns and authentic recommendations.

Influencers are highly creative marketers who understand insights and trends, and have the power to draw attention to what you sell. Whether it's a mum looking for organic baby clothes or a teenage boy searching for the latest haircut trend, an influencer can get your product to show up in their feed and shine the light on your brand. It's like word-of-mouth at scale.

How much does an Australian influencer cost?

If you're a small business hiring an influencer for the first time, avoid hiring a single macro-influencer. Err on the side of caution and engage a range of affordable nano- or micro-influencers to test the waters. Doing so gives you room to try different ideas, formats and audiences.

Table 18.1 presents a guideline of fees an influencer may charge. These are estimates only and will vary depending on who you choose, what they sell and their engagement rates. See which ones are right for your business.

Table 18.1 influencer rates per post

Follower range	Instagram	YouTube	Facebook	TikTok
Nano (1000–10000)	$50–$300	N/A*	$50–$250	$50–$300
Micro (10000–75000)	$300–$5000	$500–$3000	$250–$1500	$300–$1500
Mid-tier (75000–250000)	$5000–$8000	$3000–$5000	$1500–2500	$1500–$4000
Macro (250000–1000000)	$8000–$10000	$5000–$20000	$2500–$10000	$4000–$10000
Mega (1000000+)	$10000+	$20000+	$10000+	$10000+

*To monetise via the YouTube Partner Program (YPP), creators need at least 1000 subscribers and 4000 watch hours in the past 12 months (or 10 million Shorts views in 90 days).

Metrics that matter

Lots of founders choose influencers based on follower count, gut feel or personal preference, but forget to look at the numbers that really matter. When you know how to assess an influencer's metrics, you can compare creators objectively, choose partnerships that offer real value and avoid wasting money on influencers who look impressive but won't drive sales.

The following formulas will help you compare influencers, understand what you're paying for and make smarter decisions about who to work with and why.

1. *Engagement rate:* This shows how deeply the audience connects with the content.

$$\text{Engagement rate} = \frac{\text{likes} + \text{comments} + \text{shares} + \text{saves}}{\text{followers}} \times 100$$

Example: $(800 + 40 + 20 + 40) \div 20\,000 \times 100 = 4.5\%$

What does success look like?

- Excellent: 6%+
- Good: 4–6%
- Average: 2–4%
- Low: <2%

2. *Reach rate:* This shows how many followers actually see the content. Instagram reach measures the number of unique accounts that have seen your content at least once.

$$\text{Reach rate} = \frac{\text{reach}}{\text{followers}} \times 100$$

Example: $15\,000 \div 20\,000 \times 100 = 75\%$

What does success look like?

- Excellent: 40%+
- Good: 25–40%
- Average: 15–25%
- Low: <15%

3. *Average comments per post (depth of engagement)*: This shows how invested the audience is. 'Likes' show attention and 'comments' show trust.

Average comments per post = Total comments across selected posts ÷ Number of posts analysed

Example: 320 comments ÷ 10 posts = 32 comments per post

What does success look like? See 'Comments to likes' ratio below for the answer.

4. *Comments-to-likes ratio (depth of engagement)*: This shows how invested the audience is, not just how many people tap 'like'.

Comments-to-likes ratio = Average comments per post ÷ Average likes per post × 100

How to calculate it

Step 1: Calculate average comments per post

Total comments across selected posts ÷ Number of posts analysed

Step 2: Calculate average likes per post

Total likes across selected posts ÷ Number of posts analysed

Step 3: Calculate the ratio

Average comments per post ÷ Average likes per post × 100

Example

- Total comments across 10 posts = 320
- Total likes across 10 posts = 4000

Average comments per post = 320 ÷ 10 = 32

Average likes per post = 4000 ÷ 10 = 400

Comments-to-likes ratio = 32 ÷ 400 × 100 = 8%

What does success look like?

- Excellent: 15–20%
- Good: 10–15%
- Average: 5–10%
- Low: <5%

5. *YouTube formulas — average view duration (AVD):* This shows how long viewers stay engaged.

$$\frac{\text{Total watch time}\,(\text{minutes})}{\text{Total views}}$$

Example: 5000 total watch minutes ÷ 1000 views = 5 minutes average view duration

What does success look like?

- Excellent: 6–8 minutes+
- Good: 4–6 minutes
- Average: 2–4 minutes
- Low: <2 minutes

Note: Average view duration should be assessed relative to video length.

6. *Audience retention:* This shows what percentage of your video is watched on average.

$$\frac{\text{Average view duration}}{\text{Video length}} \times 100$$

Example: 3-minute average duration ÷ 10-minute video × 100 = 30% retention

What does success look like?

- Excellent: 60–70% retention
- Good: 45–60%
- Average: 30–45%
- Low: <30%

The creative brief

If you can't afford to hire a marketing agency to run your influencer campaigns, borrow the templates they use to run their campaigns. A clear creative brief is how agencies keep projects focused, aligned and effective. Influencer marketing has many moving parts, so taking a structured approach from the outset helps you maximise results and maintain focus. Use this sample eight-step creative brief (below) as a practical blueprint to help you plan, execute and manage an influencer campaign with confidence.

Step 1: Define your goals

Be clear about what you want to achieve. Do you want more sales, increased website traffic, brand awareness or all three? Specify exactly which product or service you're promoting and make sure your systems can support demand. Your website, payment process and fulfilment must be ready to go. Don't launch until the backend is locked in, so you can respond quickly when interest turns into sales.

Step 2: Choose your target audience

Who are you trying to reach? Be specific. You should be able to picture this person so clearly you could have a real conversation with them. If you're unsure where to start, look at who is already buying from you. That's your best and most reliable starting point. A customer avatar worksheet (see the template in figure 18.2) can help you turn a vague idea of who your audience is into a real person. That clarity will make your copy sharper, more specific and far more compelling.

	Brand: Baby Love **Product:** Organic baby clothes **Customer Avatar Worksheet**
Avatar #1	Louise
Age	35
Gender	Female
Marital status	Married
# / Age of children	Ben, 4, Riley, 1
Location	Newton, NSW
Occupation	Lawyer
Annual income	$220k
Education level	Masters of Law
What problem do we solve?	Riley has eczema, which means itchy skin, broken sleep and long nights for everyone. Our organic, non-allergenic baby clothes are designed to be gentle on sensitive skin, helping reduce irritation and scratching. When Riley is more comfortable, he sleeps better, and when Riley sleeps, Louise finally gets some rest too.

Figure 18.2 a customer avatar

When you know exactly who you're talking to and what problem you can solve, your copy moves from the abstract to the concrete and it's that specificity that makes an impact. Here's a before and after version to show the contrast.

- *Generic copy:*
  'Looking for soft, organic baby clothes? Our new range is gentle on skin, beautifully made and perfect for little ones. Shop now for cosy basics every mum will love.'
- *Targeted copy:*
  'If your baby's eczema keeps them awake (and leaves you exhausted), our non-allergenic babywear can help. Made for sensitive skin, it reduces itching and irritation so your baby can sleep more peacefully, and so can you.'

Step 3: Choose your platform

Now you know who you're targeting, you need to find out where they hang out online. Are they gamers on YouTube, retirees on Facebook or teenage girls on TikTok? Louise, our sample avatar, probably hangs out on Instagram so look for an influencer who is active on Instagram.

Step 4: Select influencers

Choose influencers who genuinely align with your brand, not just those with big follower counts. Depending on your budget, use a mix of macro-influencers to build broad awareness and micro- or nano-influencers to drive deeper engagement.

Step 5: Negotiate terms

Contact your influencer directly or through their agent with a view to building a long-term relationship. Be honest about expectations including the kinds of content you want them to create, the results you could expect and lead times required so everyone is aligned.

Step 6: Develop a strategy

Give your influencer a clear brief outlining goals, audience, key messages and content format, and then invite their input so the content feels authentic to them. Add brand guidelines so they have guardrails as to what they can and can't say.

Step 7: Execute campaign

When the campaign goes live, amplify your influencer's posts through your own channels and track engagement to see what's working and what's not.

Step 8: Analyse and optimise

Evaluate your results to see what worked, and then use these insights to refine your next campaign.

Best strategy for a small brand

If you're just starting out, it may pay to choose influencers who already need, or use, your products.

Start by offering them a simple deal:

- free product plus a small payment ($50–$200)
- exclusive discount codes
- revenue share / affiliate link.

Below is a sample outreach message inviting an author influencer to be part of the launch of an organic baby clothing range.

Email subject line: Collaboration with Baby Love Organic Clothing

Hi there,

I read your books and love how you share such warm, honest moments about motherhood on your socials. They feel real and relatable and very authentic.

I think your audience would really connect with our product — an organic, ethically-made clothing range designed for babies with eczema or sensitive skin.

I'm looking for genuine creators to collaborate with. I can offer a product bundle plus a small fee, along with an affiliate link for you and a discount code for your followers. I would love to explore a simple content partnership in the form of a Story, Reel or TikTok.

If that sounds interesting, I can send more details or some product samples over to you.

I hope we get to work together.

Thank you,
[Your name]
[Brand/Instagram handle/website]

* * *

Choosing the right influencer is less about looking for the big names and more about finding the ones who best suit your budget, audience and product. When you're clear on your goal, your audience and the metrics that really matter, you can launch your influencer campaign with confidence.

Nuggets of wisdom

▸ Hire an influencer. Research nano-influencers who already speak to your audience. Reach out, understand how they work, and launch a small campaign to test what resonates. Experiment, have fun, and see what happens.

▸ Review your own social accounts. See how you show up and compare it to those who are in the same sector. Commit to posting at least three times a week.

▸ Create your customer avatar. Identify your ideal customer, what they value and the questions they have, and create your content to answer those questions.

19

HOW TO GROW AN AUDIENCE WITH INSTAGRAM

If anyone understands how to turn Instagram into a business, it's Nat Kringoudis. Nat is a women's health practitioner with a background in Chinese Medicine and Health Sciences. In 2003 she set up a women's wellness clinic, The Pagoda Tree, and dedicated her career to helping women get accurate answers to questions about fertility and overall wellbeing. With over 95 000 followers on Instagram, she has built a thriving ecosystem that now includes masterclass communities, coaching programs, podcasts, a supplements range, bestselling books, a busy speaking schedule, and a large community of women who trust her judgement and buy what she recommends. What follows is the practical approach she used to build that empire.

Growing an audience that buys, shares and stays

In 2007, Nat Kringoudis began blogging to promote her natural health clinic. The act of writing about this ancient practice was seen by the Chinese medicine community as an unseemly act of self-promotion. Nat was not deterred. She kept on writing because her patients asked her to. Those blogs led to a content empire that positions her as the authority in her field.

The 'special sauce' that distinguishes her from other practitioners is her detailed understanding of the needs of her clients, her entertaining yet educational way of explaining complex concepts and her ability to use Instagram to promote her business. It's this last talent that has enabled her to expand her influence and reach.

As Nat said, 'I can pick up my phone at any time and broadcast to 95 000 women — more viewers than the prime-time news programs get each night — and reach them for free. For me, showing up on social media is the glue that ties all the elements of my business together.'

I asked Nat to break down the nuts and bolts of how she used Instagram, email, lead magnets, quizzes, ManyChat and other online tools to build her business. This was not hard for her because along with her healthcare business, she's also a social media coach who helps founders use Insta to promote their business.

Here is Nat's six-step process for turning Instagram followers into paying customers.

Step 1: Start a new account

'The big mistake people make when they start a new business is they open a new account and immediately add friends and family to it. These vanity metrics might make you feel good about yourself, but they are not your target audience and probably won't buy anything from you. And having them see what you post can make you feel self-conscious, and force you to play smaller than you should.'

Step 2: Start with 'why'

Getting clear about how you want to monetise it is critical. 'If you aren't crystal clear on this, you can spend a lot of time spinning your wheels and not getting anywhere.'

One of Nat's social media coaching clients, a fitness coach, once told her, 'I've got 5000 followers. By the end of this month, I want to have 100 000 followers.' Nat knew that was an unrealistic goal, but the client was adamant, did the work and showed up. The client didn't just smash that goal, she built an audience of nearly a million followers.

'But here's the problem,' said Nat. 'Only a fraction of her followers was interested in what she had to sell, so she didn't make any money from her following.'

To compound the issue, her client spent so much time making content for her million followers, who were never going to buy anything from her anyway, she had no time to spend on the fitness business.

'She was happy to be Insta famous,' said Nat, 'but she wasn't making any money. That's fine, if that's what you want. But if you want to monetise Instagram, you've got to know who your ideal customer is, and create high-quality content exclusively for them. Doing anything other than that is a waste of time and effort.'

The critical question that needs to be answered is: Are you using Instagram to be seen or to sell?

'There's no right or wrong answer, but the strategies you use to achieve each outcome will be very different,' said Nat.

Step 3: Know your avatar

'Everything I do is aimed at educating my avatar, and no-one else,' said Nat. 'We base all our avatars on the women we see at my clinic, and the clearer we are about who we are communicating with, the more of them we attract.'

Step 4: Be authentic

Nat's advice is simple: 'Don't copy or imitate others; be you and choose a topic you're passionate about that aligns with your business objective.'

The topic you choose to speak about is important because you'll be sitting with it for at least the next five to 10 years. 'That's how long it takes to build a business,' said Nat.

You need to be resilient too. 'If you want to grow on Instagram, you need to have a thick skin. The first negative comment will feel like the worst, but once you've experienced that, you'll get used to it and it won't feel nearly as raw. Those negative comments can actually help you because the people clicking on those salacious stories are building your engagement. In my opinion, there's no such thing as bad publicity.'

I asked Nat how she deals with the inevitable mental stress that comes with having a high profile. She said, 'It really helps to know who you are and what your intentions are. If you know that you are coming from the right place, that you are there to help others and share high-quality information, then you can ignore the criticism because you know that your intentions are honourable. If people take offence, I counter with, "That wasn't my intention".'

Having this mantra helps her manage the haters and focus on the followers who love what she does and value what she offers.

Step 5: Build a distinctive brand

'Being consistent in both style and messaging is important,' said Nat.

'Once you've established your brand's look and feel, then stick with it. Don't chop and change the colours, the font or the design.'

This is where most entrepreneurs fall down: their feed looks like a patchwork quilt of styles, moods, fonts, colours and ideas. There's no cohesion or visual identity.

She said, 'Your audience should know it's your content in their feed before they even see your name.'

Step 6: Post consistently

Nat's content framework follows a rinse-and-repeat seven-day plan that anyone can replicate. Here is her exact sequence.

Day 1: Monday — The educational post

This is an informative and engaging post that delivers high-quality content. There's no sales pitch or call to action. It's just pure value.

Topics Nat might cover include:

- the truth about HRT
- why your symptoms don't make sense
- what women get wrong about perimenopause
- the biggest mistake people make with supplements.

These posts position Nat as the authority on her topic and create credibility and trust.

Day 2: Tuesday — The call to action (CTA)

This post builds upon what Nat posted the day before. It reiterates the key message but also provides more detail and a call to action to take up her recommendations.

Example script:

> 'Yesterday we talked about how everyone is obsessed with HRT, but HRT is not for everyone. You had so many questions, here are all the answers and here's what I'd recommend you do next.'

Day 3: Wednesday — The quote

Nat loves quotes because they're easy to source, highly shareable and her audience loves them.

'These broaden my reach because they get seen by people who don't know me and it helps build my following.'

Day 4: Thursday — The 'podcast' reel

'We release a podcast every Thursday, but if we don't, I just record a piece to camera,' said Nat. She's got a hack for that. 'To make it look like you're being interviewed, just position your phone off to the side and talk as if someone was asking you questions.' This is a great way to share information you want to convey without waiting to be invited onto a podcast to do so. You get to demonstrate your expertise on your own terms.

Day 5: Friday — The funny post

Funny is money, as they say in the speaking business. 'Humour is a great way to show another side of you and reveal your personality. It also provides a softer counterpoint to the more serious content that you've shared earlier in the week.'

Nat said, 'If I'm looking for something to share, I post a carousel of funny quotes or images. They always get high engagement.'

Day 6: Saturday — No post

Day 7: Sunday — The brand partnership post

'We reserve Sundays for our brand partners. We might have up to eight brand deals on the go at one time. We post once a month for them.'

How this lead magnet broke sales records

Saunas are a big deal in the natural health world. Like ice baths, they can eliminate toxins, build immunity and clear out the system. Nat gets a lot of questions about them, so when a sauna company asked her to promote their products, she said yes.

She created a free guide that answered frequently asked questions: *Should I buy traditional or infrared? How long should I stay in? How many times a week? How hot should it be?*

To get a copy, followers just needed to write the word 'sauna' in the comments and they'd get sent a copy.

Nat used the ManyChat tool to handle distribution. When someone commented 'sauna', ManyChat automatically stepped in and managed the rest. It's a handy tool that does a lot of the leg work for you. The ManyChat tool:

▶ sends the guide via DM
▶ collects the recipient's email
▶ enters the email address into the database
▶ steers the participant towards taking out a paid membership.

The campaign results were impressive.

'We sold more saunas than Mel Robbins, their other brand ambassador,' she said. 'Mel has a lot more followers than me but my audience is very engaged and this topic was relevant to them. It's not the size of the audience that matters; it's how dialled in they are to what the creator is offering.'

Your goal should not be to go viral but to be helpful. When you stop chasing vanity metrics and focus on creating great content for your ideal customers, you'll get better results.

* * *

Being consistent, answering frequently asked questions and creating lead magnets that offer great value ensures you put your audience first and create the trust they need to start buying from you.

Nuggets of wisdom

▶ Create a seven-day content plan. Plot out the topics for each post a week in advance and then use Buffer, Hootsuite or Sprout Social to schedule it for you.

▶ Launch a podcast. Podcasts are great tools for creating awareness and connecting with high-powered guests in your industry. Seek out specialist podcast virtual assistants to help set it up.

▶ Trial ManyChat to help automate manual processes. It automatically replies to comments, sends follow-up messages, and delivers freebies or discount codes.

20

HOW TO USE INSTAGRAM TO GENERATE NEW LEADS

For many founders, Instagram requires a lot of work and delivers very little in return. They post, comment and share, yet nothing translates into a sale.

The founders who make Instagram work have a strategy that ensures all the work they put in gets a result. Wellness and fertility influencer Nat Kringoudis has a proprietary system that helps novice Insta business owners reduce their workload and turn clicks into cash.

Using Instagram to sell, not just be seen

For some business owners, Instagram is the end point. For Nat Kringoudis, it's the starting point. She doesn't use Instagram to sell; she uses it to generate leads.

As Nat puts it, 'My job is to get people onto Instagram so I can educate them, then move them onto my email list so I can nurture them to a sale. I don't own Instagram or my followers on it, but I do own my email list so I need to move them onto it as quickly as possible.'

Instagram plays a specific role in a larger marketing system that helps move people from attention to action. Instagram sits at the top of a funnel (see figure 20.1). In this example, we'll show what kinds of numbers are required to generate 1200 customers.

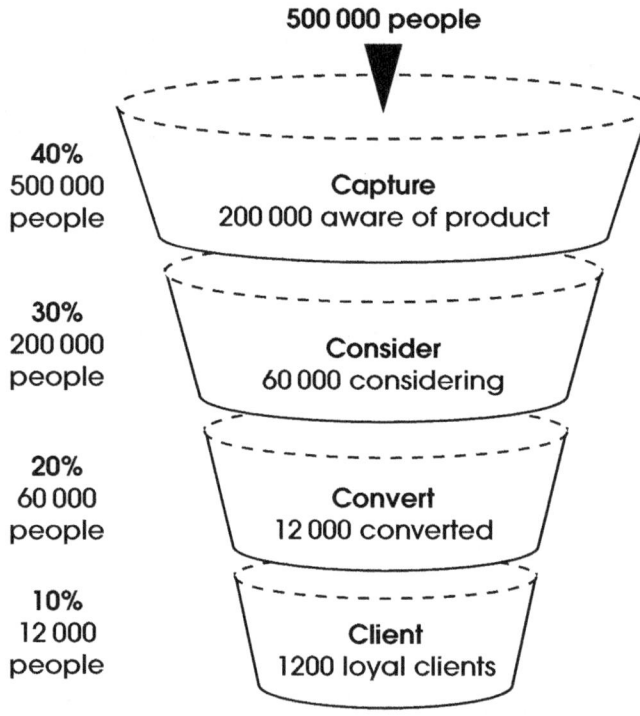

500 000 people

40%
500 000
people

Capture
200 000 aware of product

30%
200 000
people

Consider
60 000 considering

20%
60 000
people

Convert
12 000 converted

10%
12 000
people

Client
1200 loyal clients

Figure 20.1   a sample Instagram funnel

Here's how the numbers stack up:

- *Capture (40%):* Out of a potential audience of 500 000, around 200 000 people become aware of Nat through posts, reels, shares and recommendations. These people may not know her yet, but they've seen her content.
- *Consider (30%):* From there, a significant portion move into consideration. These are people who start paying attention.

They follow her, watch multiple posts, read captions and begin to recognise her voice and expertise.

- *Convert (20%):* Roughly 60 000 people take the next step. They click a link, download a guide, sign up to her email list or attend a webinar. The lead now moves from Instagram to Nat's email list, which is the overall goal of being on Instagram.

  To move someone off Instagram and onto your email list, you need to give them a reason to click. This is where the lead magnet comes in. A lead magnet is a valuable freebie designed to solve a small but urgent problem for your audience. It might be a quiz, checklist, short guide or webinar. Its goal is to attract the right people and offer enough value that they're willing to exchange their email address for it.

- *Client (10%):* From that group, around 1200 customers become long-term clients. These are the people who buy programs, products or services and stay connected over time.

Make email the mothership

The real work begins once someone joins your list. Your welcome sequence needs to keep people engaged, informed and comfortable so they feel motivated to buy.

Think of email as your mothership: Instagram starts the relationship, but email is where it deepens. The flow is simple: Instagram → Email → Membership → Sale. See figure 20.2 (overleaf).

Here's how Nat's Instagram funnel looks and when email kicks in:

- *Top of the funnel (Capture awareness via Instagram):* 'Free hormone quiz: Do you need HRT? 'Take the test!' (the lead magnet).
- *Middle of the funnel (Consider via email sequence):* Five-step email welcome sequence starts now.

- *Bottom of the funnel (Convert via email sequence):* Offer: Join the paid monthly membership group.
- *Bottom of the funnel (Client acquisition via email sequence):* Offer: Book an appointment at the clinic.

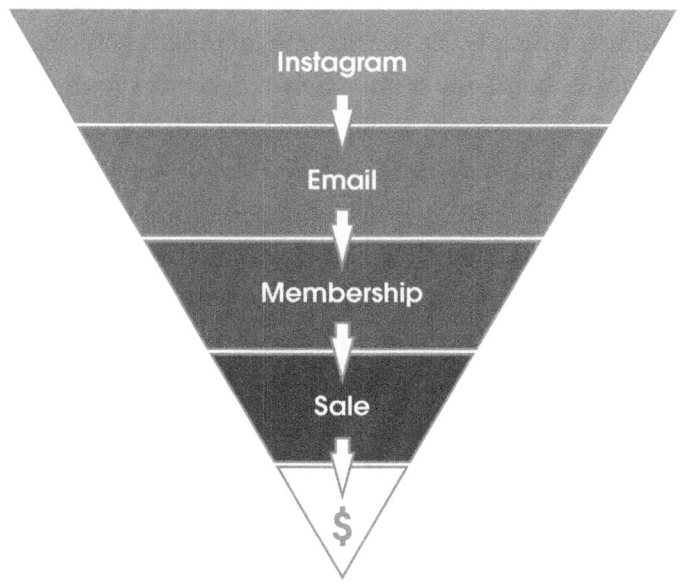

Figure 20.2   the Instagram marketing funnel

If a Welcome sequence is well constructed, it builds trust and encourages the prospect to take action. Here's how a five-part sequence might look:

- *Emailer # 1: Welcome and origin story*
  Welcome them and explain who you are and why you do what you do. This is your origin story. If you offer a lead magnet, provide an overview of why they should read it.
- *Emailer # 2: Helpful insights*
  Share tips, ideas or insights that solve their problems. Be useful and helpful but don't sell. Prove that you understand who they are and what issues they face.

- *Emailer # 3: First offer*
  Make a clear, simple offer. Don't do a hard sell. Just show them the next logical step for how you can help them.
- *Emailer # 4: Proof and results*
  Provide case studies, testimonials or real-world examples that build trust and show what's possible.
- *Emailer # 5: Second offer*
  Make the offer again, this time with more context. Some people need to see it twice before they're ready.

Diversify your sources of income

As you can see, generating leads via Instagram (or any platform) takes a bit of work. For a 'technician' who loves to do everything themselves, this could get overwhelming. Nat has a team to manage her online empire, so if you're looking to replicate this volume of work, now's a good time to call in a specialist to help you. Nat succeeds because she knows that the one area she can't delegate or outsource is 'being her', but for everything else, she brings in her team.

'They can write emails, edit videos, and manage customer service but they can't show up on Instagram as me. My role is to educate, inspire and entertain. That's the one thing I do. That's my superpower.'

Nat operates from a position of strength because she has diversified her sources of income. She earns money from sponsorships, product sales, clinic patients, podcast advertising, book royalties and speaking fees. This spread reduces risk. If one income stream slows or disappears, another can carry the load. That optionality gives Nat the freedom to choose who she works with, what she charges and how hard she works. Creating a diversified income is the cornerstone of building a sustainable lifestyle business.

There are myriad ways to make money online. The smartest creators use a mix of income streams that suit their personality, product and appetite for risk. Table 20.1 (overleaf) outlines how influencers use brand collaborations to monetise their followings.

Table 20.1 10 brand partnership and monetisation formats for influencers

Format / Acronym	Meaning	Definition / Use
1 Affiliate link	Commission-based sales link	Influencers earn a percentage commission for every sale made through their personalised link or code. Common on Instagram, TikTok and blogs.
2 Promo code	Discount code for followers	Brands offer followers a discount and track conversions via the influencer's code (e.g. 'SAUNA').
3 Brand collab	Brand collaboration	A one-off or ongoing partnership between an influencer and a brand to create content or campaigns.
4 Sponsorship / sponsored post (#ad)	Paid partnership	The influencer is paid a fee to create and post content featuring a brand or product. (Must be disclosed as #ad or #sponsored.)
5 Ambassador program	Long-term partnership	Ongoing collaboration where influencers represent a brand consistently over time.
6 Giveaway / competition	Follower engagement tactic	Brand-sponsored contests that boost visibility and engagement and grows the email list. (Not always paid for.)
7 Product seeding	Gifting campaigns	Brands provide products as value-in-kind, rather than paying a fee.
8 Whitelisting	Paid ad amplification	Influencers give brands permission to run paid ads using the influencer's account to maximise reach.

Format / Acronym	Meaning	Definition / Use
9 UGC creator work	**User-generated content (UGC) for brands**	Influencers create content for brands to use, often without posting it to their own channels.
10 Affiliate platform partnerships	**e.g. LTK, Amazon Influencer or Commission Factory**	These third-party platforms help creators manage affiliate tracking, commissions and reporting.

Treat Instagram as a business and you'll have a higher chance of making money from it. It works best when you know what you want to sell, to whom and why, and have a system for capturing those leads and converting them into paying clients.

* * *

Nuggets of wisdom

▶ Encourage followers to join your email list. You own this channel so structure your campaigns to move them onto it. Choose an email package that will support your growth so you can capture leads and track what actually converts. Check out tutorials for MailChimp, Klaviyo, Campaign Monitor and HubSpot to understand what each offers.

▶ Aim for a 3:2 value-to-sales ratio in your email sequences. In a five-email pack, three should educate, help or entertain, and two can sell. Educate, build trust and then sell.

▶ Hire a virtual assistant. If you don't have the tech skills to set up your email campaigns, hire someone who does so you can get on with doing what you do best.

21

HOW TO LEVERAGE YOUTUBE AND THOSE FIRST FIVE SECONDS

Going viral isn't the only way to win on YouTube. What matters more is understanding how attention is earned and held. This chapter draws on insights from the head of YouTube's Global Culture and Trends team to show what the platform actually rewards, why the first few seconds matter more than the algorithm, and how to turn viewers who might scroll past into fans who stay, watch and come back.

The truth about YouTube

Imagine getting paid to watch YouTube all day? My son would be a shoo-in for that job, but Kevin Allocca already has it. He's worked at Google for more than 15 years, and now heads up YouTube's Culture and Trends team that tracks what the world is watching and analyses why it spreads.

He works closely with YouTube's product and engineering teams to surface trending content; spot emerging cultural patterns; and share that intelligence with marketers, creators and media outlets so they can use those insights to shape their own video strategies.

Before joining YouTube, Kevin worked as a journalist and comedy writer, including a stint at *HuffPost*. In 2018, he published *Videocracy*, a book that explores how digital video reshaped modern culture and how we have moved from the early 'viral video' era to the creator-driven economy we see today.

He has two 'unfavourite' questions:

The first: *How do I make my video go viral?*
The second: *What's trending right now?*

'Both,' he said, 'are impossible to answer'.

'If you asked me this question 15 years ago, it would be easy,' he said. 'I'd tell you the double rainbow video is blowing up, or there's a new K-pop thing happening. But YouTube is so much bigger now. It encompasses every part of culture: podcasting, gaming, music, sport. There is no real monoculture anymore. We live in a fragmented media existence. What's trending for you will be totally different from what's trending for a 19-year-old gamer.'

As Kevin puts it, 'What makes a video go viral is a really hard question to answer, and that's the challenge everyone faces, because everyone wants their video to be found.'

Create unexpectedness

The world's leading YouTuber, MrBeast, spent months learning how to hack the YouTube algorithm. The opportunity to do that now has passed. The long tail is too long, the volume of videos too dense and the personalisation too extreme. Even if two people share the same interests and follow the same creator, they're unlikely to be served the same content.

'Unexpectedness,' said Kevin, 'is still one of the most powerful forces in digital storytelling, but also the hardest to engineer. In a world flooded with content, what makes someone stop scrolling is often the thing they *didn't* expect to see. It's the content that surprises us that stands out.'

Kevin acknowledges you can't *manufacture* unexpectedness, but you can invite it. There's an art to creating something that makes people sit up and take notice.

Lachlan and Austin Macfarlane, the film-maker brothers, are skilled at this and concede that there's a bit more to it than putting up a good thumbnail and waiting for the clicks.

'There's only one thing you need to get good at,' said Austin, 'and that's *stopping the scroll*. An audience doesn't want to watch *your* video; they want to watch the *next* one. You have to give them a reason to stop.'

'Online audiences are ruthless,' said Lachlan. 'To grab attention, every video needs a strong hook, ideally in the very first frame. It needs to be visually striking in some way. For one video, we were going to open on a wide shot of the actor walking through the forest, but we needed to grab the audience's attention, so we opened on the actor frozen mid-scream, like a statue, staring straight into the camera and that magnified our success.'

YouTube is watching you too

YouTube tracks viewing behaviour in detail: how long someone watches, whether they skip ahead, rewind, pause or leave. That data feeds into audience retention and related watch-time signals, which YouTube uses to understand how engaging a video really is. In simple terms, it shows which videos hold attention and which ones lose it quickly, and that strongly influences how widely a video is recommended.

The audience retention graph starts at 100 per cent and declines, showing exactly where viewers lost interest. 'You can literally see where they drop off,' said Lachlan. 'Once you know that, you can reverse engineer your videos to understand what keeps people watching and what makes them leave.'

So, how do you get them to stick around for longer?

Austin said, 'If viewers get past the first three to five seconds, they're more likely to stay for the entire video, which is why you need a powerful hook'.

Five ways to hook viewers in the first five seconds

Here are five budget-friendly ways to make people stop scrolling and keep watching.

1 Start with a striking visual or sound
Use an unexpected image, a loud sound effect or quick motion to jolt attention.

Example: a close-up reaction shot, a dramatic whoosh or a visual jump cut that breaks the scroll.

2 Ask a bold question
Open with a question that triggers curiosity or emotion.

Example: 'What happens if you don't sleep for three days?' or 'Can you make a three-course meal using only a toaster?'

3 Show the payoff first
Start with the result, then rewind to show how you got there.

Example: 'I built this entire cabin with no power tools.'(*Open with a sweeping shot of the finished cabin, then rewind to show how it came together from scratch.*)

---

4 Use text or captions to highlight the story

Overlay a one-line hook in large text so even silent scrollers are intrigued.

Example: 'It looks disgusting now … but wait for the final shot.'

5 Jump straight into action

Skip intros and get to the good part instantly by starting mid-scene — pouring, cutting, reacting, laughing — before adding context.

Example (cooking video):

▸ Don't do this: 'Hi guys, today I'm going to show you how to make crispy smashed potatoes.'
▸ Do this: Camera cuts to sizzling oil, potatoes crackling in the pan.
  Voiceover: 'Hear that? That's the sound of the crispiest potatoes you'll ever make.'
▸ Then pull back to show the process.

* * *

Watching videos for a living sounds like a great job but what Kevin's really doing is holding up a mirror to ourselves: showing us what we watch and care about. The advice from influencers like the Macfarlane Bros. is rather than think, 'How do I go viral?', think, 'How can I give people what they're looking for?'

Nuggets of wisdom

▶ Analyse your YouTube audience retention graphs. Get clear about what videos are working and what aren't. Do more of what works and ditch what doesn't.

▶ Don't start all your videos the same way. Audiences will get used to it and will fast forward or switch off.

▶ Ask people to subscribe to your channel and give them a concrete reason to do so. Tell them that having a more popular channel will deliver better guests, higher-quality content or fewer advertisements.

PART 4

MANAGEMENT

Bringing a management mindset to your business shifts it from being about you to being about the team you build. It influences who you hire and how you lead and sets the standard for how people show up.

Inspired management starts with creating a vibrant culture. This is more than writing slogans on the wall in fancy calligraphy. It's a living manifesto that defines what you expect, what you reward and how decisions are made.

In part 4, we'll cover how to build a culture people value, how to use language to set the tone, how to hire well, how to have the hard conversations early and how to create a business that others want to join.

22

HOW TO BUILD A CULTURE THAT MAKES PEOPLE WANT TO STAY

Hundreds of books have been written on the subject of corporate culture, yet it remains a surprisingly hard concept to define. At its simplest, culture is best defined as *how we do things around here.*

A company's culture matters because it drives every decision, behaviour and outcome in your business. Get that right and it doesn't necessarily make running a company easier, but it does give you clear frameworks and guidelines for how to move forward and deal with the various challenges that arise.

Define what you are and what you are not

The success of Seek was driven in large part because it prioritised culture. The founders knew people were critical to success, so they put culture at the heart of every decision.

In the aftermath of the 2008 global financial crisis, the company had grown rapidly and market conditions had changed. CEO Andrew Bassat wanted to use the lessons of the GFC to prepare the company for its next phase by putting the executive team's cultural framework front and centre.

Meahan Callaghan was the HR Director at the time and was tasked with identifying the right people and processes to uphold that culture. Prior to that role, she had been the HR Manager at Foxtel where she'd hired hundreds of people from all walks of life for all manner of roles — from senior television executives to casual telemarketers — and knew that culture started from the top down but was built from the bottom up.

'The starting point for building a strong culture is clarity: knowing exactly what you stand for, and what you don't,' said Meahan. 'We defined our culture by asking: What sort of company do we want to be? Who are the people we want to work with? What behaviours do we want our people to bring to work each day? What do we already know about our culture from the startup years that has driven our success, and needs to be captured in that definition?'

That clarity became the backbone of every decision. 'It defined what we rewarded, who we hired, who we fired, who we did business with, and who we didn't,' she said.

Meahan believes that being transparent about what you are, as well as what you are not, is critical to getting culture right. 'When you are honest about what you are not, you give people something real and tangible to opt into, or opt out of. Either way, the choice is clear.'

One company she worked with tried to position itself as a best employer: the one that everybody wanted to work for.

'The problem they faced,' she explained, 'was they hesitated to define themselves in any way that might be considered negative. In the end, they created a vanilla culture that meant nothing.'

She cites Macquarie Bank as a clear example of a company that created a clearly defined culture. 'From an external standpoint, they appeared to be single-minded about who they were and what they stood for. They said, "We are ruthless. If you're in the bottom 10 per cent, you'll be cut. If you make it, you'll be very rich". I'm not saying it was a great culture or a place I'd like to work, but it was clear and people knew what was expected of them.'

Meahan's advice is to avoid vague generalisations. 'If you say, "I want everyone to be a great team player with high integrity", I'd say you're relying on cliched stereotypes to define who you are, and not thinking hard enough about what you really stand for,' she said.

'The first 100 days of a startup are critical,' she said. 'You need a manifesto similar to The Ten Commandments that provide guideposts for the team to follow,' she said. 'These values may change by 5 per cent in the future, but if they change by any more than that, those who started at the company because of its core values will probably leave the company.'

'The goal,' said Meahan, 'is for the words and behaviour to be so aligned that everyone already knows what the company stands for, even before it's written down.'

How to create a culture of abundance

Ronni Kahn, founder of OzHarvest, built her organisation around a deeply held belief in abundance. That belief became the touchstone for how her not-for-profit went forward.

Rather than operating from fear or scarcity, Ronni believed there was always enough. Enough food, enough money, enough goodwill. 'From my point of view, I've never approached anyone from a place of scarcity,' she said. 'I truly believe there is abundant food and abundant money. It's about asking the right people and continuing to ask with the expectation that what we need will arrive.'

That mindset shaped how OzHarvest engaged supporters, partners and staff. It replaced competition with collaboration and fear with generosity. Over time, this attitude of abundance became the emotional backbone of the organisation, creating a culture grounded in gratitude, optimism and shared purpose. It is best represented by the fact that no matter who you are or what you do, when you step into the OzHarvest office, you will be greeted with a hug. Ronni leads with love and expects those who work with her to do the same. Her culture is well defined: people know what to expect and can decide if they want to be a part of it or not.

After more than two decades of rescuing food and passing it on to those who need it, Ronni's message is unchanged.

'We have an abundance of goodness. We will never run out. So don't ever think that if you've been nice to someone, you're using up your store. Throw a pebble in the pond and the ripples live on creating impacts you may never see.'

How happy is your team?

Before you can create a lasting culture, you need to understand the culture you already have. You can't manage what you don't measure, and without a clear baseline, any attempt to change culture will always be built on assumption rather than evidence.

Culture is what people experience day to day; it's what employees say when others ask, 'What's it like to work there?' Measuring how your team actually feels gives you a starting point for defining a new culture or reimagining the existing one.

If you want a heads-up on how your team feels about where they work, send them the following questionnaire and see what comes back. It will give you a solid benchmark for how to define your workplace culture.

Team culture pulse check

Ask your team to rate each statement on a scale of 1 to 5, where 1 means strongly disagree and 5 means strongly agree.

1. I have a clear understanding of what is expected of me in my role.
2. I have access to the tools, resources and support I need to do my job well.
3. Most days, my work allows me to use my strengths and skills effectively.
4. In the last week, my efforts and contributions have been recognised and acknowledged.
5. I feel my manager genuinely cares about me as a person, not just an employee.
6. Someone at work takes an interest in my career development and personal growth.
7. I feel comfortable sharing ideas and believe my opinions are taken seriously.
8. The purpose of this organisation makes my work feel meaningful.
9. The people I work with are committed to doing quality work.
10. I have a close friend at work.
11. In the last six months, I have received regular feedback about how I'm performing and where I can improve.
12. I have opportunities to learn, grow and develop new skills here.

Understanding how your people feel about working with and for you is the starting point in defining how your culture needs to evolve. Once you have that insight, the next challenge is to codify the behaviours and beliefs you want your culture to stand for. Few companies did this as successfully as Swisse.

What a cultural manifesto looks like

Under Radek Sali, Swisse created a culture that catapulted them from a small business with 30 employees turning over $15 million to a global business with 300 staff that sold for billions. When I asked Radek why they were so successful, he had a one-word answer: 'culture'.

Key to their success was the creation of the *Ten Commandments of Health and Happiness*, a set of principles that guided how the organisation operated. This manifesto reflected a belief that shared language and consistent action built great teams. Over time, these commandments evolved into a set of four pillars:

1. People
2. Principles
3. Passion
4. ... and then Profit.

The order mattered. The Swisse team believed that if you got the first three Ps right — People, Principles and Passion — then the fourth P, Profit, would naturally follow.

Creating a culture plan

The culture plan that emanated from the manifesto was a formal document that outlined how Swisse's culture would be created and rolled out across the organisation. It was built around the 4Ps and translated values into specific initiatives and behaviours that shaped every stage of the employee experience. Here's a snapshot of the activities each pillar contained:

1. *People: Motto: 'Building capability'*
    - Induction program
    - Health and Happiness (H+H) days off
    - Product and sales training

- Leadership programs
- Weekly team lunches

2. *Principles: Motto: 'Upholding the wellness philosophy'*
   - Monthly 'lunch and learn' sessions
   - Meditation and yoga training
   - Book club
   - Wellness Week Festival
   - Free gym membership

3. *Passion: Motto: 'Celebrating and connecting'*
   - Social and wellbeing events four times a year
   - One family day per year
   - Mid-year and end-of-year parties
   - Volunteer Day for the Celebrate Life Foundation
   - $1 coffee donation option
   - Invitations to VIP retailer events: Olympic launch, Grand Prix and the Melbourne Cup

4. *Profit: Motto: 'Ensuring value for all'*
   - International relocation and secondment opportunities
   - Succession planning
   - 'Swisse Stars' recognition awards
   - Gratitude cards
   - Job matching and salary benchmarking
   - Recruitment referral bonus scheme
   - Rostered days off

The 'People' pillar in action

To show how values were translated into day-to-day behaviour, it's useful to zoom in on one pillar in detail. The People pillar is a clear example of how the framework worked in practice and how it became the cornerstone of a broader cultural plan.

Guided by the motto 'Success is built on collective effort', it set clear expectations for how people were expected to behave. Just as importantly, it spelled out what was not acceptable. By naming both, Swisse gave its team a shared understanding for how to show up every day.

Here's what the People pillar included:

It means we:

- *respect one another and treat everyone equally*
- *celebrate individuality and acknowledge contribution*
- *treat others as they'd like to be treated.*

It means we do not:

- *work in silos or isolate ourselves from others*
- *gossip, eye-roll or undermine teammates*
- *shift blame or avoid accountability.*

The 4Ps turned abstract values into tangible behaviours, which translated into vibrant, positive language that energised staff. What began as words on a wall became something that was lived every day. Staff could point to the poster and say, 'This is how we do things around here.'

How to stamp out toxic behaviour

Carla Oates from The Beauty Chef runs a values-driven workplace. She prioritises clear communication as a method for helping her team of 26 people understand what behaviours she wants to encourage and those she wants to extinguish.

'I'm a big believer in speaking the unspoken,' she says. 'If there's an issue, talk to the person you have issues with. If you don't get anywhere, come to me or my general manager. But don't let things breed.'

Nothing tests those values faster than gossip or eye-rolling. These actions may seem trivial but the top leaders know that a toxic culture begins with micro-aggressions and that if subtle yet insidious behaviours are overlooked, and not stamped out quickly, they can spread and become an accepted — and acceptable — way of behaving.

When Carla sees eye-rolling in a leadership meeting, she handles it privately and directly. 'I'll bring the person in afterwards and say, "I noticed that you rolled your eyes when the other person was talking. I'd like to understand what that was about". Most people are surprised — and often embarrassed to be pulled up on this — because they don't even realise they are doing it, or identify as someone who would do that,' she said.

She helps them unpack the issue, and offers to sit in on a conversation if someone feels intimidated. She repeats the process with the second person so both sides feel heard.

The response is rarely defensive. 'One leader admitted, "You're right. I did do that. Thank you for pulling me up on that".' She doesn't shame anyone. 'We're all human. It's okay to get frustrated, and vent — as long as it doesn't cross into toxicity. But rolling your eyes in front of someone isn't okay.'

These small interventions protect the values she's worked so hard to create.

Janine Allis believes most businesses suffer not from big failures but from small issues no-one wants to face.

'Most people avoid confrontation. That's why small issues become big ones. If you're going to confront someone, you must know your facts. Done well, tackling the issue at the start stops bad behaviour from escalating, protects the culture and sets a standard that others follow. And when you speak up — even to someone more senior — people respect the courage it took and gives them the confidence to feel they could do it too.'

The strategic power of perks

Some leaders dismiss perks such as chef-prepared lunches, breakfast bars, pinball machines and table tennis tables as performative, arguing they make little real difference. Adam Schwab, CEO of Luxury Escapes, disagrees.

For Adam, perks like these serve a clear purpose. While they make the office a more enjoyable place to be, their real value lies in bringing people together and helping teams connect beyond their usual circles. He wants people to enjoy coming to the office, but more importantly, he wants them to know each other. As he explains, 'Google created a campus-style workplace for a reason: to promote cross-corporate collaboration. These activities and perks get people talking to people they'd never normally meet. It's great for the team, and it's great for the business.'

The free meals save employees thousands of dollars a year, but the real value is in the conversations that happen around the table: engineers talking to product managers, designers chatting with finance, ideas moving between levels and departments. When people know each other, they help each other. When they enjoy being together, they solve problems faster. They also stay longer.

As Adam said, 'You are much less likely to leave your workplace if you have one friend there.'

Luxury Escapes is in the business of selling happiness: holidays, experiences and fun, and Adam wants the internal culture to reflect that too. A workplace where people are relaxed, connected and genuinely enjoy coming to, is not just a luxury — it's a competitive advantage that delivers on multiple levels.

* * *

Culture is built in small increments: in the choices you make, the behaviour you reward and the standards you uphold. When values are clear, measured and lived daily, culture stops being an abstract construct and becomes a self-perpetuating force that is strong enough to attract the people who reflect your values, and repel the ones who don't.

Nuggets of wisdom

▶ Prepare a cultural manifesto by writing down the top 10 values you want your team to uphold. Include the behaviours you want to see as well as the behaviours you don't.

▶ Measure culture before you try to change it. You can't fix what you haven't diagnosed. Take a regular pulse-check on how your team actually feel about working for you. Test assumptions, ask for honest feedback and be willing to make changes.

▶ Call out toxic micro-aggressions before they take hold. Eye-rolling, gossip and conflict avoidance can quickly become acceptable if not extinguished early. Don't allow subtle but insidious gestures to go unchecked.

23

HOW TO CREATE A SUCCESSFUL CULTURE

Culture is what people experience when they turn up to work each day.

It's shaped in the way decisions are explained, and what happens when someone makes a mistake. Every time a leader speaks, follows through or lets something slide, the team is taking notes. They're working out what matters, what's safe and where the boundaries sit.

When language is clear and leaders mean what they say, the team can stop second guessing and focus on the job at hand. Trust builds because expectations are predictable. Over time, that creates space for people to step up, think for themselves and act with a sense of ownership.

This chapter is about building culture consciously via the words you use, the meetings you keep, and how the leaders reward risk and encourage innovation.

Choose your words carefully

Everything begins and ends with language.

Words don't just describe reality; they help create it. They shape how ideas are understood, how decisions are made and how people behave. They can mobilise a team, shut down debate, assign blame or create belief. They can also confuse, divide or deflect responsibility. In the right order, a handful of words can even turn elections.

Yes, we can.

Please explain.

We will decide who comes to this country and the manner in which they come.

I don't hold a hose, mate. ...

Make America Great Again.

Language guides behaviour, and turns principles into habits and habits into culture. Over time, the language we use sets the tone for how people think, act and treat one another, often without anyone consciously noticing it.

At Swisse, Radek Sali understood this deeply. 'Words have the power to build people up, or the potential to drag people down,' he said.

As CEO, he was deliberate about the language he used, and just as deliberate about the language his team used.

'We never used the word "I",' Radek recalls. 'It was always "we". This meant if something went wrong, the mistake wasn't attributed to an individual. The whole team owned it.'

The word 'problem' was replaced with 'challenge', and once a challenge was identified, the person who raised it was expected to suggest a solution. This small change reduced learnt helplessness and encouraged people to think for themselves.

Other shifts followed.

Staff became *team.*

Departments became *areas of business.*

The team didn't work *for* Swisse; they worked *with* it.

Deadlines were renamed *timelines*, because, as Radek said, 'No-one's going to die if we don't get things done'. Even email salutations got an overhaul.

'Dear' was replaced with 'Great day to you!' Emails were signed off with 'Celebrate Life Every Day!'

These were not cosmetic flourishes. Each word choice shifted behaviour in a specific direction: towards ownership, accountability and positivity.

Radek noted, 'Newcomers to the team found this focus on positive language a bit saccharine but soon discovered what a powerful impact it had. Errors, slip-ups and missteps were transformed into valuable opportunities for growth.'

Change the language, change the culture

Table 23.1 details how small linguistic changes at Swisse helped reframe thinking and build a culture grounded in optimism and collective responsibility.

Changing a culture takes time. Radek explains, 'In our experience, establishing a corporate language and culture typically takes about five years of consistent effort. The real power comes when the team members adjust their own language to take full ownership of those values.'

Table 23.1 change the language to reframe thinking and build a more positive culture

From	To
I / Me / My	We / Team / Us / Our
Issue / Problem	Challenge
Execute	Deliver / Roll out
Constructive criticism / Feedback	LGI (Learn, Grow, Improve)
I forgot	I'll set a reminder
I'm exhausted	I need to rest / reset

(continued)

Table 23.1 change the language to reframe thinking and build a more positive culture (*cont'd*)

From	To
Can't complain	Everything is going well
I'm busy	I'm having a productive day
Don't…	I like it when…
No worries	Definitely / Certainly / Sure thing
Why not	Sounds good
But	And
Deadline	Timeline
Brainstorm	Blue sky
Running 10 minutes late	Running 10 minutes slow

Meetings that build culture and clarity

'I love sitting in meetings,' said no-one ever. But for the founder of a fast-moving startup, keeping the team aligned is non-negotiable, and regular one-on-one meetings are one of the most effective ways to do it.

When a company is small, informal catch-ups are often enough to keep everyone aligned. As it grows, that informality breaks down, and regular, scheduled meetings become essential.

In theory, everyone agrees that meetings play a vital role in maintaining clear communication. In practice, when everyone is working flat out, meetings are often the first thing to be cancelled.

This has a quiet but insidious impact on team culture. When meetings disappear, people assume they don't matter, that their work isn't worth discussing or that decisions are being made without input. Small gripes go unresolved, clarity around priorities and processes becomes muddied and conflicts that could have been sorted out in 10 minutes are left to fester.

The irony is that the busier a business becomes, the more frequent the communication cadence needs to be. In fast-moving environments, regular meetings create a sense of calm and predictability.

As much as we deride the value of meetings, they answer the questions that most people have about their role in the organisation:

- What matters to my boss right now?
- How does my work connect to the bigger picture?
- Am I on track?
- Does anyone notice what I'm doing?

At Swisse, each meeting had a clear objective and cadence.

If you're struggling to work out how often your team should meet and what the purpose of each meeting should be, use Table 23.2 as a guide.

Table 23.2 the meeting cadence that underpinned Swisse's culture

Type of meeting	Purpose	Benefit	Frequency
One-on-ones	Provides two-way feedback between leaders and their direct reports	Keeps people accountable, supported and heard	Weekly
Executive WIP (work in progress)	Tracks key projects and decisions	Improves team alignment and execution of tasks	Weekly
Huddle (Town Hall)	Shares wins, updates and ideas across the business	Cross-pollinates teams and keeps everyone in the loop	Fortnightly
Senior team WIP	Builds independent leadership	Creates future leaders and succession options	Monthly
CEO update	Communicates vision, culture and company performance	Builds trust, transparency and morale	Quarterly
Team planning workshop	Updates goals and strategies	Aligns departments and encourages collaboration	Quarterly
Performance reviews	Creates time for reflection and planning for growth	Reinforces personal and company accountability	Twice-yearly

Meetings don't need to be formal sit-down affairs. Swisse held meetings on the run, in doorways, hallways, in cabs and over lunch. It doesn't matter where you meet or for how long, just make sure you do and don't cancel, even if you think there's nothing to discuss.

Curate a team of intrapreneurs

Once culture has clarity and cadence, the next, more confronting, question that needs to be addressed is: what are you actually encouraging people to do with that clarity? Are they simply executing instructions more efficiently, or are they thinking, testing and acting like owners?

This is where intrapreneurship comes in.

An intrapreneur is an employee who thinks and acts like an entrepreneur inside an existing organisation. They spot opportunities, question assumptions, test ideas and take responsibility for outcomes, without needing permission for every move. They don't wait to be told what to do. They look for what needs to be done. They do the right thing by the company, even if that makes it more difficult for them.

That tension between personal comfort and organisational responsibility was something Meahan saw clearly in her role as head of HR at Seek. She would ask her team: 'Are you avoiding giving feedback because it makes you uncomfortable? If so, you're putting your own needs ahead of the company's. When people do what's right for the business, everyone wins.'

Most companies don't stagnate due to a lack of talent; they stagnate because a culture of fear and self-protection sets in. When that happens, people stop showing initiative, and risk becomes something to avoid rather than manage. Over time, those once capable and courageous individuals turn into cautious administrators.

Encouraging intrapreneurship creates momentum and encourages innovation. It distributes decision-making to a wider range of stakeholders and gives people permission to take risks they may not otherwise take. Most importantly, it gives ambitious people a reason to stay.

An attitude of intrapreneurship doesn't magically appear in an organisation. It needs the right conditions to flourish: clear and transparent language about what will be rewarded and what won't; regular forums that provide feedback on the initiatives being put forward; and leaders who understand the difference between taking smart risks versus indulging reckless behaviour.

Luxury Escapes offered a clear example of what supporting intrapreneurship looks like. Its co-founder, Adam Schwab, had a blunt explanation for why so many companies stagnate.

'A lot of middle managers are averse to taking a risk. If they take a risk and it goes wrong, they get fired. If they take a risk and get it right, somebody else gets the credit.'

Innovation can't flourish in that kind of environment. Adam encouraged the opposite approach.

'We want people to take risks; not stupid risks, but smart ones with asymmetric upside. If it works, the payoff is significant. If it doesn't, it's a two-way door and we can step back.'

That thinking is embedded in the company's DNA. Reversible, two-way-door decisions are encouraged, which normalises courage and rewards bold action. One-way-door decisions are treated differently because once you commit, you can't easily undo them. These decisions affect brand, cash flow and people, and require slower, more considered thinking.

Adam makes it clear that ideas might start with one person, but they're shaped by many. 'One person may have the idea, but 100 people might work on it,' he said. Even when a senior manager comes up with an initiative like the TripPlanner — a tool that lets customers plan, organise and book an end-to-end holiday itinerary in one place — it's the product managers, engineers and commercial teams who run with it, pull it apart and rebuild it into something better.

The company runs fortnightly product showcases to keep everyone connected to the work being done by other teams.

'The product managers present what they've worked on in the last fortnight and what's coming next, so everybody can see what's happening,' Adam explained. 'It inspires others to step up and put their ideas forward because they know their work has a genuine chance of being progressed.'

* * *

Culture isn't built through grand gestures. It's created by incremental actions: the words leaders use, the meetings they commit to and the risks they reward. Together, they create an invisible framework of accountability that inspires teams to take calculated risks and act less like employees and more like business owners.

Nuggets of wisdom

▸ Create a clear lexicon that defines the language you want your team to use, and the language you want them to avoid. When everyone knows which words are encouraged and which are off-limits, expectations become explicit rather than assumed.
▸ Don't cancel meetings with your staff, even when you're busy. Cancelling meetings sends a clear signal that your people are

not an important priority. Maintain the cadence, especially when the pressure is on.

▶ Design for two-way-door decisions. Be clear about which decisions can be reversed. When people know a choice can be undone without lasting damage, they're more willing to experiment, take smart risks and act like owners, without fear of getting it wrong.

24

HOW TO PREPARE FOR A CRISIS

Most businesses don't fail because of a single event; they fail the same way people go bankrupt: gradually, and then suddenly, as Ernest Hemingway said in his novel *The Sun Also Rises*. Those failures occur for a variety of reasons: an assumption is left untested, a risk left unnamed, a decision left unchecked. Each seems insignificant on its own, until they accumulate and, gradually, and then suddenly, the business implodes.

Strong leaders don't let this happen. They think ahead, and imagine what could go wrong before it does, and take steps to prevent it from happening again. They know it's always easier to stop the wrong thing from coming in the door than removing it once it's inside.

Don't let them in

Businesses face dozens of risks. You can't prevent everything, but thinking through what might happen before it does gives you power. When you name the risk, you tame the risk.

Don't wait until the metaphorical body is on the autopsy table to work out what went wrong. Get ahead of it by running scenario plans, building contingency responses and maintaining risk registers. One of the most effective ways to manage risk is to conduct a pre-mortem.

It's like CSI for entrepreneurs: you imagine the project has already died, then work backwards to uncover what killed it.

Conducting a pre-mortem is crucial because when things go wrong, there is rarely time to think.

Pub baron Stephen Hunt learned this the hard way when a drunk and disorderly man tried to force his way into one of his venues. What Stephen and his security team didn't know was that the man had just come out of jail, had arrived to settle old debts and had a Glock 17 pistol tucked in his trousers to help him do it. He was dangerous outside the pub; imagine how lethal he would be inside it.

Stephen and his team tackled the man to the ground, wrestled the gun from him, called the authorities and went back to work. Although it was a terrifying moment, Stephen and his team didn't panic; they acted with speed, strength and precision, not because they were fearless, but because they were prepared. Stephen had already conducted a pre-mortem and taken the team through every worst-case scenario they could imagine. They had rehearsed how situations like this might unfold and what to do if and when they happened.

The core insight that the pre-mortem makes clear is that you need to work hard to keep the wrong people out. Whether they're customers, staff, partners or investors, it's easier to stop the wrong people at the door than to remove them once they're inside.

Janine Allis was very selective as to who she let into her business.

'Getting the right franchise manager was critical. I've always seen our franchise manager as the gatekeeper of the Boost Juice name. I imagine her standing in a knight's outfit, with a very sharp sword, on a plank outside the Boost castle, and I know that she will not let the wrong people into the business. The best decisions we have made involve the people who are not with us.'

Plan for the downturn before it arrives

Seek weathered the 2008 global financial crisis better than most because of the pre-mortem they ran in 2005. Their pre-mortem centred on one brutal question: *What if the jobs disappeared?*

Meahan Callaghan, Seek's HR Director at the time, remembers it well.

'We held an offsite event specifically for scenario planning and we debated everything until you just wanted to hurt yourself to get taken to hospital so you didn't have to listen anymore. But it needed to be done, and it paid off.'

When the GFC hit, it hit hard. Companies valued at millions collapsed. Thousands of employees were made redundant overnight, unemployment shot to 10 per cent, and recruiters were squeezed from both sides: overwhelmed by jobseekers clamouring for work, while scrambling to hold onto the few clients who were still hiring.

Did Seek panic? No. They pulled out the plan and put it into action.

'It was ridiculously easy because everyone knew what to do,' Meahan says. 'We didn't sack anyone or offer redundancies. We offered half pay, sourced lower cost services overseas and redeployed staff across the business.'

Being prepared gave Seek what every business craves in a crisis: time. While others prevaricated, they activated. It gave them the space to manage the crisis in a calm and controlled way, without panicking or making spur-of-the-moment decisions. This in turn gave employees and investors confidence that the business was in good hands and that they could manage whatever came next.

Meahan has seen the other side too: when companies *don't* do a pre-mortem.

'I worked with a company whose core business was custom-designed, print-on-demand T-shirts,' she said. 'They were operating in a highly competitive market, with customers able to find cheaper alternatives elsewhere, and the US — their largest market — was under pressure from rising living costs.'

In that kind of environment, it makes sense to step back and run what Meahan calls a 'what if' session, giving the team space to test different scenarios and explore possible outcomes.

'The 'what if' questions we needed to ask were: What if our American revenue halved? What if a competitor appeared tomorrow with our exact model? What if they charged $5 less? What if every artist realised they could sell on eBay more cheaply and easily than through us? What if AI could do it faster and better than us? What would we do if any of those scenarios occurred?'

To predict the future, one must be prepared to identify what that future looks like. 'Good executive planning includes managing risk, and sessions like this are critical to identifying what those risks are. Without that discipline, risk remains invisible,' she said.

Build goodwill before you need it

A pre-mortem helps you prepare for risk, but it also forces you to think about the relationships you'll need to rely on if things go wrong. Calling in a favour depends on goodwill. You can't ask for help from someone you've never invested in. Business works the same way. When crises hit, you may need to pull in some favours but if you haven't done the groundwork and built those relationships, it's very difficult to ask for support.

When COVID-19 hit in 2020, Luxury Escapes needed every ounce of goodwill they could muster. The entire travel industry was on its knees. Airlines stopped flying, hotels shut their doors, tour operators cancelled their trips.

Yet Luxury Escapes stayed strong.

It wasn't due to good luck. It was due to good planning. Long before the pandemic, Adam Schwab and his team had mapped out the worst-case scenarios: What if global travel froze? What if cash flow evaporated? What if customers panicked and wanted their money back? They built their business model with the answers to those questions in mind.

No-one could have predicted the speed of the collapse, but they were ready for the shock because they'd imagined it long before it arrived.

Pre-planning helped them build a moat that protected them from competitive threats. Customers had prepaid for their holidays, which meant Luxury Escapes held strong cash reserves. When borders slammed shut, they had millions in the bank, a buffer that bought time, optionality and calm when the rest of the industry was spiralling.

Customers could have demanded refunds but most didn't. They said, 'Hold onto it; we'll travel later.' Some waited five years to redeem their credit notes. That trust was the dividend of a decade spent building loyalty with their customers, partners and suppliers.

It was an all-team effort. The board members dropped their remuneration to zero, all senior executives took a pay cut and staff reduced their work hours. 'It was an incredibly unifying process, and allowed the business to focus on growth and deal with the immediate challenges,' he says.

Their scenario planning also underpinned how they treated their people. While other companies shed staff, Luxury Escapes redeployed theirs. 'I think we were the only travel business on earth that didn't fire anyone because of COVID,' said Adam.

The tech team grew from 30 to 140 and was assigned to a series of long-term projects they'd had on the backburner. 'We built multiple marketplaces, created a wide-ranging loyalty scheme, built the data lake, managed the AI transformation and developed our TripPlanner.'

When the market returned, the competitors had to rebuild their teams from scratch, but Luxury Escapes were ready to hit the ground running. They made it through because they could see what was coming. Their culture gave them the confidence to keep calm and carry on, and their customers gave them the time to work it out.

Create moats

Every startup has a terminal risk: that single weak point that can kill the business overnight. Tim Fung's Airtasker had to manage several on an on-going basis.

Cash flow was a constant pressure. Airtasker carried significant fixed costs but had unpredictable revenue, which meant their fundraising and expenditure had to be timed with absolute precision. One wrong move and the cash flow could have stalled, which would threaten their survival. Learning how to manage that process and bring the investors along the startup journey required delicate stakeholder management that can only be learned by doing it.

There was also the continued fear of a PR crisis that is ever present when you operate a 24/7 marketplace platform. In those early days, before the company had the brand capital it has now, Tim and his team lived with the reality that they were just one bad review away from oblivion.

'When you're dealing with thousands of people who are either booking a task or offering a service, the risk of one side being dissatisfied with something or someone is high.'

Over time, however, Tim learned that people understood the nature of two-sided communities and were more tolerant than might be expected of those who didn't uphold the values of the platform. Tim's perspective was tempered with the knowledge that the host of the party can't control everything. 'When someone behaves badly at a party, you don't shut the event down and send everyone home;

you deal with the person who's causing the issue and keep going so everyone can continue to enjoy the party.'

The biggest structural challenge was the classic chicken-and-egg problem every two-sided marketplace faces: you need customers to attract workers, and workers to attract customers. Without enough activity on both sides, the loop collapses. As Tim puts it, 'Momentum is everything. If there are too few people posting jobs or too few taskers ready to take them, the marketplace has no heartbeat.'

Keeping both sides active at the same time is a constant balancing act. It requires capital, marketing firepower and deep operational knowledge, and it's a risk the Airtasker team manages daily across every market they operate in.

They pushed through it the only way possible: relentless iteration. Launch, refine, rebuild. Then do it again. Each new country meant starting from scratch: recruiting taskers, attracting customers and funding local marketing. The learnings couldn't be cheaply replicated. As Tim said, 'It's like starting a new business every time.'

The breakthrough came when they identified the true lever: real-time activity. Once they understood that engagement depended on people being active on the marketplace simultaneously, they redesigned the platform around that insight — and the loop finally began to hold.

The irony is that the very things that once threatened Airtasker's survival eventually became its moat. Building a functioning, real-time marketplace is gruelling work. It takes patience, persistence and a willingness to grind through the hard yards. Most competitors with an eye to setting up a rival operation don't want to put the time, effort and capital into making that happen. Airtasker did, and were able to leverage their knowledge of building earlier marketplaces in other cities as a blueprint for what to do when they launched in a new market.

That institutional knowledge was hard won, which was, again, a win for Tim because it meant if they struggled to access mentorship around how to build a functioning marketplace, chances are their competitors did too. That paucity of how-to intel around building a marketplace became another source of competitive advantage.

* * *

It's clear that the startup founders who don't just survive but thrive do so not because they are lucky, or are in the right place at the right time, but because they look ahead, acknowledge the risks and create plans and procedures to ensure they are well prepared for them if and when they arrive.

Nuggets of wisdom

▸ Plan for the worst while things are calm. Run pre-mortems in the quiet times, when you have space to think clearly. When a crisis hits, there's no time to plan, so having risks named, responses rehearsed and decisions pre-made converts chaos into controlled action.

▸ Build goodwill before you need it. Invest early in customers, partners and staff so when things go wrong, you can rely on their goodwill to help get you through the tough times.

▸ Do what others aren't prepared to do. Doing difficult work can be an asset. If it's hard for you, it will be hard for your competitors too. Persisting through that discomfort is how moats are built.

25

HOW TO GET THE MOST FROM YOUR TEAM

Steven Spielberg once said, 'Ninety-nine per cent of a film's success is in the casting. If I get that right, the rest will take care of itself.'

Hiring your team works the same way. Who you let in — be they an employee, investor, customer or supplier — determines your success. Each will bring with them a bunch of baggage — habits, values, beliefs — that will very quickly become yours to manage, so choose wisely.

How to find and keep the right people

If you're a technician who prefers to do everything yourself, and believe no-one can do the job as well as you, hiring staff can feel daunting. The fear of meeting payroll, holding people accountable and having difficult conversations looms large. So does the risk of being let down by people you trusted. These are not just management challenges but personal development tests, requiring you to have the courage to admit to your own foibles and take responsibility for the role you may have played in creating conflict. Leadership is hard. It is little wonder that many founders with the potential to scale choose instead to stay small.

There's another way to look at hiring, though. With the right mindset, bringing on a team can be a panacea for a whole range of issues. Done strategically, it can eliminate the tasks you dislike doing, free up your time so you can do higher value work, strengthen your systems so there's less room for process errors, and position you as the authority in your sector so you can access more opportunities.

If you want to build a scalable business that's built to sell, you'll need to move from the *technician* zone to the *manager* zone, and ultimately into the *owner* zone. Even if you want a lifestyle business, a few strategic hires can multiply your impact and help you earn more while working less.

Who should you hire first?

Your first hire matters. It sets the tone for what happens next, reveals what the business actually needs and could either inspire you to keep hiring or put you off for life. There are lots of ways to determine who your first hires should be.

Leading business coach Kobi Simmat sees founders make their first hiring mistake by starting with job titles rather than actual needs.

'If you have ever said, "I should hire a CFO", or "I should hire a sales rep", or "I should hire an SEO person", you're coming at it from the wrong angle,' Kobi said. 'This "I should hire…" attitude compresses your imagination and makes you feel there is a one-size-fits-all first hire for every business. There isn't.'

Instead of starting with role titles, he suggests starting with the work itself; the tasks that are not getting done because you avoid them or simply don't enjoy doing them.

'Your first hire should be the person who takes your least favourite work off your plate,' said Kobi. 'List everything you don't like doing.

It might be updating the website, posting on Facebook, following up sales leads, writing blogs or networking. Prioritise the tasks you hate the most, turn them into a job description and hire someone who enjoys that kind of work. Someone, somewhere, loves doing what you hate. That person should be your first hire.'

Seek's former HR director Meahan Callaghan sees it slightly differently.

'I personally think you should hire an HR person really early. It helps create the foundation for everything that follows. If you do hire an HR professional, make sure they're aligned to your culture, because if they don't share your values, you'll have a much harder job bringing your culture to life later on when you hire more people.'

For early-stage startups, Meahan's advice is to be pragmatic. 'Hire the technical people you need to make things happen. If you're building a website, an app or a marketplace, bring in the people who can actually make that product.'

Choose all-rounders

When Janine Allis set out to hire a manager for her first Boost store in Adelaide, she knew she needed someone special. Living in Melbourne, she needed a person she could trust to run the store without close supervision.

'We were extremely lucky to find a great manager for that first store. Sharryn did not have any retail experience, but she had the passion and fire in her stomach that we were looking for. A sign of her determination emerged when she told us she was a champion speed water skier. You need enormous mental resilience and courage to be successful in that sport, and that was the kind of mindset we were looking for.'

When Vince Lebon launched his Rollie Nation shoe business, he was the archetypal jack of all trades. He did everything, from building the website and writing the sales emails to processing payments and taking customer calls. When the workload became too heavy and he needed to hire someone, he knew the qualities he was looking for. Skill and will.

'Having the right skills is critical, but will is more important. Skill can be taught, will cannot, and that's the critical quality we look for in all our new hires. Do they want to learn, grow and help the business succeed? Are they willing to pitch in and do what needs to be done, irrespective of their job title? Do they do what's right for the business?

Vince's first hire was an all-rounder who was willing to turn her hand to everything. She eventually became his executive assistant, and 14 years later, is now the senior brand manager.

MasterChef judge and online course creator Kirsten Tibballs runs a lean operation.

'I've got 13 people in the business. The marketing team are all triple-plus threats. They are skilled at videography, editing, writing, search engine marketing and social media. The others do a range of things, from writing and testing recipes, to setting up the kitchen, preparing the online classes, managing the community and more.'

A small team gives her a competitive edge.

'It keeps me nimble. We can do more, act quickly, make changes and respond faster. When you've got too many layers of approval or too much red tape, everything slows down. In the time it takes to get everyone on board, you could have already tested the idea, learned from it and moved on.'

Considering she runs a 20 000-strong masterclass community and multiple other business ventures, it's proof you don't need a big team to make a big impact. What matters is having good systems and hiring multi-talented people with the will to do what's needed to make the business a success.

Janine Allis preferred hiring an all-rounder as well.

'My first two hires were a PA and a part-time bookkeeper but they pitched in and did whatever needed doing including answering phones, delivering packages, cleaning and more. We worked from the kitchen table at home for the first two years so we all did what was needed to get done. There was no hierarchy.'

Choose people who share your values

The Beauty Chef's Carla Oates started her business in the kitchen of her Bondi home, cooking up a storm with her gut-friendly herbal elixirs. She worked solo for three years, but as demand grew, she eventually hired some senior leaders to share the load. She admits she would do it differently if she was starting over.

'I wasn't as careful around hiring at the start as I should have been. I delegated that to recruiters and I shouldn't have. Now I'm much more considered because you have to make sure all the boxes are ticked to ensure their skillsets and values align.'

When she sought out and found investors to help fund her expansion, they insisted she take on some of their people, which didn't suit the culture she had created.

'We grew really quickly. I went from eight employees to taking on investment, and those investors insisted I hire their people. They were experienced operators but they were from large corporates and they just didn't get what running a small business entailed. It was the wrong cultural fit.'

In 2021, she brought on a General Manager and a Chief Financial Officer. 'I chose those hires myself and that's when we really took off. Bringing those two professionals on board was a game changer for me.'

For the first time, she had a leadership team who genuinely shared the load.

'The three of us made a very strong trio. They were employees, but they acted like owners. If I'd known how powerful those senior hires were going to be, I would have done it much earlier. Having them take on those important roles would have let me step back and get on with what I loved doing, which was educating and communicating the vision to my customers and stakeholders. I also really enjoyed having them as collaborators. Prior to them arriving, all the decision making was on me and that was not only stressful but quite lonely as well.'

Finding the money to hire when the business is new or sales are low is always a challenge. You can't grow without staff, but you can't hire staff until you grow. What's the solution?

Carla thinks there is a middle ground. 'You can absolutely find outstanding mid-level people who are smart, passionate and aligned with your values. Some people will take a cut in salary in exchange for working with a great group of passionate people who are excited about what they do and believe in what they're selling.'

Where do you go to find good people?

Finding good staff is an age-old challenge, even for the most successful companies.

Where do you look? Seek? LinkedIn? A note pinned to the IGA community board? If you want to cut recruiter costs and reduce hiring mistakes, start closer to home. The best hires often come from people you already know, trust and enjoy being around.

Radek Sali learned this early.

'Working with family and friends can work brilliantly, if you set clear expectations and, as we did, hold them to a higher standard than everyone else. Once your culture is established, you can encourage your team to refer great people from their own networks and reward them with an incentive if the hire works out. The benefit is that you create a workplace filled with people who already share your values and want to see the business thrive.'

Like Vince, Radek didn't hire for technical skill. He hired for will.

'We weren't worried about their technical expertise. We hired those who fitted in with our culture: the kind of people who would smile, say hello to each other, stop what they were doing to have a conversation, and help each other out when needed. At the core, we hired people who really liked each other.'

Radek was often told it was unorthodox to hire people you liked to work alongside you.

'I never understood that,' he said. 'You spend half your life at work. Why wouldn't you want to spend it with people you already knew you liked? Our informal hiring process also saved us tens of thousands on recruitment fees and invariably delivered a higher quality candidate than the traditional recruitment method.'

Some outsiders joked the business looked like a cult.

'They'd come to work and see people laughing, smiling and genuinely enjoying each other's company and say, "How could everyone actually enjoy coming to work each day?"'

The culture became self-curating. 'People would join, and within a month or two they'd know whether this was, or wasn't, the place for them, and they'd either stay or leave of their own accord.'

Hire for potential, not just position

Radek also trialled an unusual strategy of hiring two people for the same role. He'd hire one seasoned operator with experience in the sector, and someone from outside the industry with fresh instincts and no attachment to 'how things are done around here'.

The experienced person brought knowledge and systems to the role and the newcomer brought curiosity and creativity. This combination of the old and the new reaped many dividends and offered a perspective that created a dynamic culture. Additionally, if someone exceptional appeared but there was no role available, they'd create one for them.

'Good people eventually pay their way. They find new opportunities, expand the business and deliver far more value than they cost.'

Radek and his team went further in terms of matching the right candidate with the right role by asking each candidate how they wanted to spend their time.

'We'd ask, "What do you really like doing? What do you do in your spare time? What do you like reading, watching, listening to?" We wanted them to find their passion and bring that energy and full self to the table so they could fulfil their potential.'

Radek's innovative approach to hiring worked.

'Even though we paid in the top 25th percentile, this policy made us one of the most productive companies in our industry. Salaries averaged 7 per cent of revenue, which was our optimal level. The real challenge wasn't cost, but finding enough good people and continuing to hire at the pace our revenue grew.'

How much is a $50 000 staff member really costing you?

Hiring is easy, firing is hard, or as it's often said, 'Hiring is guessing, firing is knowing.' Letting someone go is costly, emotionally draining and disruptive for everyone involved. It's far harder and far more expensive to move someone out of an organisation than it is to bring them in. That's why it's so important to hire the right people at the start.

It's instructive to calculate how much your staff are *really* costing you, because it's often more than you think. And if you really knew how much each staff member was costing you, you may take more interest in how you treat them.

One man who has done the calculation is leading publican and investment fund manager Stephen Hunt. He employs hundreds of staff across his pub empire and knows exactly what a staff member is worth. Here's how he calculates the true cost of a staff member.

'If you owned an investment property worth $1 million, you'd take good care of it. You'd maintain it, fix what's broken, improve what's already there and protect its long-term value. You wouldn't neglect it and hope for the best.'

The same logic applies to staff.

'Most founders don't realise that every team member they employ is effectively a million-dollar asset,' he said.

I said, 'But most startups don't have a staff member that costs them $1 million.'

'Yes, they do,' said Stephen. 'If you're paying someone more than $50 000 a year, they're actually valued at $1 million a year.'

'How does that work?' I asked.

'If you borrowed $1 million from a bank at 5 per cent interest, you would pay $50 000 a year in interest. Every $50 000 you spend on wages is effectively the same as servicing a $1 million asset. In other words, a team member on a $50 000 salary represents $1 million in capital value. If you were responsible for maintaining a million-dollar asset, would it change how carefully you looked after it? That is the true value of a $50 000 employee.'

Seen through that lens, a team member on $50 000 a year is not a minor line item, but a million-dollar investment.

'If you were responsible for a million-dollar asset, you would do everything you could to get the best return from it,' said Stephen.

'You would support it, protect it and make deliberate decisions about whether to improve it, retain it or let it go.'

So, what would change if you treated every team member earning $50 000 or more as a million-dollar asset? Would you invest more in their development, listen more carefully to their views and work harder to support them to do their best work? And just as importantly, would you act more decisively when it was clear the asset wasn't performing?

Try harder to keep good people

Knowing that every $50 000 staff member is actually a million-dollar asset supports Meahan Callaghan's assertion that we should work harder to hold onto the staff we already have. When the 2008 GFC hit, this belief became even more important and Paul Bassat, the CEO of Seek at the time, tasked Meahan with finding whatever way she could to ensure no-one lost their job. His mantra was 'we will ride this out', but that was easier said than done.

'We spent days brainstorming how to find ways to inspire people to take time off or a cut in pay but still stay. Want a year's sabbatical? Take it now. Annual leave? Take it now. Long service? Take it now. Some of it, all of it? Up to you. Would you like Monday mornings off for the next six months? You choose. Our goal was to cut costs without sacking anyone and wait for the worst of the recession to blow over.'

She said, 'It would have been easier to sack people and cut costs but when the tide turned, the business would need to rebuild from scratch.'

Instead, they chose to take a hit in the short term and hold onto their people. It was a financially risky decision, but a smarter one overall.

Meahan explained why.

'We had high-performing people, and we didn't want to lose them. If we had let them go, we would have needed to hire them again a few months later when conditions improved. They would have been snapped up by then anyway and we'd have had no way of getting those people back. People underestimate the long-term cost of losing good staff.'

That thinking reflected how she handled resignations too.

'If someone wants to leave, some managers just say, "Okay", without trying to understand why. If it's a high performer, I sit them down and ask questions. Why are you leaving? What would make you stay? If we changed X or Y, would that make a difference? People let good staff go far too easily. It's worth making the effort to hold onto them.'

Keep staff loyal

Pub baron Stephen Hunt was often asked how he kept his staff so loyal. 'I worked at it, but there were some basic strategies we put in place that helped us retain the right people.'

One of those strategies was offering an employee share options program (ESOP).

By 2015, Stephen's pub group was valued at $400 000. Four years later, it was worth more than $63 million. That kind of growth doesn't come without a cost. As the business scaled, Stephen's workload became relentless, and his health and personal life were the first casualties.

'I knew I couldn't keep going at that pace,' he admits. 'But I was totally absorbed in what I was doing and thrilled with the impact and the profit we were making, but it wasn't sustainable.'

For the business to keep growing, something had to change. Stephen realised he needed more than extra staff. He needed a true collaborator: a second-in-command who could take a significant load off his plate and operate at the same speed and intensity he did.

He began searching for a Marketing and Operations Manager: someone who could move fast, juggle multiple projects, manage people and do it all with humour and resilience. He interviewed scores of high-calibre candidates, but no-one quite fit.

Then he met Ricci-Lee.

At the time, Ricci-Lee was working as a sales representative for the Southern Cross Radio and Austereo Group. She came in each month to help Stephen develop media campaigns to promote his growing network of pubs. Over time, he noticed Ricci-Lee had the qualities he valued in a business partner.

She was proactive, creative and deeply invested in delivering outstanding customer service. More importantly, she acted like a business owner, even though she wasn't one.

Stephen realised he'd found the collaborator he was looking for: someone who could shoulder real responsibility and think beyond her job description.

Together, they designed an ESOP structure that aligned incentives and created shared ownership. Stephen explains the mechanics:

'For illustrative purposes, let's assume I give Ricci-Lee $50 000 worth of units. She now effectively owes the company $50 000 for those units. The more money we make, the quicker her debt gets paid off, the quicker she owns a share in the business — and the quicker she receives the benefits that come with ownership, like returns and dividends.'

ESOPs work because they give people skin in the game. It inspires them to think like owners, act like owners and stay loyal like owners.

Use AI to help you hire

Some startups are currently getting slammed with 3000 applications per role, with many of those résumés being generated by AI. The challenge employers now face is sifting through the chaff from the grain to see which candidates are worth pursuing. Just working your way through 3000 applications can take a week of work and still not get you any closer to choosing the right person. There has to be a better way of managing this process and Ben Fewtrell, founder of coaching company maxmyprofit.com.au and digital marketing agency digitlc.com.au has found it.

'We needed to hire a sales assistant and instead of manually reading every application, we uploaded all the résumés and cover letters into ChatGPT,' he said. 'It created an Excel spreadsheet listing each candidate and scored them across key competencies based on their experience. It saved hours of manual work and gave us a clear shortlist to review.'

Before the first interview, Ben asked each applicant to record a short video of themselves answering a few questions.

'We then transcribed each video, uploaded them so the AI could analyse responses against our criteria, identified the strongest matches and invited them to attend the next round of interviews.'

Ben recorded and transcribed those interviews, uploaded them again, and asked the AI to rank and assess candidates against the job description.

'After every round of interviews, the AI updated the spreadsheet and adjusted the rankings accordingly. From an original pool of 450, we shortlisted it down to 11 strong candidates, and found the perfect person in a fraction of the time it would take to do manually, and for a fraction of what a recruiter would charge.'

* * *

Hiring good people is not just a job. It's *the* job. Getting it wrong is financially costly to the business and emotionally draining for the business owner. It's the critical factor that will help your business thrive or die. Choose your collaborators carefully.

Nuggets of wisdom

▶ Hire for abilities, not titles. Your first hires should be people who can take on whatever needs doing, especially the work you avoid or dislike.

▶ Treat every hire like a million-dollar asset. Anyone earning $50000 a year is the equivalent of servicing a $1 million asset. If you'd protect, maintain and actively manage a million-dollar investment, your people deserve the same level of care and concern.

▶ Try hard to keep good people. Don't wait for a resignation to tell your best people they matter. High performers are expensive to lose and hard to replace, so put as much discipline and intent into retaining them as you do into hiring them.

26

HOW TO CONDUCT THE HIRING INTERVIEWS

Hiring well is an art form. Anyone can look good on paper or perform well in an interview, but assessing someone's true character off the back of a few interviews takes great skill. Done well, an interview reveals how someone thinks and behaves when no-one is looking, and their underlying character. Done poorly, it lets the wrong people slip in and can cost you everything you've worked so hard to build.

Six top tips to improve your interviewing process

Few people understand hiring like Meahan Callaghan, former HR Director at Seek.com, Afterpay, Foxtel and Mecca. She's hired thousands of people and fired a fair few too. She has seen what happens when you hire well, and when you don't. She has spent her career figuring that out and creating systems that help senior management see through the charm and polished résumés to find the people who truly fit. 'Recruitment is a series of assessments, each one designed to reveal character, competence and cultural alignment,' she said.

(continued)

Meahan uses a multi-step methodology to avoid mis-hires. Here are a few of her top tips to hiring a high-performance team.

1 Establish the non-negotiables

'Before you meet candidates, you need absolute clarity about the role, the expectations and the values that guide your decision,' said Meahan.

A strong recruitment process starts with one question: *What problem am I trying to solve by hiring this role?*

Meahan recommends you establish your non-negotiables and confirm the absolute essentials before you advertise the role.

'If the candidate needs to manage people, say how many people they'll need to manage. If they need to know JavaScript or have a forklift license, be explicit about those minimum requirements.'

Take care in choosing the questions you ask too.

'You can't ask anything where the person could claim that you made a decision based on protected areas.'

The 'protected areas' that you must avoid are race, sex, age, disability, marital status, pregnancy, religion, political opinion and more. Fair Work Australia's website contains more information on what you can and can't ask.

2 Allow enough time

Meahan believes the time allocated for most interviews is too short, which results in a surface-level interview that doesn't reveal the true nature of the candidate. She adopts a disciplined, scientific approach that takes a little longer but is more robust and delivers a better result.

Most hiring managers allocate an hour for each interview. 'That's not long enough,' said Meahan. 'If you allow 10 minutes of small talk, 10 minutes for showing them in and out of the room, that allows just 40 minutes for the real interview, so you only have time for four questions of 10-minute duration. If you want to ask six meaningful questions, you need two hours. And you need two meetings: one for technical capability, one for culture fit.'

The first interview should require the candidate to complete some role play or test. 'They don't get paid for that preparation. You need to remind them, in a nice way, if they've got the right skillset, this preparation won't take very long. If they have to spend all weekend on it, that would be a concern as it's something they should already be able to do.'

3 Ask better questions

One of the most common and least useful interview questions is, 'What are you passionate about?' said Meahan.

'If you ask that and they say "windsurfing", it tells you nothing about whether they are right for the role,' she said. A better question is, 'Tell me about a time you felt so passionate you pushed something too far, and what happened when you did?'

Meahan also looks for ambition in candidates, both for their own growth and for the success of the company. In her view, a sense of ambition is a quality you either have or you don't.

'It's important to hire people who believe in your ambition, because the company will inevitably go through ups and downs, and you need to know they can withstand the rocky patches. When Seek faced significant challenges during the dot-com bust in the early 2000s, salaries were frozen to avoid layoffs, and shares in the company were offered in lieu of salaries. Not everyone accepted the offer, but those who did went on to become extremely wealthy.' Meahan wasn't at Seek at that time, but she said those who were have often said how smart

(continued)

that decision was, and how it created an extraordinary level of loyalty. 'What it showed was that belief in the founders' ambition really mattered. If they hadn't believed in the company and where it was heading, there's no way they would have stuck around during those tough times.'

4 Use role plays and testing

Meahan believes the only way to know who you're really hiring is to test the candidate, in real time. In the age of AI-generated résumés, this is more important than ever.

One applicant for the chief marketing role didn't even look at the company's marketing collateral before his interview.

'We asked him to comment on our current campaign and he hadn't even looked at our website. That was an immediate red flag,' Meahan said. 'If you can't be bothered preparing for the job you supposedly want, that does not augur well for the future.'

She's also a firm believer in asking candidates to take reasoning tests: verbal, numeric and especially abstract tests. 'The results tell me a lot about how you think. People who do well in these tests are generally tenacious and great problem solvers who don't give up on something easily, two qualities we always looked for in our candidates.'

5 Apply the cultural test

Meahan believes the founding team has the best instincts for who will fit in on a cultural level. After the official interviews have been completed, she'll often ask one of the founders or the original employees to meet with the candidates for a casual coffee to check 'the vibe'.

'Those early hires built the DNA of the place,' she said. 'If they come back and say, "Something doesn't feel right", I factor that into our decision.'

Ronni Kahn is the final link in the hiring chain for OzHarvest.

'I always do the last interview for every new hire. The candidate might have the best skills in the world, but if they don't understand why they are coming to work for us, or don't genuinely want to be part of a purpose-led organisation where it's not about them, but about the people we serve, I don't hire them.'

Cultural fit also extends to where you want your team to work from.

Adam Schwab from Luxury Escapes has a firm work-from-office policy.

'We're a work-from-office, collaborative, high-paced, high-excitement environment. Lots of people love it, but it's not for everyone. We want to make sure it's a good fit for the candidate as much as for the business. We think working from the office is much better in terms of mentoring, especially for our younger team members. It's hard for a 20-year-old to come into a business and not have anyone to bounce off. Working from home can be very lonely and isolating for young people. I don't think that's a good way for young people to start or grow their careers.'

6 Conduct final checks

Once the formal interviews are out of the way, there are a few steps you can take to double check you've made the right choice.

The receptionist test

Meahan said the real interview often starts before a candidate even enters the room.

'People reveal themselves when they think no-one is watching,' she told me. More than once, a top-tier candidate

(continued)

has unravelled in under 10 seconds by being rude to the receptionist on their way in or way out, or by treating junior staff with disdain. These things get noticed.'

The break-bread test
Sharing a meal with a candidate often reveals more than any formal interview. Are they polite to wait staff? Do they engage with those around them? Do they ask questions and show curiosity? These small cues show what they are really like outside the interview room and will reveal more about their character than an hour of formal questioning.

The referee test
Don't just seek out the referees listed on the résumé. When Adam Schwab hires for a senior role, 'We do anonymous reference checks with people who aren't their official referees'. Take the time to scan their résumé for unexplained gaps, short stints or sideways moves and ask them to walk you through those missing years.

The airline-seat test
Once competence and character are locked in, Meahan reserves the final question for herself: 'Would I want to sit next to this person on a plane for eight hours?' If the answer is anything other than an enthusiastic 'yes', it's a no from her.

* * *

When you hire well, the benefits compound. You'll have fewer fires to extinguish, longer tenure and a harmonious work environment. When you hire badly, the cost is immediate, and can take its toll on you, the team and the company's performance. Interviews are your best chance to get it right. Take them seriously, trust your instincts and don't let the wrong people in.

Nuggets of wisdom

▶ Be ruthless about the non-negotiables. If a candidate misses a core requirement, don't assume a charming personality will make up for it.

▶ Do your due diligence. Don't rely on gut instinct. Test for the role, check their résumés, ask trusted employees to do the final interview and if you're still unsure, sleep on it. If you're still not sure, start the recruitment process again. It'll be cheaper than hiring the wrong person.

▶ Ask the receptionist for their opinion. How a candidate speaks to reception, junior staff or anyone they think doesn't matter tells you more about their character than any pre-rehearsed answer ever will.

PART 5

MONEY

Fortune may favour the brave, but it consistently rewards the founders who do their homework, understand the numbers, and walk into the room knowing exactly what they're building, what it's worth, and what they're willing to sell it for.

Once you understand the metrics, the multiples and the investor mindset, you will know which deals to say yes to, which to walk away from, when to push, when to pull and how to negotiate from a position of power.

27

HOW TO SELL A BUSINESS

Business owners spend a great deal of time thinking about money: how to make it, protect it, invest it, share it and spend it. It all informs how and why they got into business in the first place.

Along the way, business becomes something else too: a test of character, work ethic, judgement, creativity, resilience and competence.

There are many ways to measure success, and not all of them fit neatly on a balance sheet, but if your goal is to build something valuable and eventually sell it, one measure outweighs the rest: what a buyer is willing to pay.

What investors look for

It's every founder's dream: to build a business from the spare bedroom and sell it just over a decade later for nearly half a billion dollars, and that's exactly what Shaun Wilson did with Bondi Sands.

They launched in 2012, with a salon-grade self-tan that looked good, felt good and cost less than $20. Over the next decade, the brand grew into a global force, was stocked in more than 40 000 retailers and sold in 95 countries. Revenue climbed from a few thousand in 2012, to $50 million (in 2019) to $105.8 million (in 2022), and then $190 million (in 2023).

But with rapid growth came complexity. They were scaling across multiple continents, negotiating with major retailers, and ramping up their sun-care and skincare R&D operations. Shaun spent half the year overseas and knew that without deeper scientific capability, operational infrastructure and global reach, their growth would be capped. Offers to acquire them rolled in but the valuations fell short of Shaun's expectations. What mattered most was finding a partner who didn't just want the brand, but had the capability to take it to the next level.

Citi, a global investment bank, was appointed to find a buyer. They ran two sale processes. The first, in 2021, attracted multiple offers and valued the company at over $320 million. The founders rejected the offer as it did not reflect the business's ongoing hyper-growth projections. The second sales process, in 2023, brought in Kao Corporation, a $26 billion Japanese consumer giant with a long history in beauty, skincare and deep expertise in manufacturing and distribution. The challenge for Shaun and co-founder Blair James was to maintain a 'business-as-usual' poker face for the team while simultaneously running the sale process, managing late-night diligence calls and maintaining the explosive growth.

'Finding a partner who aligned with our values was our key goal,' Shaun explained. 'There's two kinds of partners: a transactional partner and a transformational partner and Kao was definitely transformational.' What really excited Shaun was Kao's ability to unlock the potential growth in R&D and new markets.

In July 2023, Kao acquired Bondi Sands for over $450 million. Shaun stayed on as CEO, Blair as Creative Director and manufacturing remained in Melbourne.

Kao was the pivotal partner that brought the scientific capability, global distribution and long-term strategic alignment that would enable the brand to become as big as Shaun knew it could be.

How to impress an investor

Investors come in all shapes and sizes. Who you partner with depends on what you want, the resources you have and what you're prepared to give in exchange for what they bring.

Working with investors, said the co-founder of Luxury Escapes, Adam Schwab, comes down to one principle: absolute transparency. 'Be as open and as honest with your investors as possible. Investors hate surprises. If something's going wrong, tell them early, explain why and outline what you plan to do to fix it.'

He said, 'There's nothing worse than investors thinking you're going to make a million bucks and then losing a million bucks.'

In the early days, he admits he thought investors were a hindrance. Over time, he learned it was quite the opposite.

'You need to treat investors as partners. They're on the ride with you. Even if they're not on the board, they deserve respect, communication and inclusion in the journey.'

If transparency is the foundation of working with investors, purpose is what keeps the partnership together. Few people understand that better than Radek Sali.

After building Swisse into a billion-dollar wellness brand, Radek turned his focus to investing in purpose-led businesses through his firm, Light Warrior Group. He approached investment with the same commercial rigour and deep sense of social responsibility he brought to Swisse.

'We look for companies that have:

- a proven founder and talented team
- a positive culture that is purpose driven
- a highly scalable business model within a growth sector
- a proven point-of-difference from competitors

- an executable business model complemented by strong financials
- the opportunity for significant equity ownership
- the ability to use our expertise and network to fast-track growth and returns.'

When forming Light Warrior Group, Radek partnered with Adam Gregory, his former colleague from Goldman Sachs, appointing him as CEO and Chief Investment Officer. Together, they assembled a team of senior professionals from institutions such as Goldman Sachs, Macquarie and UBS.

He and Gregory see Light Warrior as more than a traditional investment office.

'We didn't want to be just another family office,' Radek explains. 'We wanted to create a purpose-driven investment firm — and we're doing that.' The long-term goal is to create a movement that shapes industries and society over the next decade.

Radek reviews hundreds of pitches each year but only backs a handful. Out of 150 approaches last year, he invested in four. He accepts that not every investment will succeed. Some will stumble, others will hold steady, but a small number — two or three — will more than compensate for any losses. Light Warrior takes a seven- to 10-year view on all investments, allowing time for the right ideas to mature. 'Great things take time,' Radek said.

What your pitch deck needs to include

Radek and the Light Warrior team use seven key questions to assess potential partners.

1 Who are you?

Before Radek invests in anything, he wants to understand the person behind the pitch. What experience do they bring to the business? What are they like as a person? Are their values aligned? For Radek, the founder matters as much as the idea.

'The consequences of a business partnership can be for life,' he said. 'It's like a marriage, but harder, because you probably don't have the love and commitment that you have when you choose your life partner.'

2 What do you want from us?

Radek sits on more than a dozen boards — some commercial, others community focused — and only stays involved if he can contribute meaningfully. 'If I can't add value, there's not much point me being there,' he said.

He applies the same principle to investing. Founders must articulate why he's the right investor for them and how his involvement will enhance their business.

'You need to make me feel that I am essential to your business success,' he said, 'and make me feel that I have something unique to offer that others can't.'

3 Have you done an apprenticeship?

Before backing a founder, Radek looks for proof of experience — either formal training, a solid track record or a previous venture.

'I need to see that the founders understand the sector and can handle what's coming,' he said. 'Ideally, they've already worked in the industry, learned from others, made their early mistakes and have the experience to run it independently without a lot of oversight. The founder must demonstrate they can handle the details and challenges on their own.'

4 Does the business have a 'drum beat'?

Radek also has a strong preference for buying or investing in businesses that already exist, rather than starting from scratch. A going concern — even one that has failed but still holds a brand, customer base or infrastructure — offers a head start.

'We quickly learned that investing in ventures in the early years is hard,' he said. 'But once you have that heartbeat — a core product with commercial traction — things get easier. Not easy. Just easier. The first $10 million is always the hardest.'

Momentum, to him, is both commercial and emotional. 'I need to see your passion too,' he adds. 'We'll be doing this together and I want to have fun, so rather than just pitching, think about how you can connect with me and build a relationship.'

5 What's the worst-case scenario?

Radek respects founders who can balance optimism with realism. 'You need to acknowledge that the journey may not be rosy all the time,' he said. He expects every pitch to include a stress test of best- and worst-case outcomes — and he pushes founders to think deeply about both.

Some call this process a pre-mortem: exploring what could go wrong before it does. 'You can't avoid surprises,' he said, 'but when they do arise, you can be less surprised in how you react.'

6 Can you take on feedback?

When Radek declines to invest, he's often generous with his reasons and offers constructive feedback. What matters most to him is how founders respond.

'I want to see them take it with an open heart and use it to make their business better,' he said.

'When the CEO of Anthem pitched to us for the first time, we turned him down. He went away, thought about the feedback, applied it, kept in touch and a couple of months later came back, re-pitched, and we invested in the business.'

7 What's the return?

Return on investment comes last for Radek, not because it's unimportant, but because purpose comes first. 'People are always shocked that I don't automatically ask about how quickly I'll get my money back,' he said.

'Your idea needs to have a high likelihood of success financially, but for us, it also needs to have a great purpose behind it,' he explains. 'Whether it's wellness, inclusion or empowerment, the business must move the dial on making the community better in some way.'

Have a plan

Radek rejects the common startup mantra that says business plans are a waste of time. 'You must have a business plan,' he insists. 'I won't invest in anything that doesn't.'

To him, a plan isn't a static document; it's a living framework that gets reviewed and refined every three months. It must include these documents:

- executive summary
- financial projections
- marketing plan
- ownership structure
- operating plan
- values and culture statement.

Radek's commitment to impact also extends to reconciliation. Through Light Warrior's Reconciliation Action Plan, the group actively supports economic equity and self-determination for First Nations communities — another example of profit and purpose working hand in hand.

* * *

Most novice entrepreneurs don't know how to pitch to a potential investor. But when you know what questions investors will ask, and the kinds of answers they expect, everything gets easier.

Nuggets of wisdom

- ▸ Research your buyers early. Identify who could buy your business before you plan on selling it and build connections with them before you need to.
- ▸ Use marketplaces to benchmark value. Business brokers and M&A advisers help you see what similar businesses sell for and what they might pay for yours.
- ▸ Choose your pathway to expansion. Explore the Ansoff Matrix, a strategic planning tool, to choose your growth path. Start with safer moves (sell more to current customers or enter nearby markets) before investing in the business on higher risk options (sell new products to new markets).

28

HOW TO PITCH TO AN INVESTOR

It's rare to hear candid insights from founders and investors who've seen the full arc of business life — from building category-defining companies and navigating billion-dollar exits, to backing the next generation of founders. Matt Rockman, co-founder of Seek, is one of them.

In this chapter, he's joined by investors and founders who lift the lid on what really matters when money, control and reputation are on the line. Together, they reveal how serious investors think, what earns trust, how partnerships are formed and what to include in your pitch document to maximise your chance of attracting investors.

What this billion-dollar founder looks for when he invests

Few people are better placed to speak honestly about startups than Matt Rockman. As co-founder of Seek, he's lived the full journey — building from nothing, scaling at speed, and navigating the personal and commercial costs that come with success.

In this Q&A, Matt shares what he looks for when assessing founders and businesses, where most entrepreneurs go wrong, and why being successful is harder than it looks.

Q and A with Matt Rockman,
co-founder of Seek

Q: What's the difference between a startup and any other business?

A: A startup is early stage, high risk, less established and doesn't have a built-in customer set. It doesn't have a clear operating rhythm and the IP is not established or scaled.

Q: What do you look for in a startup before you invest?

A: Investing in the startup community is a wonderful and legitimate act and it can provide amazing returns, but it's not right for me anymore. I'm too old and too grumpy, and it's not a great fit for what I want to do with my time or balance sheet.

I buy existing businesses that offer lower risk than startups but I don't expect the same return. They've got established management teams, a good track record and a proven way of doing things.

If I can't invest, I am honest about why I can't. I'm always respectful and I don't tear them apart. I signal to them why it's not for me, or where the holes are, because some people just don't see it.

Q: What do you look for in an entrepreneur?

A: I look for founders who are mentally and physically committed to doing the work, and who have the necessary grit to churn it out and suck it up.

They need to be able to put people in the right seats on the bus and take care of things they're not good at. That takes self-awareness.

Q: What do startup entrepreneurs get wrong?

A: They run out of capital, hire the wrong team and don't have the right product–market fit. They don't solve a real problem and if they do, they are not fully aware of the competitors—both the obvious competitors, and the one-standard-deviation-away competitor—or the guys who could easily move into that space. I think people get too caught up in designing a logo, building a website and raising some money. That doesn't give you permission to succeed. There's a lot more that has to happen beyond that.

Q: Is entrepreneurship born or bred?

A: It's not anyone's God-given right to be a success. A startup career is no better or worse than having a labouring career, or having a teaching or arts career. They're all valid occupations, so don't be sucked into thinking that because you watch Instagram, you can go and raise some money, build a website and become a billionaire.

Q: What advice would you give a new entrepreneur?

A: It's harder than you think, and you must get the fundamentals right. Solve a real problem, make it compelling, offer good value, be customer obsessed and give a shit.

People are online, so go and find where they are, engage with them and direct them to your side of your proposition. The platforms change, and the cost per eyeball and marketing ROI might have changed, but the fundamentals don't.

Q: What are your tips for those looking for funding?

A: The most successful founders don't send blind emails to hundreds of investors. They research, shortlist and target those whose portfolios, stage preferences and philosophies align with their business.

> **Q: When should an entrepreneur give up?**
>
> A: You never give up, but don't flog the wrong idea that has poor market fit. You've got to work that stuff out, ask the right people, analyse the data, and have the right amount of persistence. I think a lot of startup people have a mediocre idea that was never going to succeed in the first place, and should have stopped before they ever got started.

After hearing Matt's take on what founders get wrong, the Hey Lemonade app founder journey shows what it looks like when a team gets it right. This is what happens when the founder team act with purpose, provide solid evidence and execute with precision.

How this app found funding

Hey Lemonade is a wellbeing app built around a simple idea: the right words, delivered at the right moment, can help people cope better with everyday stress. Co-founded by leading actresses Lucy Durack and Elise McCann, the app delivers short, evidence-based audio pep talks designed to support users through moments of pressure, self-doubt and overwhelm.

Developed in collaboration with psychologists and tested through scientific trials, Hey Lemonade sits at the intersection of positive psychology, technology and practical mental health support, with applications across individuals, schools and workplaces.

They knew they needed support to get started, so when they saw an advertisement for a Kickstarter grant, they applied for it and won. That win and the contacts that came with it led to a partnership with CSIRO and the opportunity to conduct a scientific trial.

The partnership with CSIRO gave them the scientific validation they were looking for.

'We did a randomised control trial led by a team of scientists. Previous studies showed the pep talks worked in a sporting or corporate context, but we wanted to know if the talks would work in a one-on-one setting.'

The research showed that after using the app, users felt calmer, more vital and better equipped to cope with stress. From there, Lucy and Elise focused on sourcing smaller, strategic funding rounds and partnering with investors who shared their belief in purpose-led and ethical tech.

'The CSIRO research was written up in a peer-reviewed piece for the *Journal of Medical Internet Research*. That was all part of our MVP. We waited for that to be finalised before we launched,' Lucy said.

'Not long after that, we won a student innovation grant from the New South Wales government, and we used that to build out our high-school version of the app, which was a completely separate app from our general public version. We tested that over a term with Year 9 and 10 kids across 15 geographically and gender-diverse schools and got really amazing results. Two months after that we launched.'

The founders were also accepted into SBE Australia's business accelerator, a program for early-stage, women-led technology companies.

'It ran for six months and helped us upgrade our entrepreneurial skills and language to show investors that we understood the landscape.'

When they needed investment advice, they turned to the producers and business leaders they knew through the entertainment industry and asked them for guidance. One of them said, 'I can give you advice, but I'd like to back you too. Here's what I recommend you do first. Do that, and then let me know how you went.'

They did what he suggested, came back, and he said, 'Great. I'll give you your first $200 000.' He introduced them to another angel investor, who also provided mentoring and support.

'We were only seeking advice from him too, but he was excited by what we offered and said, "I'm on board, too. Here's $100 000."'

They used that first $300 000 to build the MVP. 'Our investors came on board because they could see we had taken their advice seriously, and had applied the feedback they offered.'

They chose to raise funds via multiple smaller rounds rather than go for one big Series A raise because that would have taken them out of the business for six months, which they didn't want to do.

'We invited our existing investors to reinvest, and selectively approached a small number of individuals we believed would make strong strategic partners.'

They wanted investors who could see both the commercial returns and community impact that they were creating with individuals, school students and corporates.

It proves that when purpose, evidence and momentum align, the right investors don't need convincing, they start offering.

What Gabby Leibovich invests in

I interviewed Gabby Leibovich to find out what he invests in and why. Having exited Catch and Menulog and many other businesses, he's well placed to give advice to novice founders about how to source investors, and how to negotiate the best terms possible.

Q & A with Gabby Leibovich, co-founder of Catch, Menulog and Fingertip

Q: How can people get in touch with you to pitch their idea?

A: Send me a quick message on LinkedIn. I don't reply to 100 per cent of them, but I reply to most. If you sound like a dickhead, we will probably ignore you. I have coffee with lots of young entrepreneurs who ask for my help. The youngest entrepreneur I helped was an 11-year-old kid who reached out to me. He was the youngest marketplace seller on Catch.com, and he really wanted to meet the founder. I had breakfast with him and his dad and answered his questions. I also gave him my book, *Catch of the Decade.* I give everybody a copy of my book.

Q: Who have you invested in recently?

A: We invested in Brian Pham, the founder of Litecard, a marketing platform that uses mobile wallets to boost engagement and revenue. He sent me a cold-call message via LinkedIn and then we met up at a retail conference.

Q: What did you like about that business?

A: You could tell straight away that this guy was going to be successful. If he's not successful with business number one, he'll be successful with business number two. He's been going for three years, has about 10 employees, good revenue and blue-chip customers like Spotlight, JB Hi-Fi and others. He's got an interesting niche, and customers are willing to pay him for his service. He's done the hard yards.

Q: What did you see in the founder?

A: He's an immigrant born to a Vietnamese family, super intelligent and as hungry as can be. You can see that when you speak to him. I said to my brother Hezi, 'You've got to meet this guy. There's something special here. Let's see if we can join his little rocket ship.'

Q: How do you negotiate the equity position that you take?

A: After we sold Catch, we did not appreciate the value that we brought to those startups, and we were willing to join at exactly the same valuations as anyone else. We've since learned that startups are willing to give us a chunk of their business for a lot less, possibly for free, in order to get us involved and help in any way that we can, be it advice, experience, connection, marketing, branding, PR or all of the above. So, we are becoming smarter as well.

Q: How do you decide how much equity to take and what you will pay for it?

A: It's all about supply and demand/desperation. If the right person came along, like Jeff Bezos, I'd be willing to give him 50 per cent of my website business Fingertip, so it really all depends on what that person brings to the mix.

Q: As an investor, what could that founder expect to get from you?

A: My brother and I suffer from FOMO, so we would rather invest in 25 different businesses. Other investors may only invest in two or three, and get very involved. I'm on the board of Luxury Escapes, where we give more of ourselves. For the other ones we've invested in, they can call me when they like or we might catch up twice a year for a coffee. But I won't go too far afield. They'd need to come and meet me in Caulfield.

Gabby's story shows that investors look just as closely at who the person is behind the idea — their background, character and work ethic — as they do at the idea itself.

Media-for-equity partnerships: An innovative form of funding

Airtasker's growth story isn't just about building a global platform — it's about how Tim Fung mastered the art of funding without losing control. From early rounds of capital raised in a buoyant investment cycle, to trading equity for advertising in a bold media-for-equity model, Tim redefined how startups could scale without burning through cash. When he wanted to open Airtasker's international operations, the strategy evolved into a country-by-country investment structure that balanced risk with opportunity, and a global Formula One partnership that turned Airtasker's brand philosophy — celebrating skilled people — into a powerful symbol of craftsmanship.

To scale Airtasker in Australia, the company partnered with Channel 7.

'We did a media-for-equity deal where we swapped shares in our company for advertising contra. Channel 7 gave us a lot of advertising space in exchange for a share in the company. That was really successful because it helped us grow the brand, and scale the business in Australia.'

This approach became a cornerstone of Airtasker's funding model: an innovative way to trade equity for marketing reach while conserving cash. It allowed the company to grow quickly through trusted media partners rather than relying solely on traditional capital raises.

As Airtasker expanded, Tim applied the same strategy internationally. 'When we enter new markets like the United States and the UK, we've replicated that strategy. We spent about $15 million in the UK, $35 million in the United States and $11 million in Australia — a total of $61 million in value of all the advertising deals that we've done.'

He explains that Airtasker starts from scratch with its media partnerships in each country, tailoring the investment structure to match local conditions.

'Airtasker Australia is doing hundreds of millions in turnover, Airtasker UK is doing tens of millions in turnover and Airtasker USA single-digit millions, so you don't want to have the same capital ratio being applied to all three.'

Tim customises his approach based on who he's targeting. 'If you're Channel 4 in the UK, you're set up to help Airtasker UK scale. But that partnership is not relevant if we were to launch in Germany or Italy. We allocate the shares to the media partners country by country, and that's intentional, because the local media partners generally have leverage in their own country.'

This philosophy also shaped Airtasker's global brand campaign partnership with the Visa Cash App RB Formula One team, which shaped its brand communication strategy.

'We don't sponsor the cars or the drivers; we sponsor the team who do all the tasks behind the scenes that make the magic of Formula One possible. There's about 30 people just in the pit crew and another 100 people at the racetrack who do everything from IT to logistics to garage operations. We're celebrating the fact that every human being has unique skills. That's really close to Airtasker's mission.'

He elaborates: 'Even small things — like someone laying out sticky tape on the ground to mark the box the car drives into — reflect the same precision and skill we see on Airtasker. We wanted to celebrate that craftsmanship because, on Airtasker, someone might assemble Ikea furniture or mow a lawn better than you, and that craftsmanship deserves the same respect.'

The collaboration with Formula One became a symbol of Airtasker's ethos: that every small, precise task contributes to a larger success. As Tim said, 'The partnership is a metaphor for the company's mission: to recognise and celebrate the everyday skills and dedication that keep the world running.'

* * *

In the end, selling or funding a business comes down to a series of choices about who you partner with, what you are willing to trade and how much control you want to keep. Your task is to listen to your instinct and choose your investors with the same care you choose your partners, team and critical suppliers.

Nuggets of wisdom

▸ Research investors before you pitch. Use platforms like Crunchbase and PitchBook to see who's investing in your sector, at what stage and on what terms.

▸ Use LinkedIn to unlock warm introductions. Check who investors back and who they follow, and then ask for introductions. Deals move faster when someone trusted opens the door.

▸ Attend startup and angel investor conferences. Book an expo stand to gain access to cocktail functions and VIP events where you can meet those who matter.

29

HOW TO PROTECT WHAT YOU'VE WORKED FOR

When I asked founders for their secret of success, I expected to hear about the importance of strategy, grit or timing.

What I heard was: Get a great lawyer and get a great accountant.

They know better than most that you can have the best business idea in the world and outstanding execution, but if you sign the wrong documents or fail to protect yourself from miscreants, you could lose everything.

The key is to get advice early, before you've signed anything or before a deal has even been done, to ensure you set yourself up correctly from the start. That journey begins and ends with your company's constitution.

Get the constitution right

Before you can win the game, you need to know the rules — and in business, the rulebook starts with your constitution. It's the document that decides who has power, what gets approved and how decisions are made. The person who writes the rules holds the advantage. If you don't craft this carefully, with legal advice, you could lose control of the company you built. One founder I spoke to learned this the hard way.

He self-drafted the constitution, assuming it was a formality.

'At the start, the constitution felt like a piece of obligatory paperwork; something you had to complete. In reality, it is the rulebook everyone must live by, including the founder.'

What a lot of founders don't realise is the constitution is legally binding, for everyone, including the founder. They draft it, put it in a drawer and forget about it, not realising what they signed two years, or even twenty years ago, could come back to bite them in a very big way.

'When I took on investors five years later, the anti-dilute clauses were used against me and my shareholding was diluted to the point I became a minority shareholder in my own company and was eventually pushed out altogether and they took over the company I had built. It was devastating - but legal - and it was all due to the constitution I drafted at the very start.'

Another founder told me that she also nearly lost control of her business because her constitution demanded she get 100 per cent of the board's approval for any financial expenditure. If she wanted to buy a $2 pen or a $2 million warehouse she'd need to get 100 per cent of the shareholders to agree. 'In hindsight,' she said, 'I should have set the threshold figure to 51 per cent, not 100 per cent, and only seek their permission for larger expenditures.'

If that happens to you, you'll need to go back to ask the shareholders to approve the amendment to the constitution.

Ironically, if the constitution requires you to get 100 per cent of shareholder approval to amend the constitution, you'll need 100 per cent of those shareholders to agree to the change. This is where novice founders get trapped and opens the door for investors to extract concessions. Ultimately, you should retain as much control over your company as you can while ensuring the shareholders still have a say in the important decisions.

Before you sign anything, get it approved by your accountant and lawyer so you can sleep easy at night.

Get your numbers right

George Calombaris knows better than most what it feels like to have numbers that don't add up. When it was revealed that his restaurant group had underpaid staff, the media turned him into the face of wage theft. Behind the headlines was a much more complex reality, and what the media reported and what really happened were two different things.

One person who was there before, during and after it happened was George's business partner, Radek Sali. He had joined MAdE Establishment to help George and his team professionalise and scale the business. MAdE's portfolio spanned 15 restaurants, including the Jimmy Grants Greek eatery, the Hellenic Republic and many others.

When Radek's investment firm Light Warrior Group bought out George's previous investors, George's shareholding increased from 10 per cent to 30 per cent. But the prior shareholders would only deal directly with George, limiting Light Warrior's ability to conduct due diligence. Three months after the buyout, Radek appointed CEO Troy McDonagh to review the state of play and see where they stood.

'One month into Troy's tenure, he found a fundamental lack of systems and processes across the business,' said Radek. 'Of most concern were anomalies in the payroll systems.'

Crucially, the MAdE Establishment Group self-reported the payroll discrepancies to Fair Work Australia - a point often overlooked in media coverage.

As confirmed by the Fair Work Ombudsman, they investigated 'following a self-disclosure of underpayments,' with Calombaris stating they were 'upfront and honest' about the issues once discovered.

The discovery of the anomalies was progressive. In 2017, they self-reported $2.6 million that covered 162 staff, and in 2019, the extended investigation revealed it was $7.83 million to a total of 515 staff. Once the discrepancies were discovered, the monies were paid back in full.

It took until 2019 for the Fair Work investigation to close, but by then the story had become national news.

'When the story hit the media, it was insinuated that we hadn't self-reported or repaid,' said Radek. 'None of that was true. The award pay rates were, and still are, far too complicated for even the most sophisticated companies to navigate.'

Other companies to get mired in wage issues include Domino's, Australian universities, Woolworths, Commonwealth Bank, the Reserve Bank of Australia, the ABC and a raft of others. Few of the CEOs of these companies received the personal vitriol that George did.

'I was perceived as a wage thief,' George said. 'But thieves are people who intend to steal something from someone. That was never my intent.'

Radek said, 'The unions refused to correct the record because the media campaign suited their agenda. We reminded them this wasn't just about George but about 600 people who worked at MAdE Establishment. They didn't care because none of those workers were union members.'

Under intense public pressure George, along with the directors of MAdE, made the devastating decision to close the business, place it into voluntary administration and let 600 employees go.

External forces compounded the damage. COVID-19 restrictions, the Victorian bushfires, a sharp downturn in economic conditions, and the collapse of both domestic and international tourism all converged, accelerating the business's decline. The failure resulted from multiple decisions made by multiple people. George was one of many involved and was not solely responsible for what happened.

The personal fallout was severe. George lost his home, media contracts and speaking engagements. He was subjected to verbal abuse at public events, and the sustained pressure took a serious toll on his mental health.

'There wasn't a day without a journo, a pap or someone with a camera at the top of my street. That's okay, because I chose to be in the public eye. But when it affects your family, that's when you need to work out how to protect them.'

Following the 2019 underpayment controversy, George now maintains rigorous payroll compliance practices. Today, his businesses undergo regular independent audits to ensure accurate wage payments. This system ensures all staff are paid correctly and reflects his commitment to learning from the past.

Today, George's new restaurants are thriving, his team remains loyal and his reputation is slowly rebuilding. He's partnered with Shannon Bennett to launch Culinary Wonderland, an online community of over 100 chefs, each revealing their secrets on how to cook their favourite dish and sharing their insights on the best restaurants, bars and cafes to frequent when travelling around the world.

George also knows that being wildly creative doesn't excuse being financially illiterate. 'I know how to read a balance sheet,' he said. 'When we had a meeting with Deutsche Bank to negotiate a new property deal, I could tell they were looking at me, thinking, *What would this chef in his black T-shirt know about finance*? But this wasn't my first rodeo. You've got to understand what's happening on the bottom line, which I do.'

That self-awareness — knowing what you're good at and what you're not — has shaped his approach to business. 'Don't be afraid to tell someone they're better at something than you are,' he said. 'That's why you hire them.' His partnership with entrepreneur Radek taught him exactly that.

'The key is to know yourself, be honest about your strengths and partner with people who can do what you can't.'

George's experience is a reminder that brilliance and creativity aren't enough. His story demonstrates the importance of accountability, governance and the value of trusted advisers.

Be 'greedy long'

Goldman Sachs understood one of the most powerful principles in business: play the long game — or be 'greedy long', as its former senior partner Gus Levy put it — because if you do the right thing now, you can earn far more later.

Prior to being appointed as the investment bank to manage the Swisse sales process, Goldman Sachs had pitched for a much smaller job and lost out to a competitor. When they were invited to pitch for the big gig of selling Swisse, they could have declined the invitation. Instead, they came back, humble, persistent and willing to do whatever was needed to help Swisse achieve their goal. They won not because they were the cheapest or the flashiest, but because they had shown that they could rise above that earlier rejection and were prepared to invest in the relationship.

Their approach was simple: understand the fundamentals, take the time to learn the business and do the work properly. They dug into the Swisse history, backed the turnaround strategy (when so many didn't) and guided the team through a disciplined global sale process that attracted 40 bidders — an extraordinary number for a private deal.

As tensions rose and last-minute bidders pushed the price higher, Goldman held the line and put the needs of getting Swisse the very best deal above their own of getting a good deal and moving on to the next. Their mantra was 'greedy long': do the right thing by the client in the short term and the long-term rewards will take care of themselves.

It did. Swisse sold for $2.1 billion, one of the biggest private sales in Australian history.

Playing the long game paid off for Goldman Sachs in ways they didn't expect. They recovered the $70 million loan they had extended to Swisse to fund the turnaround process, and earned just under $100 million in interest and merger and acquisition fees. Biostime liked the way they did business too. They asked Goldmans to fund the debt Biostime used to acquire Swisse and later took over managing their financial affairs.

'Greedy long' certainly paid off for Goldman Sachs.

Measure the inputs, not the output

Shaun Wilson, co-founder of Bondi Sands, believed in playing the long game too. He implemented a simple but rarely practised strategy: reward the work, not just the win. Most founders obsess over outputs — revenue, profit, units sold — but Shaun knew those numbers tempt people to take shortcuts. So, he re-engineered the system to change what got measured and what metrics were rewarded. Most firms reward results, or outputs. Shaun created a system that measured inputs: the number of distribution points secured, the number of facings on the shelf, the end-cap displays they negotiated, the volume and variety of training delivered to retail staff, the way the product was presented at the cash register and other inputs.

Shaun visited stores constantly, doing mystery shops, talking to staff, checking displays. 'If someone asks a pharmacy assistant about a tanning product, I want the first words out of their mouth to be "Bondi Sands".' That was another of the outputs he wanted to measure and reward.

Then came the hard part: building the systems to support this new process. To work, and be accurate, it needed to offer real-time visibility across every market, live reporting on stock flow and margins, detailed scorecards to measure staff performance, balance-sheet exposure and rolling reports on sell-through.

'The system cost \$400 000 to install and created months of disruption,' said Shaun.

Output dipped and stress spiked, but Shaun played the long game. 'We knew the next financial year would be better for it.'

And it was. Measuring inputs, not just outputs, inspired the team, improved forecasting and ensured every decision the company made was based on facts and figures.

* * *

Focus on the work, not the win. The founders who play the long game are the ones who prevail in the long run. They put the right rules in place early, surround themselves with trusted advisers, measure what truly drives performance and make decisions that protect the business for the future.

Nuggets of wisdom

▶ Appoint a trusted accountant and lawyer. If you don't know any, ask your industry association for recommendations and check reviews before engaging them.

▶ Don't self-draft your constitution. Find out what best practice looks like, and ask your legal and accounting advisors to look it over.

▶ Play the long game. Give a bit to get a bit, take the losses on the chin and reset to have another crack when conditions are different. Don't do something permanently stupid because of a temporary setback.

30

HOW TO SECURE YOUR INTELLECTUAL PROPERTY

Intellectual property is a complex area, but it's a topic you need to address early in your startup journey. Yes, it's intimidating and hiring patent attorneys can be expensive, but not having the IP conversation will cost you a lot more in the long run if you don't take care of it in the short term.

Protecting what you've created doesn't have to be hard or costly but it does have to be done, or you risk losing everything you've worked so hard to create.

What's in a name?

It's getting harder than ever to protect what you've created. Whether it's a line of code, a colour, a formula or a framework, if it's good enough, and gets traction, you can rest assured that someone somewhere will try to take it off you.

But what happens when *you* are the brand? What elements of your own existence do you need to protect? Hollywood's legal eagles are scrambling to work out how A-list actors and celebrities can protect themselves from AI replicating their personality rights, image rights and voice rights, but protecting the commercial use of even your own name may be a reality you need to factor into your thinking.

If you're an influencer, founder or creator tying your personal identity to a product, tread carefully. Your name carries equity, risk and legal complexity, and once it's attached to something, it's very hard to get back.

The fashion and wellness world offers a few cautionary tales. If Alannah Hill, Peter Alexander and Marcus Blackmore had their time again, I wonder if they'd still use their personal names to build their corporate brands. When the venture capitalists stepped in, each one eventually lost the right to use their own name for future endeavours. Naming the business after yourself feels obvious and easy at the start, but if the goal is to sell your business in some shape or form in the future, it can make the exit far more complicated. That's why it is so important to work out what you want from the business at the start, because creating an eponymous brand could create a lot of opportunities in the short-term but it may cost you in other ways in the long-term.

Should you put your own name on your brand?

If using your own name was always a good idea, Facebook would be called Mark, Square would be called Dorsey, and Tesla would be called Musk, which is actually a cool name for a cologne. (I'm surprised he hasn't made that yet.)

Radek Sali, a prolific hirer of influencers, has seen the trap repeatedly. His advice is simple and blunt: 'Think twice about being the face of your brand. It's okay at the beginning to help you get traction, but once you've got some momentum, spread the risk and bring in other names and faces. You will change over the years and the needs of the company will change too.'

Using your own name or face to build a brand can be both a shortcut and a trap. Influencers grow fast because audiences follow the person, not the product, but stepping back later becomes much harder. The Macfarlane Bros are navigating that transition.

'Austin and I think long term,' said Lachlan. 'We've always wanted to be film directors, but when we started making YouTube shorts, we didn't have access to actors, so we found ourselves in front of the screen.'

Their new project, a *Twilight Zone*-style anthology web series, marks the beginning of that shift. Initially, they planned to star in every episode. Now, they're limiting their appearances to maintain brand continuity only. 'We probably have to be in it for brand reasons, with our recognisable faces, but we're more focused on being behind the camera now.'

For them, this evolution is about scale. 'Content creators often have their face and personality tied to their brand, which can make it a challenge to scale,' said Lachlan. 'You have to be in front of the camera and also be the one having the meetings, doing the admin and shooting the content. It's weird because the CEO isn't usually the one doing the PR too.'

Their aim is to reverse that dynamic. 'We feel it should be a video *by* the Macfarlane Bros, not *of* the Macfarlane Bros.'

They've already begun making the transition. For their next project, they've hired a cinematographer and a 15-person crew so they can spend more time where they always wanted to be: behind the camera.

How Bondi Sands got its name

Shaun Wilson always wanted his Bondi Sands brand to feel uniquely Australian. He and co-founder Blair James agreed that 'Bondi' would be the first word in the brand name; they just couldn't work out what the second word would be. Bondi *Body* felt too generic. Bondi *Tan* felt too restrictive. Bondi *Beach* too obvious. They needed a word that could scale and carry a global concept across cultures and continents to become a category-defining brand.

The breakthrough came from the least expected place. A friend of Blair's had joined them in the earliest days of getting started. All three were driving home from a photo shoot (the shoot was conducted before the product even had a name, which took courage) when he turned to them and said, 'What about Bondi Sands?'

That was it! They had found their name. They registered it and got to work. That third person, the man who came up with the name, reluctantly chose to end his involvement with Bondi Sands after that because he didn't have the $50 000 capital to invest and didn't want the stress of building a startup. He returned to his former work as a tradesperson, and watched from the sidelines and cheered as his two mates went big and exited with a $450 million payout, a portion of which could have been his. That's gotta hurt.

The name game

Sometimes the biggest breakthroughs come disguised as setbacks. Online wine retailer Vinomofo had a difficult start. They were all set to launch a cool wine site called Vinomojo. They had the web pages up, the socials ready to go and a teaser campaign in place. Three days before launch, they received a cease-and-desist letter from a legal firm representing Mojo Wines, a public company also in the wine sector. Their message was unmistakeable: if you use that name we will sue you.

What to do? Push ahead and gamble that the company wouldn't make good on their threat? Scrap everything and start again? Both were costly options; neither was appealing.

They could have called it a day and declared it all too hard, but they didn't want to give up everything they had already created. Instead, they called an emergency meeting—which may or may not have involved a little bit of alcohol, because they were a little bit stressed—to see if they could find a solution.

After a few hours of pitching new names to each other and coming up with nothing that stuck, one of them said, 'Let's just call it Vinomofo for the motherfuckers who are trying to stop us from launching!' They laughed about it but then realised how good that name really was because it summed up exactly what they felt about the big mofo that was trying to shut them down. They shortened it for obvious reasons but kept the rest and went on to launch with one of the riskiest names in business. They, and their customers, loved it because it showcased that 'up yours' energy that has come to define the brand.

That distinctive and slightly risqué name generated millions in earned media and has been marketing gold ever since.

How to choose your product and business name

Carla Oates, founder of The Beauty Chef, learned early that expensive legal advice doesn't always equate to good business advice.

When she launched her now-iconic Glow powder, the name felt perfect. It captured everything the product promised: radiance, vitality, inner beauty. But she quickly discovered she wasn't the only one who thought so.

'There are so many powders that have come out called Glow now,' she said. 'It's hilarious. People often ask, "Why didn't you trademark the brand Glow?" Well, we did try, but it's very difficult to trademark a descriptive word.'

Glow was never going to be easy to protect. It's a common descriptor word used in everyday language and across multiple product categories—glow up, glow stick, glow in the dark, healthy glow—and because the term describes

315

a quality or outcome rather than a specific commercial source, it lacks inherent distinctiveness, making it weak as a standalone trademark.

'That's why a made-up word that has no defined meaning can be a good way to name a business,' she said.

'I never thought anyone would copy us because it was so niche,' she said. 'But now there are hundreds of glow powders: Super Glow, Skin Glow, Inner Glow. People don't realise the ingredients in each are completely different. Some just throw in cheap fillers and call it the same thing.'

Despite this, Carla's lawyers encouraged her to pursue the trademark. 'I shouldn't have. I wasted a lot of money trying to protect it, when I could have invested that money on more important priorities.'

Would she do things differently if she had her time again? 'Probably,' she said. 'I'd pick a name that was less descriptive, and something that could be protected.'

Still, she knows her brand is her strongest defence. 'That's where brand is so important. While everyone might call their product Glow, there's nothing like *The Beauty Chef's* Glow. When your brand halo is strong, people buy into that, not just the name.'

Her lesson for founders is simple: don't expect lawyers to make branding decisions for you, and don't waste money fighting to own a word that the world already uses.

Protect what's yours

A good name can build a brand, but only if you can protect it. Glow had to let its name go; it was too common and too hard to defend.

Bondi Sands didn't have that luxury. Once the brand took off, the name became an asset, and opportunists circled fast. Some tried to trademark it overseas before Shaun could register it in those countries.

The biggest wake-up call came from China. Shaun had already launched in Australia but had not yet secured the trademark in Asia, assuming he had time because the brand had not launched there yet. He didn't. A cheeky local Chinese company registered Bondi Sands first, then tried to sell the name back to him for $70 000.

'They watched the brand grow and waited,' he said. 'We had to take action to stop it. After weeks of negotiation with the counterfeiter, and $20 000 in legal fees, we paid them $25 000 to go away, but we got off pretty lightly as their demands could have been a lot worse.'

It wasn't the last time someone tried to siphon off their success.

A manufacturer in Asia began producing its own tanning mitts, stamped them with the Bondi Sands logo and sold them at half price. Shaun was alerted to the scam when a stockist emailed him saying, 'Great price on those mitts—can we get some at that rate?'

Shaun understood the lesson quickly: if you don't lock down your IP, someone else will.

* * *

Protecting your IP costs money, but not protecting it costs more. When it does come time to hire an IP expert, shop around. Not all patent attorneys are the same. Don't default to the biggest firm, ask lots of questions, even the dumb ones, challenge their assumptions, get second and third opinions, and then hire the best you can afford.

One missed document, one blown deadline or one box left unticked is all it takes for a copycat to walk in and take what you've built.

Nuggets of wisdom

▶ Choose your business and brand names carefully. Avoid generic or descriptive names that will limit your product offering or geographic expansion.

▶ Protect your product. File a provisional patent first. It's a low-cost way to protect how your product works and gives you 12 months to test the market before you have to file a full patent.

▶ Watch for copycats. Set up Google Alerts to flag competitive or deceptive brands that crop up online.

31

HOW TO PREPARE YOUR BUSINESS FOR SALE

If you want to build a business others want to buy, it pays to understand what a potential buyer looks for. Buyers don't just want to know how your business performs today — they want to know how it will perform tomorrow. They look for proof of growth, resilience and systems that can survive without the founder. These indicators, known as 'value drivers', tell a buyer whether your business is profitable, scalable and investable. If you get this right at the start, you can sell your business for a higher price at the end.

Know your metrics

Top business coach Kobi Simmat said, 'Most entrepreneurs enter a business without much thought as to how they will exit the business. They also tend to build a business around their technical skill: bakers open bakeries, plumbers start plumbing companies, chefs open restaurants.'

There's nothing wrong with that, but many spend too much time working *in* the business, rather than *on* the business. 'Technicians get so involved in doing the work,' said Kobi, 'they don't stop to think about what they really want from the business, or what they want the business to do for them in the long term.'

This is okay for those early years, when you are fuelled by energy and optimism. But as the years go by, and you get older, your energy fades, fatigue sets in and that's when the internal dialogue kicks in: *I'm tired. I wouldn't mind doing something else. Maybe I should sell?* Only then do they realise the business isn't ready to be sold, and that all the work needed to prepare it should have been done much earlier.

Kobi recommends you have a plan for how to exit before those feelings take over. 'Begin with the end in mind. Act as if you're going to sell the business from the minute you begin it. If you do, you'll build better systems, hire differently and create a company that is far more valuable, in half the time.'

He regrets not doing this. 'I started my business when I was 29 years old, and wasted a good 10 years working out what I wanted the business to do for me and why I was in business to start with.'

It helps to have a target price in mind for what you'd like to sell the business for. You can estimate this in advance using a simple formula buyers rely on when valuing companies, known as a business multiple.

Understand the multiples

Business buyers use a 'multiple' to estimate what a company is worth. It expresses value as a ratio of profit or revenue, such as:

- Enterprise value ÷ EBITDA, or
- Enterprise value ÷ revenue

EBITDA stands for *Earnings Before Interest, Tax, Depreciation and Amortisation*. It's commonly used because it shows how the business performs at its core, before financing and accounting effects. It's a widely used metric that reflects both earnings and market perception and translates financial performance into a credible value estimate: *value = profit × multiple*.

Multiples vary by country and industry, reflecting growth, risk and buyer demand. Table 31.1 lists a few to demonstrate how it is calculated.

Table 31.1 examples of business multiples

Industry	Multiple (EBITDA)
Retail	2x–4x
Hospitality	2x–3x
Consulting / Professional services	3x–6x
Technology / IT-enabled	4x–8x
Healthcare / Financial services	4x–6x

Examples:

- A retail business with $800 000 EBITDA at 3× is valued at $2.4 million.
- A consulting business with $1 million EBITDA at 5× is valued at $5 million.
- A tech firm with $1.2 million EBITDA at 6× is valued at $7.2 million.

10 growth metrics that determine your sale price

Once you understand how multiples work, you need to know the levers that drive them.

Here are 10 growth metrics Kobi says buyers look to when assessing the true strength of a business. There are many more, but we'll use these ones to kickstart the process. They will vary depending on the business or sector you are in. Together, they offer a complete picture of business health and future potential.

1 Net profit

Formula: net profit = total revenue – total expenses

This is the money left after everything's paid. It tells a buyer how much real profit the business produces.

Example:

A landscaping firm earns $600 000 in sales and spends $480 000 on labour, materials and admin.

Net profit = $600 000 – $480 000 = $120 000, or 20 per cent margin.

Buyers look for a consistent margin above 20 per cent.

2 Asset turnover

Formula: asset turnover = total revenue ÷ total assets

This shows how efficiently your business uses its assets to generate income.

Example:

A cleaning company owns $200 000 of equipment and vehicles and earns $1 000 000 in revenue.

$1 000 000 ÷ $200 000 = 5

This means every dollar of assets produces $5 in sales.

3 Strike rate

Formula: strike rate = (number of sales ÷ number of leads) × 100

Your strike rate reveals how well you convert opportunities into paying customers.

Example:

Out of 20 sales calls, a consultant closes five deals.

(5 ÷ 20) × 100 = 25% strike rate

Buyers love systems that consistently produce strong conversion rates.

4 Annual contract value (ACV)

Formula: ACV = total contract value ÷ contract term (in years)

This shows the average yearly revenue per customer contract.

Example:

A software firm signs five clients on two-year deals worth $50 000 each.

5 × $50 000 = $250 000 ÷ 2 years = $125 000 ACV

Growing ACV demonstrates loyalty and trust.

5 Monthly recurring revenue (MRR)

Formula: MRR = total subscribers × average monthly spend

This shows how stable and predictable your income is from month to month, a key indicator of future cash flow.

Example:

A pet-care subscription has 2500 members paying $20 per month.

2500 × $20 = $50 000 MRR

Buyers will pay more for a business that offers stable, repeatable revenue.

6 Average revenue per customer (ARPC)

Formula: ARPC = total revenue ÷ total customers

This tracks how effectively you monetise each client.

Example:

An e-commerce store makes $900 000 from 3000 buyers.

$900 000 ÷ 3000 = $300 per customer

Rising ARPC signals successful upselling and a strong brand.

7 Customer churn

Formula: customer churn = (MRR lost during the period ÷ starting MRR) × 100

Churn measures how much recurring revenue is lost through customer cancellations or downgrades, excluding any new sales or upgrades.

Example:

Start of month MRR = $50 000

MRR lost during the month = $5000

(5000 ÷ 50 000) × 100 = 10% churn

Buyers typically look for monthly churn well below 10%, with lower churn signaling stronger customer retention and lower risk.

8 Customer retention rate

Formula: retention rate = [(customers at end – new customers) ÷ customers at start] × 100

This shows how many customers stick around.

Example:

Start: 1000 customers

End: 1200 customers (300 new)

[(1200 – 300) ÷ 1000] × 100 = 90% retention

Strong retention figures indicate how loyal customers are.

9 Customer lifetime value (CLV)

Formula: CLV = annual revenue per customer × average customer lifespan

This predicts total profit from one customer relationship.

Example:

Each gym member spends $600 a year and stays for four years.

$600 × 4 = $2400 CLV

Buyers value businesses with rising CLV because it means predictable long-term returns.

10 Customer acquisition cost (CAC)

Formula: CAC = total marketing spend ÷ new customers acquired

This reveals what it costs to get one paying customer.

Example:

Spend $40 000 on ads, gain 1000 customers.

$40 000 ÷ 1000 = $40 CAC

Buyers prefer the *lifetime value* of a customer to be at least three times the CAC.

* * *

A business that runs smoothly without you and scales predictably will always command a premium. Treat these tools and formulas as a fitness test for your business. The stronger you score, the easier it will be to sell it. Build as if you'll sell tomorrow because the habits that make your business saleable are the same ones that make it successful.

Nuggets of wisdom

▸ Build to sell from day one. Design systems, processes and roles so the business can run without you. Buyers pay more for companies that don't depend on the founder.

▸ Track the metrics that matter to buyers. Focus on the levers that buyers care about and place your energy where it matters.

▸ Grow with the multiple in mind. Not all revenue is equal. Predictable income, strong margins and low churn lift your multiple far more than raw sales alone.

WHAT'S NEXT?

In the end, this book isn't really about the founders you've just met — it's about what you do with the information they have imparted. You've seen that tech tools come and go, and trends spike and fade, but the real constants are courage, persistence, clear thinking and taking concerted action. Keep what resonates, ignore what doesn't, steal the scripts, borrow the strategies and adapt the playbooks until they fit your life, your market and your idea of success. You don't need anyone's permission, a perfect plan or a viral moment; you just need to start, keep learning and keep going, even when it gets hard. You get one life. I hope you get to do something magical with it.

Good luck and thank you for reading.

For more resources, bonus content and free training, visit:

bernadetteschwerdt.com.au
copyschool.com

Find me on social media: @bernadetteschwerdt @copyschool

Bernadette Schwerdt:

Facebook: facebook.com/bernadetteschwerdt
Instagram: instagram.com/bernadetteschwerdt
LinkedIn: linkedin.com/in/bernadetteschwerdt/

Australian School of Copywriting:

Facebook: facebook.com/copyschool

Instagram: instagram.com/copyschool

LinkedIn: linkedin.com/company/australian-school-of-copywriting/

YouTube: youtube.com/@schoolofcopywriting

Copywriting Life group:

facebook.com/groups/thecopywritinglife

ACKNOWLEDGEMENTS

This book would not exist without the generosity of the entrepreneurs who gave me their time, insights and hard-won wisdom. You are busy people, and I'm deeply grateful for the openness with which you shared your stories.

My thanks to Radek Sali for opening his address book, making introductions and connecting me with such an extraordinary network of people.

To Gabby Leibovich, for the many introductions and for trusting me as your ghostwriter on my very first project. That experience opened up an entirely new world of writing for me.

To the many entrepreneurs — listed and unlisted — who have chosen me as their ghostwriter and book coach: thank you for your trust, your candour and the privilege of helping you tell your stories.

To my family, thank you for giving me the time and space to write.

To my nieces and nephews — Laura, Helena, Bella, Lana, Dylan and Ethan — for your invaluable insights on covers, guests, titles and more. You insisted on being named, so I am doing as instructed.

To my beautiful mum and my dad, for giving me a lifelong love of words and for supporting me in everything I do.

To the team at Wiley — Lucy Raymond, Chris Shorten, Leigh McLennon, Ingrid Bond, Sandra Balonyi and Renee Aurish — thank you for your passion for books and your commitment to the genteel art of reading.

To Matt Davies, for being an early reader and a sounding board.

To Monique Gibson, my long-standing PA — with me from the very beginning and still going strong. Your trust, dedication and kindness are so appreciated. And to Ami-Leigh O'Donnell for keeping my socials on track.

To my stepchildren, Maddi and Cameron for bringing such joy into our lives.

To my son, Darcy, for giving me a portal into the world of Gen Z, fixing my phone, cooking dinner and for loving words as much as I do. And for being the most awesome son a mother could hope for. I'll beat you at Scrabble one day.

And finally, to my husband Phil, my creative muse, first reader and biggest supporter. Thank you for making me laugh, creating perspective, and driving to Daylesford for afternoon tea when you don't really want to, but do anyway. That's love.

Printed and bound by CPI Group (UK) Ltd, Croydon, CR0 4YY

19/05/2026

14883265-0003